ON THE CONTRARY

First Warbler Classics Edition

On the Contrary first published in 1961 by Farrar, Straus and Cudahy

"America the Beautiful" originally appeared in *Commentary*; "Naming Names" in *Encounter*; "Artists in Uniform," "Mister Rodriguez of Lisbon," and "Settling the Colonel's Hash" in *Harper's Magazine*; "The American Realist Playwrights" in *Harper's Magazine* and *Encounter*; "The Vassar Girl" in *Holiday*; "Tyranny of the Orgasm" in the *New Leader*; "Letter from Portugal" and "The *Vita Activa*" in *The New Yorker*; "An Academy of Risk," "Characters in Fiction," and "The Fact in Fiction" in *Partisan Review*; "A Letter to the Editor of *Politics*" and "Gandhi" in *Politics*; "Mlle. Gulliver en Amérique," "No News," "Re-called to Life," and "Up the Ladder from *Charm* to *Vogue*" in *The Reporter*; "My Confession" in *The Reporter* and *Encounter*.

ISBN 978-1-7351212-2-2 (paperback)
ISBN 978-1-7351212-3-9 (e-book)

warblerpress.com

Printed in the United States of America. This edition is printed with chlorine-free ink on acid-free interior paper made from 30% post-consumer waste recycled material.

ON THE CONTRARY
Articles of Belief, 1946-1961

MARY McCARTHY

Contents

I

POLITICS AND THE SOCIAL SCENE

A Letter to the Editor of *Politics*

November, 1946

Sir:

MAY I ADD SOMETHING to your comment on the Hiroshima *New Yorker*? The editors of that magazine imagined, and you yourself in your comment take for granted, that the Hersey piece was an indictment of atomic warfare. Its real effect, however, was quite the opposite. What it did was to minimize the atom bomb by treating it as though it belonged to the familiar order of catastrophes—fires, floods, earthquakes—which we have always had with us and which offer to the journalist, from Pliny down to Mr. Hersey, an unparalleled wealth of human-interest stories, examples of the marvelous, and true-life narratives of incredible escapes. The grandness of the disaster and the smallness of the victims are ideally suited to the methods of journalism, which exaggerates and foreshortens simultaneously. The interview with the survivors (*Mrs. Margaret O'Reilly, of 1810 Oak Street, housewife, speaking to reporters, said: "When I first smelled smoke, I threw an old coat on and woke the baby," etc.*) is the classic technique for reporting such events—it serves well enough to give some sense, slightly absurd but nonetheless correct, of the continuity of life. But with Hiroshima, where the continuity of life was, for the first time, put into question, and by man, the existence of any survivors is an irrelevancy, and the interview with the survivors is an insipid falsification of the truth of atomic warfare. To have done the atom bomb justice, Mr. Hersey would have had to interview the dead.

But of this Mr. Hersey is, both literally and temperamentally, incapable. He is *The New Yorker's* reporter-at-large, not Virgil or Dante—hell is not his sphere. Yet it is precisely in this sphere—that is, in the moral world—that the atom bomb exploded. To treat it journalistically, in terms of measurable destruction, is, in a sense, to deny its existence, and this is what Mr. Hersey has accomplished for the *New Yorker* readers. Up to August 31 of this year, no one dared think of Hiroshima—it appeared to us all as a kind of hole in human history. Mr. Hersey has filled that hole with busy little Japanese Methodists; he has made it familiar and safe, and so, in the final sense, boring. As for the origin of the trouble, the question of intention and guilt—which is what made Hiroshima more horrifying, to say the least, than the Chicago Fire—the bombers, the scientists, the government appear in this article to be as inadvertent as Mrs. O'Leary's cow.

There is no question that *The New Yorker's* editors did not deliberately plan the August 31 issue as an anniversary celebration of the atom bomb (though one wonders whether they were not competing just a little with it in this journalistic coup that allowed a single article to obliterate the contents of the magazine). The point is that *The New Yorker* cannot be against the atom bomb, no matter how hard it tries, just as it could not, even in this moral "emergency," eliminate the cigarette and perfume advertising that accompanied Mr. Hersey's text. Since *The New Yorker* has not, so far as we know, had a rupture with the government, the scientists, and the boys in the bomber, it can only assimilate the atom bomb to itself, to Westchester County, to smoked turkey, and the Hotel Carlyle. ("Whenever I stay at the Carlyle, I feel like sending it a thank-you note," says a middle-aged lady in an advertisement.) It is all one world.

MARY McCARTHY

America the Beautiful
The Humanist in the Bathtub

September, 1947

A VISITING EXISTENTIALIST WANTED recently to be taken to dinner at a really American place. This proposal, natural enough in a tourist, disclosed a situation thoroughly unnatural. Unless the visiting lady's object was suffering, there was no way of satisfying her demand. Sukiyaki joints, chop suey joints, Italian table d'hôte places, French provincial restaurants with the menu written on a slate, Irish chophouses, and Jewish delicatessens came abundantly to mind, but these were not what the lady wanted. Schrafft's or the Automat would have answered, yet to take her there would have been to turn oneself into a tourist and to present America as a spectacle—a *New Yorker* cartoon or a savage drawing in the *New Masses*. It was the beginning of an evening of humiliations. The visitor was lively and eager; her mind lay open and orderly, like a notebook ready for impressions. It was not long, however, before she shut it up with a snap. We had no recommendations to make to her. With movies, plays, current books, it was the same story as with the restaurants. *Open City, Les Enfants du Paradis*, Oscar Wilde, a reprint of Henry James were *pâté de maison* to this lady who wanted the definitive flapjack. She did not believe us when we said that there were no good Hollywood movies, no good Broadway plays—only curios; she was merely confirmed in her impression that American intellectuals were "negative."

Yet the irritating thing was that we did not feel negative. We admired and liked our country; we preferred it to that imaginary

America, land of the *peaux rouges* of Caldwell and Steinbeck, dumb paradise of violence and the detective story, which had excited the sensibilities of our visitor and of the up-to-date French literary world. But to found our preference, to locate it materially in some admirable object or institution, such as Chartres, say, or French café life, was for us, that night at any rate, an impossible undertaking. We heard ourselves saying that the real America was elsewhere, in the white frame houses and church spires of New England; yet we knew that we talked foolishly—we were not Granville Hicks and we looked ludicrous in his opinions. The Elevated, half a block away, interrupting us every time a train passed, gave us the lie on schedule, every eight minutes. But if the elm-shaded village green was a false or at least an insufficient address for the *genius loci* we honored, where then was it to be found? Surveyed from the vantage point of Europe, this large continent seemed suddenly deficient in objects of virtue. The Grand Canyon, Yellowstone Park, Jim Hill's mansion in St. Paul, Jefferson's Monticello, the blast furnaces of Pittsburgh, Mount Rainier, the yellow observatory at Amherst, the little-theatre movement in Cleveland, Ohio, a Greek revival house glimpsed from a car window in a lost river-town in New Jersey— these things were too small for the size of the country. Each of them, when pointed to, diminished in interest with the lady's perspective of distance. There was no sight that in itself seemed to justify her crossing of the Atlantic.

If she was interested in "conditions," that was a different matter. There are conditions everywhere; it takes no special genius to produce them. Yet would it be an act of hospitality to invite a visitor to a lynching? Unfortunately, nearly all the "sights" in America fall under the head of conditions. Hollywood, Reno, the sharecroppers' homes in the South, the mining towns of Pennsylvania, Coney Island, the Chicago stockyards, Macy's, the Dodgers, Harlem, even Congress, the forum of our liberties, are spectacles rather than sights, to use the term in the colloquial sense of "Didn't he make a holy spectacle of himself?" An Englishman of almost any political opinion can show a visitor through the Houses of Parliament with a sense of pride or at least of indulgence toward his national foibles and traditions. The American, if he has a spark of national feeling, will be humiliated by the very prospect of a foreigner's visit to Congress—these, for the most part, illiterate hacks whose fancy vests are spotted with gravy, and whose speeches, hypocritical, unctuous, and slovenly, are spotted also with the gravy of political patronage, these persons are a reflection on the democratic process rather than of it; they expose it in its underwear. In European legislation, we are told, a great deal of shady business goes on in private, behind the scenes. In America, it is just the opposite, anything good, presumably, is accomplished *in camera*, in the committee rooms.

It is so with all our institutions. For the visiting European, a trip through the United States has, almost inevitably, the character of an exposé, and the American, on his side, is tempted by love of his country to lock the inquiring tourist in his hotel room and throw away the key. His contention that the visible and material America is not the real or the only one is more difficult to sustain than was the presumption of the "other" Germany behind the Nazi steel.

To some extent a citizen of any country will feel that the tourist's view of his homeland is a false one. The French will tell you that you have to go into their homes to see what the French people are really like. The intellectuals in the Left Bank cafés are not the real French intellectuals, etc., etc. In Italy, they complain that the tourist must not judge by the *ristorantes*; there one sees only black-market types. But in neither of these cases is the native really disturbed by the tourist's view of his country. If Versailles or Giotto's bell-tower in Florence do not tell the whole story, they are still not incongruous with it; you do not hear a Frenchman or an Italian object when these things are noticed by a visitor. With the American, the contradiction is more serious. He must, if he is to defend his country, repudiate its visible aspect almost entirely. He must say that its parade of phenomenology, its billboards, super-highways, even its skyscrapers, not only fail to represent the inner essence of his country but in fact contravene it. He may point, if he wishes, to certain beautiful objects, but here too he is in difficulties, for nearly everything that is beautiful and has not been produced by Nature belongs to the eighteenth century, to a past with which he has very little connection, and which his ancestors, in many or most cases, had no part in. Beacon Street and the Boston Common are very charming in the eighteenth-century manner, so are the sea captains' houses in the old Massachusetts ports, and the ruined plantations of Louisiana, but an American from Brooklyn or the Middle West or the Pacific Coast finds the style of life embodied in them as foreign as Europe; indeed, the first sensation of a Westerner, coming upon Beacon Hill and the gold dome of the State House, is to feel that at last he has traveled "abroad." The American, if he is to speak the highest truth about his country, must refrain from pointing at all. The virtue of American civilization is that it is unmaterialistic.

This statement may strike a critic as whimsical or perverse. Everybody knows, it will be said, that America has the most materialistic civilization in the world, that Americans care only about money, they have no time or talent for living; look at radio, look at advertising, look at life insurance, look at the tired business man, at the Frigidaires and the Fords. In answer, the reader is invited first to look instead into his own heart and inquire whether he personally feels himself to be represented by these things, or whether he does not, on the contrary, feel them to be irrelevant to him, a necessary evil, part of the conditions of life. Other people, he will assume, care about them very much: the man down the street, the entire population of Detroit or Scarsdale, the back-country farmer, the urban poor or the rich. But he himself accepts these objects as imposed on him by a collective "otherness" of desire, an otherness he has not met directly but whose existence he infers from the number of automobiles, Frigidaires, or television sets he sees around him. Stepping into his new Buick convertible, he knows that he would gladly do without it, but imagines that to his neighbor, who is just backing *his* out of the driveway, this car is the motor of life. More often, however, the otherness is projected farther afield, onto a different class or social group, remote and alien. Thus the rich, who would like nothing better, they think, than for life to be a perpetual fishing trip with the trout grilled by a native guide, look patronizingly upon the whole apparatus of American civilization as a cheap Christmas present to the poor, and city people see the radio and the washing machine as the farm-wife's solace.

It can be argued, of course, that the subjective view is prevaricating, possession of the Buick being nine-tenths of the social law. But who has ever met, outside of advertisements, a true parishioner of this church of Mammon? A man may take pride in a car, and a housewife in her new sink or wallpaper, but pleasure in new acquisitions is universal and eternal; an Italian man with a new gold tooth, a French bibliophile with a new edition, a woman with a new baby, a philosopher with a new thought, all these people are rejoicing in progress, in man's power to enlarge and improve. Before men showed off new cars, they showed off new horses; it is alleged against modern man that he as an individual craftsman did not make the car; but his grandfather did not make the horse either. What is imputed to Americans is something quite different, an abject dependence on material possessions, an image of happiness as packaged by the manufacturer, content in a can. This view of American life is strongly urged by advertising agencies. We know the "others," of course, because we meet them every week in full force in *The New Yorker* or the *Saturday Evening Post*, those brightly colored families of dedicated consumers, waiting in unison on the porch for the dealer to deliver the new car, gobbling the new cereal ("Gee, Mom, is it good for you too?"), lining up to bank their paychecks, or fearfully anticipating the industrial accident and the insurance-check that will "compensate" for it. We meet them also, more troll-like underground, in the subway placards, in the ferociously complacent One-A-Day family, and we hear their courtiers sing to them on the radio of Ivory or Supersuds. The thing, however, that repels us in these advertisements is their naïve falsity to life. Who are these advertising men kidding, besides the European tourist? Between the tired, sad, gentle faces of the subway riders and the grinning Holy Families of the Ad-Mass, there exists no possibility of even a wishful identification. We take a vitamin pill with the hope of feeling (possibly) a little less tired, but the superstition of buoyant health emblazoned in the bright, ugly pictures has no more power to move us than the blood of St. Januarius.

Familiarity has perhaps bred contempt in us Americans: until you have had a washing machine, you cannot imagine how little difference it will make to you. Europeans still believe that money brings happiness, witness the bought journalist, the bought politician, the bought general, the whole venality of European literary life, inconceivable in this country of the dollar. It is true that America produces and consumes more cars, soap, and bathtubs than any other nation, but we live among these objects rather than by them. Americans build skyscrapers; Le Corbusier worships them. Ehrenburg, our Soviet critic, fell in love with the Check-O-Mat in American railway stations, writing home paragraphs of song to this gadget—while deploring American materialism. When an American heiress wants to buy a man, she at once crosses the Atlantic. The only really materialistic people I have ever met have been Europeans.

The strongest argument for the un-materialistic character of American life is the fact that we tolerate conditions that are, from a materialistic point of view, intolerable. What the foreigner finds most objectionable in American life is its lack of basic comfort. No nation with any sense of material well-being would endure the food we eat, the cramped apartments we live in, the noise, the traffic, the crowded subways and buses. American life, in large cities, at any rate, is a perpetual assault on the senses and the nerves; it is out of asceticism, out of unworldliness, precisely, that we bear it.

This republic was founded on an unworldly assumption, a denial of "the facts of life." It is manifestly untrue that all men are created equal; interpreted in worldly terms, this doctrine has resulted in a pseudo-equality, that is, in standardization, in an equality of things rather than of persons. The inalienable rights to life, liberty, and the pursuit of happiness appear, in practice, to have become the inalienable right to a bathtub, a flush toilet, and a can of Spam. Left-wing critics of America attribute this result to the intrusion of capitalism; right-wing critics see it as the logical dead end of democracy. Capitalism, certainly, now depends on mass production, which depends on large-scale distribution of uniform goods, till the consumer today is the victim of the manufacturer who launches on him a regiment of products for which he must make house-room in his soul. The buying impulse, in its original force and purity, was not nearly so crass, however, or so meanly acquisitive as many radical critics suppose. The purchase of a bathtub was the exercise of a spiritual right. The immigrant or the poor native American bought a bathtub, not because he wanted to take a bath, but because he wanted to be in a *position* to do so. This remains true in many fields today; possessions, when they are desired, are not wanted for their own sakes but as tokens of an ideal state of freedom, fraternity, and franchise. "Keeping up with the Joneses" is a vulgarization of Jefferson's concept, but it too is a declaration of the rights of man, and decidedly unfeasible and visionary. Where for a European, a fact is a fact, for us Americans, the real, if it is relevant at all, is simply symbolic appearance. We are a nation of twenty million bathrooms, with a humanist in every tub. One such humanist I used to hear of on Cape Cod had, on growing rich, installed two toilets side by side in his marble bathroom, on the model of the two-seater of his youth. He was a clear case of Americanism, hospitable, gregarious, and impractical, a theorist of perfection. Was his dream of the conquest of poverty a vulgar dream or a noble one, a material demand or a spiritual insistence? It is hard to think of him as a happy man, and in this too he is characteristically American, for the parity of the radio, the movies, and the washing machine has made Americans sad, reminding them of another parity of which these things were to be but emblems.

The American does not enjoy his possessions because sensory enjoyment was not his object, and he lives sparely and thinly among them, in the monastic discipline of Scarsdale or the barracks of Stuyvesant Town. Only among certain groups where franchise, socially speaking, has not been achieved, do pleasure and material splendor constitute a life-object and an occupation. Among the outcasts—Jews, Negroes, Catholics, homosexuals—excluded from the communion of ascetics, the love of fabrics, gaudy show, and rich possessions still anachronistically flaunts itself. Once a norm has been reached, differing in the different classes, financial ambition itself seems to fade away. The self-made man finds, to his anger, his son uninterested in money; you have shirtsleeves to shirtsleeves in three generations. The great financial empires are a thing of the past. Some recent immigrants—movie magnates and gangsters particularly—retain their acquisitiveness, but how long is it since anyone in the general public has murmured, wonderingly, "as rich as Rockefeller"?

If the dream of American fraternity had ended simply in this, the value of humanistic and egalitarian strivings would be seriously called into question. Jefferson, the Adamses, Franklin, Madison, would be in the position of Dostoevsky's Grand Inquisitor, who, desiring to make the Kingdom of God incarnate on earth, inaugurated the kingdom of the devil. If the nature of matter is such that the earthly paradise, once realized, becomes always the paradise of the earthly, and a spiritual conquest of matter becomes an enslavement of spirit, then the atomic bomb is, as has been argued, the logical result of the Enlightenment, and the land of opportunity is, precisely, the land of death. This position, however, is a strictly materialist one, for it asserts the Fact of the bomb as the one tremendous truth: subjective attitudes are irrelevant; it does not matter what we think or feel; possession again in this case is nine-tenths of the law.

It must be admitted that there is a great similarity between the nation with its new bomb and the consumer with his new Buick. In both cases, there is a disinclination to use the product, stronger naturally in the case of the bomb, but somebody has manufactured the thing, and there seems to be no way *not* to use it, especially when everybody else will be doing so. Here again the argument of the "others" is invoked to justify our own procedures: if we had not invented the bomb, the Germans would have; the Soviet Union will have it in a year, etc., etc. This is keeping up with the Joneses indeed, our national propagandists playing the role of the advertising men in persuading us of the "others'" intentions.

It seems likely at this moment that we will find no way of not using the bomb, yet those who argue theoretically that this machine is the true expression of our society leave us, in practice, with no means of opposing it. We must differentiate ourselves from the bomb if we are to avoid using it, and in private thought we do, distinguishing the bomb sharply from our daily concerns and sentiments, feeling it as an otherness that waits outside to descend on us, an otherness already destructive of normal life, since it prevents us from planning or hoping by depriving us of a future. And this inner refusal of the bomb is also a legacy of our past; it is a denial of the given, of the power of circumstances to shape us in their mold. Unfortunately, the whole asceticism of our national character, our habit of living in but not through an environment, our alienation from objects, prepare us to endure the bomb but not to confront it.

Passivity and not aggressiveness is the dominant trait of the American character. The movies, the radio, the super-highway have softened us up for the atom bomb; we have lived with them without pleasure, feeling them as a coercion on our natures, a coercion seemingly from nowhere and expressing nobody's will. The new coercion finds us without the habit of protest; we are dissident but apart.

The very "negativeness," then, of American intellectuals is not a mark of their separation from our society, but a true expression of its separation from itself. We too are dissident but inactive. Intransigent on paper, in "real life" we conform; yet we do not feel ourselves to be dishonest, for to us the real life is rustling paper and the mental life is flesh. And even in our mental life we are critical and rather unproductive; we leave it to the "others," the best-sellers, to create.

The fluctuating character of American life must, in part, have been responsible for this dissociated condition. Many an immigrant arrived in this country with the most materialistic expectations, hoping, not to escape from a world in which a man was the sum of his circumstances, but to become a new sum of circumstances himself. But this hope was self-defeating; the very ease with which new circumstances were acquired left insufficient time for a man to live into them: all along a great avenue in Minneapolis the huge stone chateaux used to be dark at night, save for a single light in each kitchen, where the family still sat, Swedish-style, about the stove. The pressure of democratic thought, moreover, forced a rising man often, unexpectedly, to recognize that he was *not* his position: a speeding ticket from a village constable could lay him low. Like the agitated United Nations delegates who got summonses on the Merritt Parkway, he might find the shock traumatic: a belief had been destroyed. The effect of these combined difficulties turned the new American into a nomad, who camped out in his circumstances, as it were, and was never assimilated to them. And, for the native American, the great waves of internal migration had the same result. The homelessness of the American, migrant in geography and on the map of finance, is the whole subject of the American realists of our period. European readers see in these writers only violence and brutality. They miss not only the pathos but the nomadic virtues associated with it, generosity, hospitality, equity, directness, politeness, simplicity of relations—traits which, together with a certain gentle timidity (as of very *unpracticed* nomads), comprise the American character. Unobserved also is a peculiar nakedness, a look of being shorn of everything, that is very curiously American, corresponding to the spare wooden desolation of a frontier town and the bright thinness of the American light. The American character looks always as if it had just had a rather bad haircut, which gives it, in our eyes at any rate, a greater humanity than the European, which even among its beggars has an all too professional air.

The openness of the American situation creates the pity and the terror; status is not protection; life for the European is a career; for the American, it is a hazard. Slaves and women, said Aristotle, are not fit subjects for tragedy, but kings, rather, and noble men, men, that is, not defined by circumstance but outside it and seemingly impervious. In America we have, subjectively speaking, no slaves and no women; the efforts of *PM* and the Stalinized playwrights to introduce, like the first step to servitude, a national psychology of the "little man" have been, so far, unrewarding. The little man is one who is embedded in status; things can be done for and to him generically by a central directive; his happiness flows from statistics. This conception mistakes the national passivity for abjection. Americans will not eat this humble pie; we are still nature's noblemen. Yet no tragedy results, though the protagonist is everywhere; dissociation takes the place of conflict, and the drama is mute.

This humanity, this plain and heroic accessibility, was what we would have liked to point out to the visiting Existentialist as our national glory. Modesty perhaps forbade and a lack of concrete examples—how could we point to ourselves? Had we done so she would not have been interested. To a European, the humanity of an intellectual is of no particular moment; it is the barber pole that announces his profession and the hair oil dispensed inside. Europeans, moreover, have no curiosity about American intellectuals; we are insufficiently representative of the brute. Yet this anticipated and felt disparagement was not the whole cause of our reticence. We were silent for another reason: we were waiting to be discovered. Columbus, however, passed on, and this, very likely, was the true source of our humiliation. But this experience also was peculiarly American. We all expect to be found in the murk of otherness; it looks to us very easy since *we* know we are there. Time after time, the explorers have failed to see us. We have been patient, for the happy ending is our national belief. Now, however, that the future has been shut off from us, it is necessary for us to declare ourselves, at least for the record.

What it amounts to, in verity, is that we are the poor. This humanity we would claim for ourselves is the legacy, not only of the Enlightenment, but of the thousands and thousands of European peasants and poor townspeople who came here bringing their humanity and their sufferings with them. It is the absence of a stable upper class that is responsible for much of the vulgarity of the American scene. Should we blush before the visitor for this

deficiency? The ugliness of American decoration, American entertainment, American literature—is not this the visible expression
of the impoverishment of the European masses, a manifestation
of all the backwardness, deprivation, and want that arrived here
in boatloads from Europe? The immense popularity of American
movies abroad demonstrates that Europe is the unfinished negative
of which America is the proof. The European traveler, viewing with
distaste a movie palace or a Motorola, is only looking into the terrible concavity of his continent of hunger inverted startlingly into
the convex. Our civilization, deformed as it is outwardly, is still an
accomplishment; all this had to come to light.

America is indeed a revelation, though not quite the one that was
planned. Given a clean slate, man, it was hoped, would write the
future. Instead, he has written his past. This past, inscribed on billboards, ball parks, dance halls, is not seemly, yet its objectification
is a kind of disburdenment. The past is at length outside. It does not
disturb us as it does Europeans, for our relation with it is both more
distant and more familiar. We cannot hate it, for to hate it would be
to hate poverty, our eager ancestors, and ourselves.

If there were time, American civilization could be seen as a
beginning, even a favorable one, for we have only to look around us
to see what a lot of sensibility a little ease will accrue. The children
surpass the fathers and Louis B. Mayer cannot be preserved intact
in his descendants… Unfortunately, as things seem now, posterity
is not around the corner.

Gandhi

Winter, 1949

"WELL, DID YOU HEAR they got the Mahatma," said a woman faculty member, settling down at the lunch table in the Sarah Lawrence faculty cafeteria. Her manner was bright and newsy, and she put the word Mahatma in comical quotation marks, as though to say the Swami, the old rope-trick artist. "The Mahatma," echoed another woman teacher, holding her fork in the air, twinkling, merry, reminiscent, thinking, it would seem, of the long series of fads her newspaper memory spanned—Coué, King Tut, Aimee McPherson, the cloche hat. There was a moment of silence before the conversation was reopened and raised to a "responsible" plane. "Nehru is much more realistic," said a male history professor in a conclusive bass. No one articulated any further thoughts. Our end of the table—the new, younger teachers—glared at the others in defiant speechlessness: if Gandhi's life, not to mention his death, was powerless to defend him against this complacency, what was there for us to say?

When I came home in the evening my little boy and the colored maid were talking about Gandhi too as she moved about, setting the table, and he sat on the floor, pasting stamps in his album. The little boy was angry, and the old maid was sad. "They ought to have let him live out his life and finish his work in peace," she iterated sorrowfully, as if the right she claimed for him were too feeble and beaten to be anything but a plaintive mild assertion. "The *dirty* things..." said Reuel.

A little boy, an old domestic worker, myself and a few friends, we, I presume, must be the people who were meant by the newspaper and the radio commentators who declared, "The world was shocked to hear, etc., etc." For the world, actually, was not shocked at all, and if we few protested Gandhi's death, it was only out of raging impotence. We could not bring him back to life or punish his assassin or even influence others (the faculty realists at the lunch table) to feel the slightest regret for what had happened.

And the fact is that a protest against such a death as Gandhi's, or Trotsky's, or Carlo Tresca's, can only be made to God. It is God, metaphorically speaking, i.e., some ideal assumption of an unwritten law governing human conduct, that we call to account for such an outrage; it is this assumption, indeed, that is injured. A crime like this cannot be felt toward in a positive or practical manner; insofar, in fact, as we are positive and practical people, it is impossible for us fully to react to it. After all, as one of those wise heads said in the faculty cafeteria, he was seventy-eight years old; in other words, it was time for him to die anyway. There is no *action*, moreover, which can answer such a crime. The futility of writing letters to the newspapers, holding memorial meetings, even catching the criminal, has been fully demonstrated in the Trotsky and Tresca cases; action somehow misses the mark. And today, if Stalin's régime were to be overthrown and the entire NKVD brought to justice, Trotsky's murder would remain unrequited, since it was not Stalin or the NKVD who struck him with the alpenstock but one man who came into his library and talked with him face to face.

The horror of Gandhi's murder lies not in the political motives behind it or in its consequences for Indian policy or for the future of non-violence; the horror lies simply in the fact that any man could look into the face of this extraordinary person and deliberately pull a trigger. The Crucifixion and other historical precedents notwithstanding, many of us still believe that outstanding goodness is a kind of armor, that virtue, seen plain and bare, gives pause to criminality. But perhaps it is the other way around, and particularly today, on the left. One wonders why the Nazis did not kill Niemöller, for instance, when in Stalin's hands his opposite number would certainly be dead. Prudential reasons do not explain it; it was imprudent, in the long run, to kill six million Jews. But the Nazis, in general, seem to have shrunk in an old-fashioned way from murdering their more prominent or distinguished opponents—those opponents who were "symbols." Not so on the left. On the left, it is Gandhi who can be killed or Trotsky, men *integri vitae sceleris-que puri*, while Stalin, apparently, bears a charmed life. Obviously, anyone with a matured plan and sufficient resolution could long ago have succeeded in killing this tyrant if some mysterious factor were not involved; he seems to have been protected, not only by his plain-clothes men, but more powerfully by the *mana* of his crimes.

In Gandhi's death, as in Trotsky's and Carlo Tresca's (no one yet knows who ordered his murder—the Stalinists, the Fascists, or some offended racketeer), the very amiability and harmlessness of the victim appears to have formed part of the motive: Gandhi on his way to a prayer-meeting, the Old Man in his study, Tresca stepping out from a spaghetti dinner—the homely and domestic attitudes in which these sages were caught emphasize the horror of the attacks and suggest a reason for them; to the murderer, the serenity of the victim comes as the last straw. It is as though the very fact that these men were patently not dangerous had incensed the killer against them: for the past two years, Gandhi's influence had been very noticeably declining; Trotsky and Tresca too, no longer "counted" as political forces in the world. Their murders, therefore, have an almost gratuitous character; it is as though the announced motive were not the real one. Was Gandhi murdered, as his assassin claimed, because of what he stood for in the Indian question or rather because what he stood for in his life—simplicity, good humor, steadfastness—affronted his assassin's sense of human probability?

There is clearly some reciprocal relation between the fact that we (children, old women, and *Politics* subscribers) refuse, in a certain sense, to credit the killer's deed and a refusal on the killer's part to credit the existence of such a man as Gandhi in the world. And the good-natured derision of my colleagues at the luncheon table, as they "cut him down to size," between mouthfuls, is different only in degree from the angry unconcern of the murderer, who immediately told reporters that he was not "at all sorry." This crime and the Trotsky and Tresca crimes too are acts, as it were, of intellectual or artistic criticism; the killer eliminates these venerable men from the human scene as the modern academic critic dismisses the "good" characters in a novel—glaring improbabilities.

Mlle. Gulliver en Amérique

January, 1952

IN JANUARY, 1947, SIMONE de Beauvoir, the leading French *femme savante,* alighted from an airplane at LaGuardia Field for a four months' stay in the United States. In her own eyes, this trip had something fabulous about it, of a balloonist's expedition or a descent in a diving bell. Where to Frenchmen of an earlier generation, America was the incredible country of *les peaux rouges* and the novels of Fenimore Cooper, to Mlle. de Beauvoir America was, very simply, movieland—she came to verify for herself the existence of violence, drugstore stools, boy-meets-girl, that she had seen depicted on the screen. Her impressions, which she set down in journal form for the readers of *Les Temps Modernes,* retained therefore the flavor of an eyewitness account, of confirmation of rumor, the object being not so much to assay America as to testify to its reality.

These impressions, collected into a book, made a certain stir in France; now, three years later, they are appearing in translation in Germany. The book has never been published over here; the few snatches excerpted from it in magazine articles provoked wonder and hostility.

On an American leafing through the pages of an old library copy, the book has a strange effect. It is as though an inhabitant of Lilliput or Brobdingnag, coming upon a copy of *Gulliver's Travels,* sat down to read, in a foreign tongue, of his own local customs codified by an observer of a different species: everything is at once familiar and distorted. The landmarks are there, and some of the institutions and personages—Eighth Avenue, Broadway, Hollywood, the Grand Canyon, Harvard, Yale, Vassar, literary celebrities concealed under initials; here are the drugstores and the cafeterias and the busses and the traffic lights—and yet it is all wrong, schematized, rationalized, like a scale model under glass. Peering down at himself, the American discovers that he has "no sense of *nuance*," that he is always in a good humor, that "in America the individual is nothing," that all Americans think their native town is the most beautiful town in the world, that an office girl cannot go to work in the same dress two days running, that in hotels "illicit" couples are made to swear that they are married, that it almost never happens here that a professor is also a writer, that the majority of American novelists have never been to college, that the middle class has no hold on the country's economic life and very little influence on its political destiny, that the good American citizen is never sick, that racism and reaction grow more menacing every day, that "the appearance, even, of democracy is vanishing from day to day," and that the country is witnessing "the birth of fascism."

From these pages, he discovers, in short, that his country has become, in the eyes of Existentialists, a future which is, so to speak, already a past, a gelid eternity of drugstores, juke boxes, smiles, refrigerators, and "fascism," and that he himself is no longer an individual but a sort of Mars man, a projection of science fiction, the man of 1984. Such a futuristic vision of America was already in Mlle. de Beauvoir's head when she descended from the plane as from a space ship, wearing metaphorical goggles: eager as a little girl to taste the rock-candy delights of this materialistic moon civilization (the orange juice, the ice creams, the jazz, the whiskeys, the martinis, and the lobster). She knows already, nevertheless, that this world is not "real," but only a half-frightening fantasy daydreamed by the Americans.

She has preserved enough of Marxism to be warned that the spun-sugar façade is a device of the "Pullman class" to mask its exploitation and cruelty: while the soda fountains spout, Truman and Marshall prepare an anti-Communist crusade that brings back memories of the Nazis, and Congress plots the ruin of the trade unions. "The collective future is in the hands of a privileged class, the Pullman class, to which are reserved the joys of large-scale enterprise and creation; the others are just wheels in a big steel world; they lack the power to conceive an individual future for themselves; they have no plan or passion, hope or nostalgia, that carries them beyond the present; they know only the unending repetition of the cycle of seasons and hours."

This image of a people from Oz or out of an expressionist ballet, a robot people obedient to a generalization, corresponds, of course, with no reality, either in the United States or anywhere else; it is the petrifaction of a fear very common in Europe today—a fear of the future. Where, in a more hopeful era, America embodied for Europe a certain millennial promise, now in the Atomic Age it embodies an evil presentiment of a millennium just at hand. To Mlle. de Beauvoir, obsessed with memories of Jules Verne, America is a symbol of a mechanical progress once dreamed of and now repudiated with horror; it is a Judgment on itself and on Europe. No friendly experience with Americans can dispel this deep-lying dread. She does not wish to know America but only to ascertain that it is there, just as she had imagined it. She shrinks from involvement in this "big steel world" and makes no attempt to see factories, workers, or political leaders. She prefers the abstraction of "Wall Street."

This recoil from American actuality has the result that might be expected, a result, in fact, so predictable that one might say she willed it. Her book is consistently misinformed in small matters as well as large. She has a gift for visual description which she uses very successfully to evoke certain American phenomena: Hollywood, the Grand Canyon, the Bronx, Chinatown, women's dresses, the stockyards, the Bowery, Golden Gate, auto camps, Hawaiian dinners, etc. In so far as the U.S. is a vast tourist camp, a vacationland, a Stop-in Serv-Urself, she has caught its essence. But in so far as the United States is something more than a caricature of itself conceived by the mind of an ad man or a Western Chamber of Commerce, she has a disinclination to view it. She cannot, for example, take in the names of American writers even when she has their books by her elbow: she speaks repeatedly of James Algee (Agee), of Farrel (Farrell), O'Neil (O'Neill), and of Max Twain—a strange form of compliment to authors whom she professes to like. In the same way, Greenwich Village, which she loves, she speaks of throughout as "Greeni-wich," even when she comes to live there.

These are minor distortions. What is more pathetic is her credulity, which amounts to a kind of superstition. She is so eager to appear well informed that she believes anything anybody tells her, especially if it is anti-American and pretends to reveal the inner workings of the capitalist mechanism. The Fifth Avenue shops, she tells us, are "reserved for the capitalist international," and no investigative instinct tempts her to cross the barricade and see for herself. Had she done so, she might have found suburban housewives, file clerks, and stenographers swarming about the racks of Peck & Peck or Best's or Franklin Simon's, and colored girls mingling with white girls at the counters of Saks Fifth Avenue. A Spanish painter assures her that in America you have to hire a press agent to get your paintings shown. An author tells her that in America literary magazines print only favorable reviews. A student tells her that in America private colleges pay better salaries than state universities, so that the best education falls to the privileged classes, who do not want it, and so on. At Vassar, she relates, students are selected "according to their intellectual capacities, family, and fortune." Every item in this catalogue is false. (Private colleges do not pay better salaries—on the contrary, with a few exceptions, they pay notoriously worse; family plays no part in the selection of students at Vassar, and fortune only to the extent that the tuition has to be paid by someone— friend, parent, or scholarship donor; you do not have to hire a press agent; some literary magazines make a positive specialty of printing unfavorable reviews.)

Yet Mlle. de Beauvoir, unsuspecting, continues volubly to pass on "the low-down" to her European readers: there is no friendship between the sexes in America; American whites are "stiff" and "cold"; American society has lost its mobility; capital is in "certain hands," and the worker's task is "carefully laid out." "True, a few accidental successes give the myth of the self-made man a certain support, but they are illusory and tangential..."

The picture of an America that consists of a small ruling class and a vast inert, regimented mass beneath it is elaborated at every opportunity. She sees the dispersion of goods on counters but draws no conclusion from it as to the structure of the economy. The American worker, to her, is invariably the French worker, a consecrated symbol of oppression. She talks a great deal of American conformity but fails to recognize a thing that Tocqueville saw long ago; that this conformity is the expression of a predominantly middle-class society; it is the price paid (as yet) for the spread of plenty. Whether the diffusion of television sets is, in itself, a good is another question; the fact is, however, that they *are* diffused; the "Pullman class," for weal or woe, does not have a corner on them, or on the levers of political power.

The outrage of the upper-class minority at the spectacle of television aerials on the shabby houses of Poverty Row, at the thought of the Frigidaires and washing machines in farmhouse and working-class kitchens, at the new cars parked in ranks outside the factories, at the very thought of installment buying, unemployment compensation, social security, trade-union benefits, veterans' housing, at General Vaughan, above all at Truman the haberdasher, the symbol of this cocky equality—their outrage is perhaps the most striking phenomenon in American life today. Yet Mlle. de Beauvoir remained unaware of it, and unaware also, for all her journal tells us, of income taxes and inheritance taxes, of the expense account and how it has affected buying habits and given a peculiar rashness and transiency to the daily experience of consumption. It can be argued that certain angry elements in American business do not know their own interests, which lie in the consumers' economy; even so, this ignorance and anger are an immense political fact in America.

The society characterized by Mlle. de Beauvoir as "rigid," "frozen," "closed" is in the process of great change. The mansions are torn down and the real-estate "development" takes their place: serried rows of ranch-type houses, painted in pastel colors, each with its picture window and its garden, each equipped with deep-freeze, oil furnace, and automatic washer, spring up in the wilderness. Class barriers disappear or become porous; the factory worker is an economic aristocrat in comparison to the middle-class clerk; even segregation is diminishing; consumption replaces acquisition as an incentive. The America invoked by Mlle. de Beauvoir as a country of vast inequalities and dramatic contracts is rapidly ceasing to exist.

One can guess that it is the new America, rather than the imaginary America of economic royalism, that creates in Mlle. de Beauvoir a feeling of mixed attraction and repulsion. In one half of her sensibility, she is greatly excited by the United States and precisely by its material side. She is fascinated by drugstore displays of soap and dentifrices, by the uniformly regulated traffic, by the "good citizenship" of Americans, by the anonymous camaraderie of the big cities, by jazz and expensive record players and huge collections of records, and above all—to speak frankly—by the orange juice, the martinis, and the whiskey. She speaks elatedly of "my" America, "my" New York; she has a child's greedy possessiveness toward this place which she is in the act of discovering.

Toward the end of the book, as she revises certain early judgments, she finds that she has become "an American." What she means is that she has become somewhat critical of the carnival aspects of American life which at first bewitched her; she is able to make discriminations between different kinds of jazz, different hotels, different night clubs. Very tentatively, she pushes beyond appearance and perceives that the American is not his possessions, that the American character is not fleshly but abstract. Yet at bottom she remains disturbed by what she has seen and felt, even marginally, of the American problem. This is not one of inequity, as she would prefer to believe, but of its opposite. The problem posed by the United States is, as Tocqueville saw, the problem of equality, its consequences, and what price shall be paid for it. How is wealth to be spread without the spread of uniformity? How create a cushion of plenty without stupefaction of the soul and the senses? It is a dilemma that glares from every picture window and whistles through every breezeway.

If Americans, as Mlle. de Beauvoir thinks, are apathetic politically, it is because they can take neither side with any great conviction—how can one be *against* the abolition of poverty? And how, on the other hand, can one champion a leveling of extremes? For Europeans of egalitarian sympathies, America *is* this dilemma, relentlessly marching toward them, a future which "works," and which for that very reason they have no wish to face. Hence the desire, so very evident in Mlle. de Beauvoir's impressions and in much journalism of the European left, not to know what America is really like, to identify it with "fascism" or "reaction," not to admit, in short, that it has realized, to a considerable extent, the economic and social goals of President Franklin D. Roosevelt and of progressive thought in general.

No News, *or,* What Killed the Dog

July, 1952

THE TERM "CULTURAL FREEDOM" is on everybody's tongue today.
It is contended that we in America have it and the Russians don't,
that we in America don't have it, that we are losing it; a committee
exists to defend it, yet even within that committee there appears to
be disagreement as to what cultural freedom is and hence whether
it is imperiled, say by Senator McCarthy or by the activities of
Communist schoolteachers or by both or neither.

Twenty years ago, by contrast, a definition of cultural freedom
would not have been difficult. It would have had to do with freedom of expression: the right of ideas and works of art to circulate
without interference. The campaign for cultural freedom after the
First World War was a series of engagements against censorship:
there was the battle of *Jurgen*, of *Ulysses*, the battle of evolution at
the Scopes trial in Tennessee, the battle of the school textbooks in
Chicago.

Judge Woolsey's decision on *Ulysses* in 1934 was felt to be the
turning point. It was a conclusive victory for the conceptions of
the Renaissance and the Reformation, for the human nude, for the
hymnody of the flesh, for the freedom of inquiry, for science, for
the rights of secularism, for a Faustian conception of man. In the
public libraries, locked cases were opened and banned volumes
came out into the light. Everywhere, on all fronts, the censors fled
in confusion. At the customs, modernist sculptures were photographed, in victory parade, entering without duty, as legitimate
works of art; museums hung controversial paintings, around which

a curious public marveled. With the removal of the fig leaf, not only the human nude was licensed, but distortions and refractions of the human nude came under the same franchise; with the classic, and under its humanist sanction, came the anti-classic, the experimental.

Today, this victory is held by many people, including its own veterans, to be secure in America. The banning of the Italian movie "The Miracle" or the suppression of *Memoirs of Hecate County* is regarded as an isolated episode, unfortunate but atypical—so atypical, in fact, that it can even be mildly condoned. An occasional breakthrough of Philistinism is felt to be only natural on the part of a defeated enemy. Even when instances multiply, comparisons with the Soviet Union or with the book-burning Nazis reinforce the sense of general national well-being, of a cultural health so buoyant as to require no special attention: "Ain't no news, boss; it's jest that your dog died." Or, in the words of the French popular song based on that old blackface monologue, *tout va très bien,*[1] it is felt, on the cultural front, and sporadic fire from the enemy, like Representative Dondero, the man who hates modern art, is listened to with amused annoyance, like the sound of an old musket going off. President Truman may call modern artists "nutty" and have a Philistine taste in music, but, unlike Premier Stalin, he does not exact uniformity from artists as the price of survival.

So much must certainly be granted by any rational person: cultural freedom, in the old-fashioned sense of the freedom of works of art and ideas to circulate, is still more or less intact in the United

---

1   The song was popular around 1940. After an absence, Mme. la Marquise calls up her château to get the news from the butler. Everything's fine, she's told; it's just that her gray mare is dead. Full of concern, she asks how it happened, and one servant after another takes the phone to tell her that everything is fine, except for a few little nothings connected with the mare's death.

It turns out that the mare died when the stable caught fire from the burning château; the château caught fire when a candlestick was knocked over during the search for the bullet that killed M. le Marquis, who had shot himself on receiving the news that he was ruined financially. However, aside from these little events leading to the death of the gray mare, everything is fine, fine, fine.

States. Howard Fast may serve a jail term, but his books are in currency. Fast is even able to take a full-page ad in the *New York Times* book section to promote the sale of his latest. The Communist leaders may be jailed, but the Communist books and pamphlets which constitute, presumably, the theoretic basis for their actions are still available to the public. The impounding of "Red" literature which was characteristic of the A. Mitchell Palmer raids of 1919–1920 does not characterize our own period. Indeed, many people who favor outlawing the Communist Party favor at the same time the teaching of Communist classics in colleges (by anti-Communist pedagogues), as a sort of preventive medicine. *Tout va très bien.*

Communist texts may be propounded, but Communists may not teach—it is this singularity of our period that permits some defenders of cultural freedom to take pride in the state of our native liberties. The little abuses that can be pointed out can be regarded in this light as the *necessary* by-products of a free, pluralistic society, since one of freedom's prerogatives is the prerogative not to be perfect, to make mistakes (always called "honest" mistakes), to be overzealous and excessive. "To err is human," etc. And the right to err, bountifully conferred on officialdom, comes to be taken as a sign of a living, healthy social organism.

Finally, in this sequence, freedom to criticize is held to compensate for the freedom to err—this is the American system. If one points out, for example, the many absurdities and cruelties of the McCarran Act, the arbitrary refusal of visas without any kind of due process, the separation of families for some "crime" committed by one member in the long-ago past, one is assured, gently, that one has the freedom to criticize, as though this freedom, *in itself,* as it attaches to a single individual, counterbalanced the unjust law on the books. This sacred right of criticism is always invoked whenever abuses are mentioned, just as the free circulation of ideas and works of art is offered as evidence of a basic cultural freedom. Whenever we hear of some injustice, we remind ourselves that the *Daily Worker* and the *Compass* may be found on newsstands, that

Owen Lattimore's *Ordeal by Slander* was a best-seller.

The ideas circulate and the individual is imprisoned—this, I fear, is the paradox toward which our society is floating, almost against its will. I have heard it said in all innocent plausibility that the Committee for Cultural Freedom ought not to criticize Senator McCarthy because McCarthyism is not a cultural phenomenon but an "event" in the sphere of politics, quite independent of culture, i.e., of books and statuary. The ideas circulate but the individual is impounded; this is true of present-day America, even in the realm of sexual morals, where there is great license of expression combined with limitations on action. Homosexual literature circulates and enjoys wide popularity, but homosexuality is a crime, for which one can be arrested. In politics, one finds the same contradiction— in the case of Howard Fast, in the case of the Communist leaders, in the case of the Hollywood screenwriters. The ideas circulate; the individual holding them may be jailed.

This is something very new and quite the contrary of what happened in the 1920s, when a book was prosecuted in court while the author remained relatively undisturbed. Even in the case of Mr. Lattimore, one observes something of the same thing. It is his biography, his personal conversations and meetings, whom he lunched with, what he wrote in a private letter, that are the principal targets of Congressional investigation; his right to express his ideas is conceded. The whole tendency of his Congressional investigators is to brush aside his books and articles and get down to "brass tacks."

This is classical liberalism's uneasy response to the challenge offered it by Communism. The Communist stands in a novel relation to ideas. He does not express ideas in the old, individualistic way, as effusions of his personality. Rather, he is an implementation of ideas; an idea, so to speak, disappears into him and is subsumed. He becomes an idea in action, an applied idea, which society now moves to suppress as it once moved to suppress an offensive picture or a doctrine embodied in a book. It is the Communist now who is under the counter, while the book is on the display table. The Communist's concealment of his ideas and motives makes him very difficult for classical liberalism to defend. Yet when he is reproached with this concealment, he insists that capitalist society will penalize him if he expresses his convictions openly. This is true enough; yet it leads into mazes of ambiguity, since society's proscription of him and its perplexity before him rest, to a large extent, on the conspiratorial character of his work. He presents himself as a danger precisely because of the lying façade he shows society; yet was it society, originally, which invited him into the role of a conspirator?

In any case, here and now, there is a natural desire on the part of the ordinary straightforward citizen to expose him, to make him acknowledge what he is; this was felt by many people about the Hiss case. It was not that one wanted Hiss to be punished for passing the papers but simply to declare what he was, to tell the truth. Yet the professional Communist, and by dutiful imitation the fellow-traveler, will never divulge his ideas. He would rather go to jail than proclaim them, as in the past a liberal or social revolutionary would rather go to jail than *not* proclaim them. One feels a kind of fury with Lattimore for the fact that he will not proclaim what seems sufficiently obvious from his writings, that he was some species of fellow-traveler. This is not an indictable crime, but the man will not acknowledge it. Hence an understandable desire to wring the facts from him, by means of his biography, by means of letters and conversations and luncheons; one can even understand a temptation to frame him, though one should not of course yield to it. What one is after (I am speaking as a liberal) is not the ruin of Lattimore but the reconstitution of the old clear-cut unambiguous relation between a man and his beliefs.

This is perhaps a lost hope, a form of romanticism. Certainly, in some of its manifestations, it borders on the demand for "confessions" that rules in totalitarian societies. In the activities of such Red-hunting publications as *Counterattack* and *Red Channels*, there is something very similar to the psychological pressure exerted by the MVD on its victims: the erring radio performer or night-club artist, blacklisted, is permitted to perform again if he confesses to having been the dupe or tool of the Communists, denounces his fellow-sinners, and makes his peace with society.

But even here there is a distinction. In the Soviet Union, a man is ordered to confess to crimes that were never committed by him or anyone else—sabotage, poisoning of wells, plots with the German General Staff, attempts on the life of Stalin, and so on, and to involve others, equally innocent, in his imaginary outrages. With *Red Channels* and *Counterattack*, on the contrary, the accused is expected to accept as a crime something of his own doing (membership in an organization) which is not a crime but which he must now see as one if he is to be restored to good standing. In short, he is to take his definition of what is criminal from these ex-FBI agents who have appointed themselves guardians of his conscience.

This idea is, of course, monstrous, yet it is not without its parallels in the intellectually more reputable world, where a man is expected to confess to having made a "grave" mistake about China before he can be received back into the fold. On the other hand, it is still reasonable to expect that a man will acknowledge kinship with his own ideas and deeds, even those that are now unpopular. Despite the changed political climate and all the rest of it, we are not really oversimplifying, as some people charge, if we ask Hiss to admit that he passed the papers—assuming, of course, that he did. As liberals, we must not demand that he concur retroactively in our view of this action, but we feel we have a certain claim to be told the bare, factual truth about it. To think otherwise, surely, would be to conceive of lying as a right.

And yet, as we see, police methods are failing to elicit the desired result. Alger Hiss is in the penitentiary, but he continues to tantalize us. We wanted the truth and all we got was his body, a mere husk in convict clothing. Many people remain unconscious of this distinction, except as they experience a sense of vague frustration toward such persons as Hiss, Remington, and Lattimore; a sense of the unconsummated hangs over all these trials. Hence, there remains in this country an enormous anxiety on the subject of Communism, which is admittedly not a menace in any practical internal sense. This anxiety is a response not only to an external

military danger but to this experience of bafflement in dealing with
the underground man, the fair-faced conspirator—Hamlet's emotion toward Claudius, who could smile and smile and be a villain
still. Like Hamlet, faced with this depthless possibility, we turn to
making mousetraps to catch the conscience of the king, the usurper
of the liberal succession.

Every amateur endeavors to become a specialist in the detec-
tion of Communism. The ideas expressed by an individual become
suspect, not in themselves but as clues to a hidden involvement.
Certain constellations of ideas are automatically suspicious: a
person who favors racial equality, say, plus progressive education,
plus peace, minus Senator McCarthy and the McCarran Act, minus
teachers' oaths, is regarded as a poor security risk, not only by the
government, not only by his acquaintances and employers, but even
by himself. He must try either to suppress some of these clues or
to produce a counter-clue. A denunciation of Stalinism used to be
thought sufficient, but nowadays in some quarters it is not enough.
Something more positive is asked for: approval of Chiang or of the
"work" of the McCarran Committee; otherwise you may be labeled
as "objectively" pro-Communist, whatever your subjective beliefs.
Such guarantees of "objective" solidarity are demanded not only by
the extreme right but by the so-called left. In order to perform or
work for the Columbia Broadcasting System you have to sign a loyalty oath which is presented with your contract, while in the circle
of Carey McWilliams and the *Nation* you are required to believe
in Lattimore's total injured innocence if you are to escape being
detected as a McCarthyite. In other circles, approval of progressive
education or a belief in cultural anthropology or in the Sullivan
school of psychiatry or in the abstract school of American painting
is mandatory if you do not wish to admit that you are a reactionary.
In some places, on the opposite side of the fence, the idea that Louis
Budenz is a saint is an article of faith.

These are private forms of the loyalty oath prescribed in the
cultural sphere: you have to be "cleared" culturally to work with
various groups. If you are a doctor practicing in a Catholic hospital

in Poughkeepsie, you must furnish guarantees that you are not associated with a birth-control organization; this is, succinctly, a demand for loyalty. You will have difficulty entering the country if at any time you belonged to a subversive organization, never mind what your opinions are now. If you wish a passport to travel abroad, your trip must be deemed "in the best interests of the United States." Hence, if a citizen cannot show a total and positive belongingness, he may be subject, without trial, to what amounts to house arrest within the territory of the United States. This happened to Corliss Lamont and Paul Robeson and may happen to anyone. When Secretary Wallace, an official of the government, was making speeches in England that Secretary Forrestal did not like, Forrestal recommended that his passport be withdrawn. Those who criticize such procedures are told that no citizen has a Constitutional right to a passport, just as no doctor has a Constitutional right to practice in a Poughkeepsie hospital. Undoubtedly; but it is not an issue of rights but of what is desirable in an open society.

The evil done by the passport policy and by exclusions and detentions under the McCarran Act is not only specific but pervasive. Apologists for the American Way of Life find themselves condoning injustices, defensively, lest they seem to be giving aid to Communism, while various groups are encouraged by government precedent to exact total conformity on their own.

I recently talked to a man, an anti-Communist demi-intellectual, who had been nine months getting cleared by the government because through some bureaucratic error he had been listed as a former Communist Party member. This person, far from deploring what had happened to him, positively welcomed it. "I am glad to suffer," he said piously, "if our society can be safe." He did not dare resent even in his soul this concrete injustice lest he fall into the mortal sin of being "objectively" pro-Communist. Such a person, when pressed, will admit that there is no internal Communist menace now, but will express great fears of the "softness" of the American mentality, which lies open to decay, like a carious sweet tooth. In the course of our conversation, he expressed the thought that *The New Yorker* ought to be investigated by Congress, not because it was subversive but because it was "soft."

The idea of a society, stern, resolute, dedicated, hard, has made tremendous headway with certain intellectuals and demi-intellectuals, particularly of the ex-fellow-traveler and ex-party-member type. They see the mass of ordinary people, who fortunately at this moment do not share these fears and obsessions and retain a sense of proportion, as so much damp plasticine to be molded into a harder form through constant indoctrination. These so-called "experts" have carried with them into the democratic camp the emergency mentality of totalitarianism, like a germ in its dormant phase that has incubated in the fetid atmosphere of the world crisis. For these people, cultural freedom, in the sense of the genuine freedom of individuals, must be deferred until some future date when everybody will be in total agreement; on that date, it can be afforded. It is such people, sad to say, in a new *trahison des clercs*, who threaten cultural freedom from within as they make common cause with the enemy from without—with Senator McCarthy, Senator McCarran, *Counterattack*, *Red Channels*, and all those who demand a clean bill of health, a sterile biography. They make this alliance, sometimes with repugnance, sometimes with an air of sorrow, but sternly, as good citizens, pointing always, in justification, to the cases of Hiss and Judith Coplon and Remington and the Rosenbergs, who have made the alliance "necessary."

Yet it is just such real conspirators who generally present aseptic biographies and who elude all our attempts to elicit the truth from them by confrontation and material evidence. If we execute the Rosenbergs, we still will not have their confessions. We can punish them for their overt actions, but they will retain the secret of their thoughts and motives, remaining to the last a quiet ordinary Bronx couple, keeping themselves to themselves. What we will do, however, if we persist in our demands for loyalty, a positive citizenship, testimonials, confessions of error, in the investigative methods of McCarthy and McCarran, will be to create new underground men behind the façade of conformity, new lies, new evasions, new human beings who float like glittering icebergs on the surface of society, with the perilous eight-ninths submerged. We will live in a society of surfaces, where papers and books circulate freely, like so many phantom abstractions, while their human authors and readers have been suppressed or excluded from the country.

This article is based on a speech given by the author at the American Committee for Cultural Freedom conference in March, 1952.

The Contagion of Ideas

Summer, 1952

THE DECLARATION OF INDPENDENCE speaks of certain unalienable rights given to Man by God—the rights to life, liberty, and the pursuit of happiness. Yet nothing is clearer than that these rights are far from unalienable. They can be taken from a man by other men; they can be surrendered by a whole people to the state; if they are to be preserved at all, the state, presumably, must secure them. In the days of the Founding Fathers, these rights had a certain sacred character that flowed from a belief in God; they were hallowed in the individual by the supposed intention of the Creator and were hardly to be distinguished from the sacredness of life itself. God meant man to be free, paradoxically, to obey his conscience; indeed, man's freedom imposed on him the *duty* of obeying the inner voice, in defiance, if necessary, of law and common opinion.

Today, in a secular society that no longer believes in God, we retain a lip-belief in the doctrine of inherent rights without knowing what we mean by them or where they are supposed to come from. In practice, we look to the state as the source of rights and the patenter of new rights that have suddenly come to light—the right to teach, the right to a government job, and so on, though it is evident that no one has the right to teach inherent in him as a human being. But when we look to the state as the source of rights, these rights lose their sacred character and become mere privileges which the state can withdraw at any time from individuals or groups that displease it. This is the situation of the Communists in the United States today; their liberty is looked upon by the public as a privilege accorded them by the government that they have misused and that therefore ought to be taken away from them. Liberty, as it is conceived by current opinion, has nothing inherent about it; it is a sort of gift or trust bestowed on the individual by the state pending *good behavior*. We see this notion applied not only to Communists but to racketeers like Frank Costello and Erickson, who are deprived of their freedom to remain silent before Congressional committees; their Constitutional rights are suspended, as long as they remain uncooperative. Thus a Communist is free to testify to his party-associations; Costello is free to testify to his illegal gambling transactions; but neither is free to be silent. In the same way, other, more parvenu rights fade overnight into privileges—the right to strike, for example, or the right to teach in the public schools turns out to depend on the teacher's or the trade union's "good behavior," i.e., on political criteria. In short, these so-called rights are not, realistically speaking, rights at all but resemble, rather, licenses, like hunting licenses, licenses to carry firearms, or driving licenses, which keep having to be renewed and are subject to all sorts of restrictions and limitations. This is very clear in the case of a passport: nobody, it is claimed, has a right to a passport inherent in him as a citizen, and if this right does not exist, then a passport becomes simply a travel permit which can be canceled for infractions of discipline, exactly like a license to drive.

Once the state is looked upon as the *source* of rights, rather than their bound protector, freedom becomes conditional on the pleasure of the state. You may say that in practice this has always been true and always will be: the state has always decided how much freedom shall be had and by whom. Yet the difference between a democracy and a tyranny or despotism is that in theory the citizen of a democracy possesses inherent rights, and this theory becomes the working hypothesis, i.e., the practice of a democratic state. However, without a belief in a Creator as the divine provider of rights, the theory tends to shift and to be stood, even, on its head, i.e., to turn into a doctrine of privileges vested in the state and dealt out by it to citizens who can prove their worthiness to enjoy them. That is what is happening today; rights and privileges have become so confused that to talk of rights at all is to invite a demonstration that there are none, for every right can be shown to be contingent and not absolute. If you argue today's vexed cases in terms of rights, you will lose the argument every time, strangely enough, to advocates of "freedom." Nobody, they will tell you, has a right to a Hollywood swimming pool, nobody has a right to perform on television or the radio, nobody has a right to a government job, nobody has a right to a passport, nobody has a right to teach in a public school, nobody has a right to conspire against the government. Conversely, a Hollywood screen-producer has a right to fire whom he chooses, radio and television companies have a right to be responsible to their advertisers, and the advertisers have a right to be responsible to the public, and the public has a right to complain of Communist performers on the air; a school board has the right to refuse to allow subversives to teach the children in its care; the government has the right to keep Communists out of its services, to refuse passports to citizens according to its own judgment, to revoke visas of entry, and in general to withhold the rights of citizenship from those who would take them from others. Agreed, but what exactly are these "rights" we are speaking of? Closely examined, they seem to be not rights but powers. What is meant is that nobody has the power to keep the government from denying a passport or to keep an employer from firing a Communist, to prevent a school board from screening the teachers it selects for its children; and, conversely, no schoolteacher or radio-performer has, in himself, the power to retain his job. Powers, once they have been weakened, cease to be thought of as rights, or a right, on the defensive, is an enfeebled power. Take the right of an employer to hire and fire; this right, once universally recognized and seemingly, almost, a "natural" right, now exists chiefly in small business and in households, where no union power is massed to limit it; similarly, the "right to work," which a few years ago meant the right to a job, now has shifted to mean the right of a worker *not* to belong to a union and is really the old employer's right to hire and fire presented in a proletarian disguise. Rights which appear natural and unquestioned take on a highly unnatural look when the power that bred them wanes. I might like to assert the right of a Communist to perform on the radio, but I lack the power to implement it, a power that could only be created by a *demand* for Communists on the air. Since there is not likely soon to be a demand for Communists, on the air, or in the schools, or in the government service, it becomes rather futile to urge their "right" to be employed in these fields. In default of a real demand, can a synthetic one be improvised, in the interests of pluralism? Is a university president with liberal ideas obligated by his principles to hire a token Communist on his faculty—in fairness to minorities? Should a breakfast-food company be obliged to keep a Communist artiste on its payroll, to show that it does not discriminate? No. Communism is not a commodity that we can force entrepreneurs to stock. When the argument is put in this way, scarcely anyone today would defend the right of a Communist, qua Communist, to a job in entertainment or education. Where the problem really presents itself is not in terms of general propositions but in specific cases. For example, should Paul Robeson be allowed to sing on the radio? Here it is easy for the liberal to answer yes, the more so since there is a real demand for Robeson as a singer. And the question for the university president is not whether he should hire new Communists in order to prove himself a liberal, but whether he should get rid of the ones he already has on his staff. Here again, the answer is not difficult. Most liberal college presidents would object to firing a teacher simply because he was a Communist, though few would be likely to insist, in public, on the college's "right" to keep him. The usual course is to deny that the teacher concerned is a Communist, thus avoiding the whole question of the "right to teach," since this right, openly invoked, will be disputed and the college will probably lose its right, i.e., its power, to harbor him.

To my mind, this situation would be greatly clarified if we thought, not just in terms of rights, but of goods, if we endeavored to treat individuals not in terms of what was owing to them by society or the state, but in terms of what an open society owed to its own image. If we thought of liberty not only as a right but as a good, we would be more hesitant to deprive people of it than we are when we think of it as a privilege or license within the bestowal of the state. If liberty is a good, a primary, axiomatic good, then the more that can be had of it, the better, and we should tend, even in situations of danger, to think of maximums rather than minimums. When weighing such questions as that of the right to a passport or of the right to Communists to teach or even of Frank Costello not to testify, we would ask ourselves how much liberty our free society ought to extend, if it is to live up to its name, rather than how much liberty was owing to this or that individual. Advocates of the curtailment of liberties tend to reason in broad scholastic syllogisms; they seldom feel it necessary to show, concretely, how the exercise of a given liberty will endanger the body politic. The Communist conspiracy, in theory, menaces the internal security of the United States; therefore, it is reasoned, every Communist is a dangerous conspirator, potentially, and must be treated as though he were one in fact. The case of Dr. Fuchs, a *secret* Communist sympathizer, who transmitted atomic information, is used as an argument for jailing *open* Communists, who would never, in any case, be employed on an atomic energy project. Or it is maintained that though the Communists are not an internal danger now, they would be dutybound, in wartime, to disrupt the armed services and sabotage defense industries; what is overlooked in this chain of reasoning is that we *are* at war with Communist forces in Korea, and yet Harry Bridges' powerful West Coast maritime union, admittedly Communist-dominated, has been unable to halt a single shipment of war materials to the battlefront.

To argue these questions on theoretical grounds is to lose sight of common sense—the common sense which, after all, is the rationale of a democracy; a belief in common sense is the informing spirit of all democratic institutions, from the jury system to universal suffrage. No emergency can justify the national suspension of common sense, yet just that is being urged on us as a necessary measure to cope with Communism. We are told, for instance, that Communists' minds are not free and that therefore they are not "fit" to be teachers, but no attempt is made to show this on a common-sense level or to indicate, in contrast, for that matter, what minds are free. The same argument could be used against permitting Catholics to teach. I myself would think it a poor idea to have our schools staffed by large numbers of Communists, but nobody is proposing that. The question is whether, in our energetically anti-Communist society, it is worthwhile to construct a whole apparatus of repression to stamp out the few Communist teachers who have managed to survive in our school systems. Those who would say yes would pretend that the infection of a single school child's mind ought to be avoided, for moral reasons, at the cost of a whole society. But this is the purest scholasticism. In the thirties, when the Communists were a genuine power in the intellectual world, we liberals thought it our duty to expose them in the schools and colleges where they pontificated. I do not think we were wrong, but I think we are wrong today if we fail to acknowledge that the situation has changed and that the student today, far from being in danger of being indoctrinated by Communism, is in danger of being stupefied by the complacent propaganda for democracy that accompanies him to school, follows him through school, goes home with him, speaks to him in the movies and on television, and purrs him to sleep from the radio. The strange thing is that this current indoctrination for democracy has very much the same tone—pious, priggish, groupy—that we objected to in the Stalinism of the popular-front period.

Advocates of "realism" (as opposed to "idealism") in the treatment of Communists seem bent on ignoring the realities of the current situation. Those who, like Sidney Hook, advocate the refusal of teaching jobs to avowed Communists while insisting that mere fellow-travelers should have the right to teach, are courting the very result they deprecate—the growth of an underground Communism that does not acknowledge its name. Clearly, it would be more sensible to ban fellow-travelers from the schools while allowing avowed Communists, under that label, to have their representative say. In my academic experience, the fellow-traveler is far more insidious to deal with than the Party member, for the fellow-traveler invariably calls himself a "liberal" and points to some small difference he maintains with official Marxism to certify his claim to that title; students are frequently taken in by him, to the point where they become fellow-travelers themselves while imagining that they are liberals or else conceive a lasting repulsion for what they suppose to be liberal attitudes. When a science instructor recently left her job at a woman's college, the housekeeper found her Party card in her bedroom safe; no one had ever suspected her of Communism because she had never expressed any political views, though there were a number of vocal fellow-travelers on the faculty, which was considered very "pink." Now a policy that would guard students from this woman's influence while permitting fellow-travelers to teach has only one merit: that of bureaucratic simplicity. It is easier, from an administrative point of view, to clean out "card-carrying" Communists, whose names are known to the FBI, than to draw a line between a fellow-traveler and a liberal. And it might be easier, then, to fire all liberals, to avoid making mistakes. Easiest of all, finally, would be to use machines to teach—a solution not so remote as it sounds.

There is a great deal of talk today about the "dilemma" confronting the liberal. He must choose, it is said, between his traditional notions of freedom and the survival of the free world. This dilemma is totally spurious—the invention of illiberal people. If there were a strong Communist Party in America, allied to the Soviet Union, the choice for the liberal might be painful, as it might have been had there been a strong Fascist Party allied to the Nazis during the last war. As it is, the liberal's only problem is to avoid succumbing to the illusion of "having to choose."

To heighten this illusion, which common sense rejects, the strength of the Communists is claimed to lie not in their numbers but somewhere else, somewhere less evident to the ordinary, uninitiated person. The initiated anti-Communists subscribe to a doctrine that one might call Gresham's Law as transferred to the field of ideas—the notion that bad ideas drive out good. According to this notion, Communism is an idea that is peculiarly contagious. The Communists may be few in number, but their ideas are felt to have a mysterious potency that other ideas do not possess. Nobody contends, for instance, that Communist teachers constitute a majority or even a considerable minority in our schools. Nor does anybody point to a single primary school child who has been indoctrinated with Communism or suggest how, even in theory, such indoctrination might be accomplished. No; it is enough to show that a primary school teacher belongs or has belonged to a subversive organization; from this, I quote, arises "the danger of infection," as if Communism were a sort of airborne virus that could be wafted from a teacher to her pupils, without anybody's seeing it and even though the whole hygiene of school and family and civic life today was such, one would think, as to sterilize the child against such "germs."

Everyone who has had any experience of teaching knows how difficult it is to indoctrinate a pupil with anything—with the use of algebraic symbols, the rules of punctuation, the dates of American history; yet a Communist teacher, presumably, can "infect" *her* pupils with Marxism-Leninism-Stalinism by, to quote one writer, "the tone of her voice." She is able, moreover, to cite another popular image, to "plant the seeds" of Communism, undetected by parents or school superintendents or principals or fellow-teachers; she does it "by suggestion." The inference is that a single Communist teacher has more persuasion in her little finger than a school system consisting of ninety-nine others has in its whole organized body, more persuasion than all the forces of radio, movies, television, and comic books combined.

Yet no one, as I say, has produced (so far as I know) a single case history of a primary school child in the United States who has been indoctrinated with Communism. "Tragic cases," however, are often alluded to of somewhat older young people whose lives have been ruined by being exposed to a Communist teacher or professor. There may have been a few such cases in the thirties, tragic or not, yet we

do not hear that such well-known figures as Hiss or Chambers or
Remington or Elizabeth Bentley "got that way" because of a teacher.
The most Elizabeth Bentley can say, in her autobiography, is that at
Vassar she was exposed to godless and atheistic influences that softened her up for Communism. But to save the soul of one Elizabeth
Bentley, or a dozen, should all non-believing teachers be eliminated
from our colleges? The direct "causation" of Communism cannot
be established, but surely a large number of Communists, present and ex-, would claim that they became so in reaction against
their conservative parents and teachers; the revolutionary as rebel
against authority is a familiar psychological cliché. Then should
conservative teachers be eliminated?

The truth is that most young people who became Communists
in the United States in the thirties and early forties did so either in
response to the misery of the depression or in response to the threat
of fascism as exemplified by Hitler. The few in this country who
become Communists today probably do so in the mistaken hope
that Communism offers protection against a third world catastro-
phe: war. It is not a question, really, of the contagion of ideas but
of a relation that is felt to exist between certain ideas and an actual
situation, to which the ideas seem applicable. When an anti-Communist argues that Communist ideas are highly contagious and that
mere contact with a Communist is therefore dangerous for a school
child or student, he is making an implicit confession. He is admit-
ting to the fear that Communist ideas are catching, not just because
they are "bad" and tend to drive out "good" ideas, but because they
have a more evident correspondence with the realities of social
inequity than he suspects his own ideas have. If Communist ideas
are contagious or, rather, if we feel uneasily that they are, is not this
precisely because they contain a "germ" of truth? We can laugh at
Soviet "equality," Soviet "justice," Soviet "economic democracy," but
only in the Soviet context; in France, Italy, China, Indonesia, the
American South, these words have the power to shame us. We are
afraid of export Communism, though not of the Soviet domestic
article, because our own export, democracy, is competing under

the same labels, and we know that our own capitalist society to a Chinese peasant or a Sicilian peasant or even an American Negro might appear even more unjust and unequal than the Soviet product.

The fear and hatred of Communism expressed in America today is not just a revulsion from the crimes of Stalin, from the deportation camps and forced labor and frame-up trials; it is also a fear and hatred of the original ideals of Communism. In a certain sense, the crimes of Stalin come as welcome news to America: they are taken as proof that socialism does not "work." Inequality, we would like to believe, is a law of nature, and by "we" I do not mean only wealthy businessmen or blackguards like Senator McCarthy or Southern racists. As the richest nation in the world, we have developed the psychology of rich people: we are afraid of poverty, of "agitators," of any jarring notes in the national harmony. The behavior of our local Communists outrages our sense of majesty, while abroad, all over the globe, our Congressmen are filling satchels with instances of foreign ingratitude. Like all rich people, we feel we are not appreciated, and we suffer from ideas of reference; if anybody speaks about "privilege" or "exploitation," we think they must mean us; if we see a film in which the poor are good and the rich are bad, we wonder whether it is not Communist-inspired. We do not like to hear attacks on segregation, on the use of the atomic bomb, on NATO, unless we are sure that the person talking is "on our side."

It is this guilty fear of criticism, at bottom, this sense of being surrounded by an unappreciative world, that is the source of our demands for loyalty, from teachers, from public performers, from veterans getting subsidized housing, from all those, in short, whom we regard as our pensioners. Certainly, the administration of loyalty oaths, like a mass vaccination against Communism, does not make any practical sense. And if we are particularly sensitive about our schools, it is because we fear that children, with their natural lack of bias, their detached and innocent faculty of observation, will be all too ready to prick up their ears if they hear our society criticized, even implicitly, in the "tone" of a teacher's voice. Our children, we feel, may listen to *her* more than they will listen to us, because they have already noticed the injustices of our society and want to know the why of it, instead of being told that "God made it that way." People with bad consciences always fear the judgment of children.

We did not behave this way toward fascists and fascist sympathizers during the war. We did not make a national effort to root them out of our schools and colleges or demand that they take loyalty oaths; on the whole, we did nothing to disturb them or to prevent the spread of their ideas. This was not because we found their doctrines more tolerable than we find the doctrines of Communism. On the contrary. Their ideas seemed to us so crazy and disgusting that we could not imagine anybody's being taken in by them, though in fact some people were. But this was, as we used to call it, the "lunatic fringe." The proof that we do not regard Communists as lunatics is precisely this fear we have that their ideas may be catching, this fear, as I say, of the "germ" of truth. And this germ phobia will be with us as long as we ourselves try to sell the white lie of democracy abroad, to the starving nations who in fact are the "children"—the ignorant and uneducated—whose allegiance we question, rightly, and whose judgment of us we, rightly, dread.

This was a speech delivered to a group of teachers.

Artists in Uniform

March, 1953

The Colonel went out sailing,
He spoke with Turk and Jew...

"POUR IT ON, COLONEL," cried the young man in the Dacron suit excitedly, making his first sortie into the club-car conversation. His face was white as Roquefort and of a glistening, cheeselike texture; he had a shock of tow-colored hair, badly cut and greasy, and a snub nose with large gray pores. Under his darting eyes were two black craters. He appeared to be under some intense nervous strain and had sat the night before in the club car drinking bourbon with beer chasers and leafing through magazines which he frowningly tossed aside, like cards into a discard heap. This morning he had come in late, with a hangdog, hangover look, and had been sitting tensely forward on a settee, smoking cigarettes and following the conversation with little twitches of the nose and quivers of the body, as a dog follows a human conversation, veering its mistrustful eyeballs from one speaker to another and raising its head eagerly at its master's voice. The colonel's voice, rich and light and plausible, had in fact abruptly risen and swollen, as he pronounced his last sentence. "I can tell you one thing," he had said harshly. "They weren't named Ryan or Murphy!"

A sort of sigh, as of consummation, ran through the club car. "Pour it on, Colonel, give it to them, Colonel, that's right, Colonel," urged the young man in a transport of admiration. The colonel fingered his collar and modestly smiled. He was a thin, hawklike,

black-haired handsome man with a bright blue bloodshot eye and a
well-pressed, well-tailored uniform that did not show the effects of
the heat—the train, westbound for St. Louis, was passing through
Indiana, and, as usual in a heat wave, the air-conditioning had not
met the test. He wore the Air Force insignia, and there was something in his light-boned, spruce figure and keen, knifelike profile
that suggested a classic image of the aviator, ready to cut, piercing,
into space. In base fact, however, the colonel was in procurement,
as we heard him tell the mining engineer who had just bought him
a drink. From several silken hints that parachuted into the talk, it
was patent to us that the colonel was a man who knew how to enjoy
this earth and its pleasures: he led, he gave us to think, a bachelor's life of abstemious dissipation and well-rounded sensuality. He
had accepted the engineer's drink with a mere nod of the glass in
acknowledgment, like a genial Mars quaffing a libation; there was
clearly no prospect of his buying a second in return, not if the train
were to travel from here to the Mojave Desert. In the same way,
an understanding had arisen that I, the only woman in the club
car, had become the colonel's perquisite; it was taken for granted,
without an invitation's being issued, that I was to lunch with him in
St. Louis, where we each had a wait between trains—my plans for
seeing the city in a taxicab were dished.

From the beginning, as we eyed each other over my volume of
Dickens ("*The Christmas Carol*?" suggested the colonel, opening
relations), I had guessed that the colonel was of Irish stock, and
this, I felt, gave me an advantage, for he did not suspect the same
of me; strangely so, for I am supposed to have the map of Ireland
written on my features. In fact, he had just wagered, with a jaunty,
sidelong grin at the mining engineer, that my people "came from
Boston from way back," and that I—narrowed glance, running, like
steel measuring-tape, up and down my form—was a professional
sculptress. I might have laughed this off, as a crudely bad guess like
his *Christmas Carol*, if I had not seen the engineer nodding gravely,
like an idol, and the peculiar young man bobbing his head up and
down in mute applause and agreement. I was wearing a bright

apple-green raw silk blouse and a dark-green rather full raw silk skirt, plus a pair of pink glass earrings; my hair was done up in a bun. It came to me, for the first time, with a sort of dawning horror, that I had begun, in the course of years, without ever guessing it, to look irrevocably Bohemian. Refracted from the three men's eyes was a strange vision of myself as an artist, through and through, stained with my occupation like the dyer's hand. All I lacked, apparently, was a pair of sandals. My sick heart sank to my Ferragamo shoes; I had always particularly preened myself on being an artist in disguise. And it was not only a question of personal vanity—it seemed to me that the writer or intellectual had a certain missionary usefulness in just such accidental gatherings as this, if he spoke not as an intellectual but as a normal member of the public. Now, thanks to the colonel, I slowly became aware that my contributions to the club-car conversation were being watched and assessed as coming from *a certain quarter*. My costume, it seemed, carefully assembled as it had been at an expensive shop, was to these observers simply a uniform that blazoned a caste and allegiance just as plainly as the colonel's khaki and eagles. "*Gardez*," I said to myself. But, as the conversation grew tenser and I endeavored to keep cool, I began to writhe within myself, and every time I looked down, my contrasting greens seemed to be growing more and more lurid and taking on an almost menacing light, like leaves just before a storm that lift their bright undersides as the air becomes darker. We had been speaking, of course, of Russia, and I had mentioned a study that had been made at Harvard of political attitudes among Iron Curtain refugees. Suddenly, the colonel had smiled. "They're pretty Red at Harvard, I'm given to understand," he observed in a comfortable tone, while the young man twitched and quivered urgently. The eyes of all the men settled on me and waited. I flushed as I saw myself reflected. The woodland greens of my dress were turning to their complementary red, like a color-experiment in psychology or a traffic light changing. Down at the other end of the club car, a man looked up from his paper. I pulled myself together. "Set your mind at rest, Colonel," I remarked dryly. "I know Harvard very well and they're conservative to the point of dullness. The only thing crimson is the football team." This disparagement had its effect. "So…?" queried the colonel. "I thought there was some professor…" I shook my head. "Absolutely not. There used to be a few fellow-travelers, but they're very quiet these days, when they haven't absolutely recanted. The general atmosphere is more anti-Communist than the Vatican." The colonel and the mining engineer exchanged a thoughtful stare and seemed to agree that the Delphic oracle that had just pronounced knew whereof it spoke. "Glad to hear it," said the colonel. The engineer frowned and shook his fat wattles; he was a stately, gray-haired, plump man with small hands and feet and the pampered, finical tidiness of a small-town widow. "There's so much hearsay these days," he exclaimed vexedly. "You don't know *what* to believe."

I reopened my book with an air of having closed the subject and read a paragraph three times over. I exulted to think that I had made a modest contribution to sanity in our times, and I imagined my words pyramiding like a chain letter—the colonel telling a fellow-officer on the veranda of a club in Texas, the engineer halting a works-superintendent in a Colorado mine shaft: "I met a woman on the train who claims… Yes, absolutely…" Of course, I did not know Harvard as thoroughly as I pretended, but I forgave myself by thinking it was the convention of such club-car symposia in our positivistic country to speak from the horse's mouth.

Meanwhile, across the aisle, the engineer and the colonel continued their talk in slightly lowered voices. From time to time, the colonel's polished index-fingernail scratched his burnished black head and his knowing blue eye forayed occasionally toward me. I saw that still I was a doubtful quantity to them, a movement in the bushes, a noise, a flicker, that was figuring in their crenelated thought as "she." The subject of Reds in our colleges had not, alas, been finished; they were speaking now of another university and a woman faculty-member who had been issuing Communist statements. This story somehow, I thought angrily, had managed to appear in the newspapers without my knowledge, while these men were conversant with it; I recognized a big chink in the armor of my authority. Looking up from my book, I began to question them sharply, as though they were reporting some unheard-of natural phenomenon. "When?" I demanded. "Where did you see it? What was her name?" This request for the professor's name was a head-long attempt on my part to buttress my position, the implication being that the identities of all university professors were known to me and that if I were but given the name I could promptly clarify the matter. To admit that there was a single Communist in our academic system whose activities were hidden from me imperiled, I instinctively felt, all the small good I had done here. Moreover, in the back of my mind, I had a supreme confidence that these men were wrong: the story, I supposed, was some tattered piece of misinformation they had picked up from a gossip column. Pride, as usual, preceded my fall. To the colonel, the demand for the name was not specific but generic: what *kind* of name was the question he presumed me to be asking. "Oh," he said slowly with a luxurious yawn, "Finkelstein or Fishbein or Feinstein." He lolled back in his seat with a side glance at the engineer, who deeply nodded. There was a voluptuary pause, as the implication sank in. I bit my lip, regarding this as a mere diversionary tactic. "Please!" I said impatiently. "Can't you remember exactly?" The colonel shook his head and then his spare cheekbones suddenly reddened and he looked directly at me. "I can tell you one thing," he exclaimed irefully. "They weren't named Ryan or Murphy."

The colonel went no further; it was quite unnecessary. In an instant, the young man was at his side, yapping excitedly and actually picking at the military sleeve. The poor thing was transformed, like some creature in a fairy tale whom a magic word releases from silence. "That's right, Colonel," he happily repeated. "I know them. *I* was at Harvard in the business school, studying accountancy. I left. I couldn't take it." He threw a poisonous glance at me, and the colonel, who had been regarding him somewhat doubtfully, now put on an alert expression and inclined an ear for his confidences. The

man at the other end of the car folded his newspaper solemnly and
took a seat by the young man's side. "They're all Reds, Colonel," said
the young man. "They teach it in the classroom. I came back here to
Missouri. It made me sick to listen to the stuff they handed out. If
you didn't hand it back, they flunked you. Don't let anybody tell you
different." "You are wrong," I said coldly and closed my book and
rose. The young man was still talking eagerly, and the three men
were leaning forward to catch his every gasping word, like three
astute detectives over a dying informer, when I reached the door
and cast a last look over my shoulder at them. For an instant, the
colonel's eye met mine and I felt his scrutiny processing my green
back as I tugged open the door and met a blast of hot air, blowing
my full skirt wide. Behind me, in my fancy, I saw four sets of shrug-
ging brows.

In my own car, I sat down, opposite two fat nuns, and tried to
assemble my thoughts. I ought to have spoken, I felt, and yet what
could I have said? It occurred to me that the four men had perhaps
not realized why I had left the club car with such abruptness: was
it possible that they thought I was a Communist, who feared to be
unmasked? I spurned this possibility, and yet it made me uneasy.
For some reason, it troubled my *amour-propre* to think of my
anti-Communist self living on, so to speak, green in their collective
memory as a Communist or fellow-traveler. In fact, though I did
not give a fig for the men, I hated the idea, while a few years ago
I should have counted it a great joke. This, it seemed to me, was a
measure of the change in the social climate. I had always scoffed
at the notion of liberals "living in fear" of political demagoguery
in America, but now I had to admit that if I was not fearful I was
at least uncomfortable in the supposition that anybody, anybody
whatever, could think of me, precious me, as a Communist. A
remoter possibility was, of course, that back there my departure
was being ascribed to Jewishness, and this too annoyed me. I am in
fact a quarter Jewish, and though I did not "hate" the idea of being
taken for a Jew, I did not precisely like it, particularly under these
circumstances. I wished it to be clear that I had left the club car for

intellectual and principled reasons; I wanted those men to know that it was not I, but my principles, that had been offended. To let them conjecture that I had left because I was Jewish would imply that only a Jew could be affronted by an anti-Semitic outburst; a terrible idea. Aside from anything else, it voided the whole concept of transcendence, which was very close to my heart, the concept that man is more than his circumstances, more even than himself.

However you looked at the episode, I said to myself nervously, I had not acquitted myself well. I ought to have done or said something concrete and unmistakable. From this, I slid glassily to the thought that those men ought to be punished, the colonel, in particular, who occupied a responsible position. In a minute, I was framing a businesslike letter to the Chief of Staff, deploring the colonel's conduct as unbecoming to an officer and identifying him by rank and post, since unfortunately I did not know his name. Earlier in the conversation, he had passed some comments on "Harry" that bordered positively on treason, I said to myself triumphantly. A vivid image of the proceedings against him presented itself to my imagination: the long military tribunal with a row of stern soldierly faces glaring down at the colonel. I myself occupied only an inconspicuous corner of this tableau, for, to tell the truth, I did not relish the role of the witness. Perhaps it would be wiser to let the matter drop...? We were nearing St. Louis now; the colonel had come back into my car, and the young accountant had followed him, still talking feverishly. I pretended not to see them and turned to the two nuns, as if for sanctuary from this world and its hatred and revenges. Out of the corner of my eye, I watched the colonel, who now looked wry and restless; he shrank against the window as the young man made a place for himself amid the colonel's smart luggage and continued to express his views in a pale breathless voice. I smiled to think that the colonel was paying the piper. For the colonel, anti-Semitism was simply an aspect of urbanity, like a knowledge of hotels or women. This frantic psychopath of an accountant was serving him as a nemesis, just as the German people had been served by their psychopath, Hitler. Colonel, I adjured him, you have chosen, between him and me; measure the depth of your error and make the best of it! No intervention on my part was now necessary; justice had been meted out. Nevertheless, my heart was still throbbing violently, as if I were on the verge of some dangerous action. What was I to do, I kept asking myself, as I chatted with the nuns, if the colonel were to hold me to that lunch? And I slowly and apprehensively revolved this question, just as though it were a matter of the most serious import. It seemed to me that if I did not lunch with him—and I had no intention of doing so—I had the dreadful obligation of telling him why.

He was waiting for me as I descended the car steps. "Aren't you coming to lunch with me?" he called out and moved up to take my elbow. I began to tremble with audacity. "No," I said firmly, picking up my suitcase and draping an olive-green linen duster over my arm. "I can't lunch with you." He quirked a wiry black eyebrow. "Why not?" he said. "I understood it was all arranged." He reached for my suitcase. "No," I said, holding on to the suitcase. "I can't." I took a deep breath. "I have to tell you. I think you should be *ashamed* of yourself, Colonel, for what you said in the club car." The colonel stared: I mechanically waved for a redcap, who took my bag and coat and went off. The colonel and I stood facing each other on the emptying platform. "What do you mean?" he inquired in a low, almost clandestine tone. "Those anti-Semitic remarks," I muttered, resolutely. "You ought to be *ashamed*." The colonel gave a quick, relieved laugh. "Oh, come now," he protested. "I'm sorry," I said. "I can't have lunch with anybody who feels that way about the Jews." The colonel put down his attaché case and scratched the back of his lean neck. "Oh, come now," he repeated, with a look of amusement. "You're not Jewish, are you?" "No," I said quickly. "Well, then…" said the colonel, spreading his hands in a gesture of bafflement. I saw that he was truly surprised and slightly hurt by my criticism, and this made me feel wretchedly embarrassed and even apologetic, on my side, as though I had called attention to some physical defect in him, of which he himself was unconscious. "But I might have been," I stammered. "You had no way of knowing. You oughtn't to talk like that." I recognized, too late, that I was strangely reducing the whole matter to a question of etiquette: "Don't start anti-Semitic talk before making sure there are no Jews present." "Oh, hell," said the colonel, easily. "I can tell a Jew." "No, you can't," I retorted, thinking of my Jewish grandmother, for by Nazi criteria I was Jewish. "Of course I can," he insisted. "So can you." We had begun to walk down the platform side by side, disputing with a restrained passion that isolated us like a pair of lovers. All at once, the colonel halted, as though struck with a thought. "What *are* you, anyway?" he said meditatively, regarding my dark hair, green blouse, and pink earrings. Inside myself, I began to laugh. "Oh," I said gaily, playing out the trump I had been saving. "I'm Irish, like you, Colonel." "How did you know?" he said amazedly. I laughed aloud. "I can tell an Irishman," I taunted. The colonel frowned. "What's your family name?" he said brusquely. "McCarthy." He lifted an eyebrow, in defeat, and then quickly took note of my wedding ring. "That your maiden name?" I nodded. Under this peremptory questioning, I had the peculiar sensation that I get when I am lying; I began to feel that "McCarthy" was a nom de plume, a coinage of my artistic personality. But the colonel appeared to be satisfied. "Hell," he said, "come on to lunch, then. With a fine name like that, you and I should be friends." I still shook my head, though by this time we were pacing outside the station restaurant; my baggage had been checked in a locker; sweat was running down my face and I felt exhausted and hungry. I knew that I was weakening and I wanted only an excuse to yield and go inside with him. The colonel seemed to sense this. "Hell," he conceded. "You've got me wrong. I've nothing against the Jews. Back there in the club car, I was just stating a simple fact: you won't find an Irishman sounding off for the Commies. You can't deny that, can you?"

His voice rose persuasively; he took my arm. In the heat, I wilted and we went into the air-conditioned cocktail lounge. The colonel ordered two old-fashioneds. The room was dark as a cave and produced, in the midst of the hot midday, a hallucinated feeling, as though time had ceased, with the weather, and we were in eternity together. As the colonel prepared to relax, I made a tremendous effort to guide the conversation along rational, purposive lines; my only justification for being here would be to convert the colonel. "There *have* been Irishmen associated with the Communist party." I said suddenly, when the drinks came. "I can think of two." "Oh, hell," said the colonel, "every race and nation has its traitors. What I mean is, you won't find them in numbers. You've got to admit the Communists in this country are ninety per cent Jewish." "But the Jews in this country aren't ninety per cent Communist," I retorted.

As he stirred his drink, restively, I began to try to show him the reasons why the Communist movement in America had attracted such a large number, relatively, of Jews: how the Communists had been anti-Nazi when nobody else seemed to care what happened to the Jews in Germany; how the Communists still capitalized on a Jewish fear of fascism; how many Jews had become, after Buchenwald, traumatized by this fear...

But the colonel was scarcely listening. An impatient frown rested on his jaunty features. "I don't get it," he said slowly. "Why should you be for them, with a name like yours?" "I'm *not* for the Communists," I cried. "I'm just trying to explain to you—" "For the Jews," the colonel interrupted, irritable now himself. "I've heard of such people but I never met one before." "I'm not 'for' them," I protested. "You don't understand. I'm not for *any* race or nation. I'm against those who are against them." This word, *them*, with a sort of slurring circle drawn round it, was beginning to sound ugly to me. Automatically, in arguing with him, I seemed to have slipped into the colonel's style of thought. It occurred to me that defense of the Jews could be a subtle and safe form of anti-Semitism, an exercise of patronage: as a rational Gentile, one could feel superior both to the Jews and the anti-Semites. There could be no doubt that the Jewish question evoked a curious stealthy lust or concupiscence. I could feel it now vibrating between us over the dark table. If I had been a good person, I should unquestionably have got up and left.

"I don't get it," repeated the colonel. "How were you brought up? Were your people this way too?" It was manifest that an odd reversal had taken place; each of us regarded the other as "abnormal" and was attempting to understand the etiology of a disease. "Many of my people think just as you do," I said, smiling coldly. "It seems to be a sickness to which the Irish are prone. Perhaps it's due to the potato diet," I said sweetly, having divined that the colonel came from a social stratum somewhat lower than my own.

But the colonel's hide was tough. "You've got me wrong," he reiterated, with an almost plaintive laugh. "I don't dislike the Jews. I've got a lot of Jewish friends. Among themselves, they think just as I do, mark my words. I tell you what it is," he added ruminatively, with a thoughtful prod of his muddler, "I draw a distinction between a kike and a Jew." I groaned. "Colonel, I've never heard an anti-Semite who didn't draw that distinction. You know what Otto Kahn said? 'A kike is a Jewish gentleman who has just left the room.'" The colonel did not laugh. "I don't hold it against some of them," he persisted, in a tone of pensive justice. "It's not their fault if they were born that way. That's what I tell them, and they respect me for my honesty. I've had a lot of discussions; in procurement, you have to do business with them, and the Jews are the first to admit that you'll find more chiselers among their race than among the rest of mankind." "It's not a race," I interjected wearily, but the colonel pressed on. "If I deal with a Jewish manufacturer, I can't bank on his word. I've seen it again and again, every damned time. When I deal with a Gentile, I can trust him to make delivery as promised. That's the difference between the two races. They're just a different breed. They don't have standards of honesty, even among each other." I sighed, feeling unequal to arguing the colonel's personal experience.

"Look," I said, "you may be dealing with an industry where the Jewish manufacturers are the most recent comers and feel they have to cut corners to compete with the established firms. I've heard that said about Jewish cattle-dealers, who are supposed to be extra sharp. But what I think, really, is that you notice it when a Jewish firm fails to meet an agreement and don't notice it when it's a Yankee." "Hah," said the colonel. "They'll tell you what I'm telling you themselves, if you get to know them and go into their homes.

You won't believe it, but some of my best friends are Jews," he said, simply and thoughtfully, with an air of originality. "They may be *your* best friends, Colonel," I retorted, "but you are not theirs. I defy you to tell me that you talk to them as you're talking now." "Sure," said the Colonel, easily. "More or less." "They must be very queer Jews you know." I observed tartly, and I began to wonder whether there indeed existed a peculiar class of Jews whose function in life was to be "friends" with such people as the colonel. It was difficult to think that all the anti-Semites who made the colonel's assertion were the victims of a cruel self-deception.

A dispirited silence followed. I was not one of those liberals who believed that the Jews, alone among peoples, possessed no characteristics whatever of a distinguishing nature—this would mean they had no history and no culture, a charge which should be leveled against them only by an anti-Semite. Certainly, types of Jews could be noted and patterns of Jewish thought and feeling: Jewish humor, Jewish rationality, and so on, not that every Jew reflected every attribute of Jewish life or history. But somehow, with the colonel, I dared not concede that there was such a thing as a Jew: I saw the sad meaning of the assertion that a Jew was a person whom other people thought was Jewish.

Hopeless, however, to convey this to the colonel. The desolate truth was that the colonel was extremely stupid, and it came to me, as we sat there, glumly ordering lunch, that for extremely stupid people anti-Semitism was a form of intellectuality, the sole form of intellectuality of which they were capable. It represented, in a rudimentary way, the ability to make categories, to generalize. Hence a thing I had noted before but never understood: the fact that anti-Semitic statements were generally delivered in an atmosphere of profundity. Furrowed brows attended these speculative distinctions between a kike and a Jew, these little empirical laws that you can't know one without knowing them all. To arrive, indeed, at the idea of a Jew was, for these grouping minds, an exercise in Platonic thought, a discovery of essence, and to be able to add the great corollary, "Some of my best friends are Jews," was to find the philosopher's cleft between essence and existence. From this, it would seem, followed the querulous obstinacy with which the anti-Semite clung to his concept; to be deprived of this intellectual tool by missionaries of tolerance would be, for persons like the colonel, the equivalent of Western man's losing the syllogism: a lapse into animal darkness. In the club car, we had just witnessed an example: the colonel with his anti-Semitic observation had come to the mute young man like the paraclete, bearing the gift of tongues.

Here in the bar, it grew plainer and plainer that the colonel did not regard himself as an anti-Semite but merely as a heavy thinker. The idea that I considered him anti-Semitic sincerely outraged his feelings. "Prejudice" was the last trait he could have imputed to himself. He looked on me, almost respectfully, as a "Jew-lover," a kind of being he had heard of but never actually encountered, like a centaur or a Siamese twin, and the interest of relating this prodigy to the natural state of mankind overrode any personal distaste. There I sat, the exception which was "proving" or testing the rule, and he kept pressing me for details of my history that might explain my deviation in terms of the norm. On my side, of course, I had become fiercely resolved that he would learn nothing from me that would make it possible for him to dismiss my anti-anti-Semitism as the product of special circumstances: I was stubbornly sitting on the fact of my Jewish grandmother like a hen on a golden egg. I was bent on making *him* see himself as a monster, a deviation, a heretic from Church and State. Unfortunately, the colonel, owing perhaps to his military training, had not the glimmering of an idea of what democracy meant; to him, it was simply a slogan that was sometimes useful in war. The notion of an ordained inequality was to him "scientific."

"Honestly," he was saying in lowered tones, as our drinks were taken away and the waitress set down my sandwich and his corned-beef hash, "don't you, brought up the way you were, feel about them the way I do? Just between ourselves, isn't there a sort of inborn feeling of horror that the very word, Jew, suggests?" I shook my head, roundly. The idea of an *innate* anti-Semitism was in keeping with the rest of the colonel's thought, yet it shocked me more than anything he had yet said. "No," I sharply replied. "It doesn't evoke any feeling one way or the other." "Honest Injun?" said the colonel. "Think back; when you were a kid, didn't the word, Jew, make you feel sick?" There was a dreadful sincerity about this that made me answer in an almost kindly tone. "No, truthfully, I assure you. When we were children, we learned to call the old-clothes man a sheeny, but that was just a dirty word to us, like 'Hun' that we used to call after workmen we thought were Germans."

"I don't get it," pondered the colonel, eating a pickle. "There must be something wrong with you. Everybody is born with that feeling. It's natural; it's part of nature." "On the contrary," I said. "It's something very unnatural that you must have been taught as a child." "It's not something you're *taught*," he protested. "You must have been," I said. "You simply don't remember it. In any case, you're a man now; you must rid yourself of that feeling. It's psychopathic, like that horrible young man on the train." "You thought he was crazy?" mused the colonel, in an idle, dreamy tone. I shrugged my shoulders. "Of course. Think of his color. He was probably just out of a mental institution. People don't get that tattletale gray except in prison or mental hospitals." The colonel suddenly grinned. "You might be right," he said. "He was quite a case." He chuckled.

I leaned forward. "You know, Colonel," I said quickly, "anti-Semitism is contrary to the Church's teaching. God will make you do penance for hating the Jews. Ask your priest; he'll tell you I'm right. You'll have a long spell in Purgatory, if you don't rid yourself of this sin. It's a deliberate violation of Christ's commandment, 'Love thy neighbor.' The Church holds that the Jews have a sacred place in God's design. Mary was a Jew and Christ was a Jew. The Jews are under God's special protection. The Church teaches that the millennium can't come until the conversion of the Jews; therefore, the Jews must be preserved that the Divine Will may be accomplished. Woe to them that harm them, for they controvert God's Will!" In the course of speaking, I had swept myself away with the solemnity of the doctrine. The Great Reconciliation between God and His chosen people, as envisioned by the Evangelist, had for me at that moment a piercing, majestic beauty, like some awesome Tintoretto. I saw a noble spectacle of blue sky, thronged with gray clouds, and a vast white desert, across which God and Israel advanced to meet each other, while below in hell the demons of disunion shrieked and gnashed their teeth.

"Hell," said the colonel, jovially, "I don't believe in all that. I lost my faith when I was a kid. I saw that all this God stuff was a lot of bushwa." I gazed at him in stupefaction. His confidence had completely returned. The blue eyes glittered debonairly, the eagles glittered; the narrow polished head cocked and listened to itself like a trilling bird. I was up against an airman with a bird's-eye view, a man who believed in nothing but the law of kind: the epitome of godless materialism. "You still don't hold with that bunk?" the colonel inquired in an undertone, with an expression of stealthy curiosity. "No," I confessed, sad to admit to a meeting of minds. "You know what got me?" exclaimed the colonel. "That birth-control stuff. Didn't it kill you?" I made a neutral sound. "I was beginning to play around," said the colonel, with a significant beam of the eye, "and I just couldn't take that guff. When I saw through the birth-control talk, I saw through the whole thing. They claimed it was against nature, but I claim, if that's so, an operation's against nature. I told my old man that when he was having his kidney stones out. You ought to have heard him yell!" A rich, reminiscent satisfaction dwelt in the colonel's face.

This period of his life, in which he had thrown off the claims of the spiritual and adopted a practical approach, was evidently one of those "turning points" to which a man looks back with pride. He lingered over the story of his break with church and parents with a curious sort of heat, as though the flames of old sexual conquests stirred within his body at the memory of those old quarrels. The looks he rested on me, as a sharer of that experience, grew more and more lickerish and assaying. "What got *you* down?" he finally inquired, settling back in his chair and pushing his coffee cup aside. "Oh," I said wearily, "it's a long story. You can read it when it's published." "You're an author?" cried the colonel, who was really very slow-witted. I nodded, and the colonel regarded me afresh. "What do you write? Love stories?" He gave a half-wink. "No," I said. "Various things. Articles. Books. Highbrowish stories." A suspicion darkened in the colonel's sharp face. "That McCarthy," he said. "Is that your pen name?" "Yes," I said, "but it's my real name too. It's the name I write under *and* my maiden name." The colonel digested this thought. "Oh," he concluded.

A new idea seemed to visit him. Quite cruelly, I watched it take possession. He was thinking of the power of the press and the indiscretions of other military figures, who had been rewarded with demotion. The consciousness of the uniform he wore appeared to seep uneasily into his body. He straightened his shoulders and called thoughtfully for the check. We paid in silence, the colonel making no effort to forestall my dive into my pocketbook. I should not have let him pay in any case, but it startled me that he did not try to do so, if only for reasons of vanity. The whole business of paying, apparently, was painful to him; I watched his facial muscles contract as he pocketed the change and slipped two dimes for the waitress onto the table, not daring quite to hide them under the coffee cup—he had short-changed me on the bill and the tip, and we both knew it. We walked out into the steaming station and I took my baggage out of the checking locker. The colonel carried my suitcase and we strolled along without speaking. Again, I felt horribly embarrassed for him. He was meditative, and I supposed that he too was mortified by his meanness about the tip.

"Don't get me wrong," he said suddenly, setting the suitcase down and turning squarely to face me, as though he had taken a big decision. "I may have said a few things back there about the Jews getting what they deserved in Germany." I looked at him in surprise; actually, he had not said that to me. Perhaps he had let it drop in the club car after I had left. "But that doesn't mean I approve of Hitler." "I should hope not," I said. "What I mean is," said the colonel, "that they probably gave the Germans a lot of provocation, but that doesn't excuse what Hitler did." "No," I said, somewhat ironically, but the colonel was unaware of anything satiric in the air. His face was grave and determined; he was sorting out his philosophy for the record. "I mean, I don't approve of his methods," he finally stated. "No," I agreed. "You mean, you don't approve of the gas chamber." The colonel shook his head very severely. "Absolutely not! That was terrible." He shuddered and drew out a handkerchief and slowly wiped his brow. "For God's sake," he said, "don't get me wrong. I think they're human beings." "Yes," I assented, and we walked along to my track. The colonel's spirits lifted, as though, having stated his credo, he had both got himself in line with public policy and achieved an autonomous thought. "I mean," he resumed, "you may not care for them, but that's not the same as killing them, in cold blood, like that." "No, Colonel," I said.

He swung my bag onto the car's platform and I climbed up behind it. He stood below, smiling, with upturned face. "I'll look for your article," he cried, as the train whistle blew. I nodded, and the colonel waved, and I could not stop myself from waving back at him and even giving him the corner of a smile. After all, I said to myself, looking down at him, the colonel was "a human being." There followed one of those inane intervals in which one prays for the train to leave. We both glanced at our watches. "See you some time?" he called. "What's your married name?" "Broadwater," I called back. The whistle blew again. "Brodwater?" shouted the colonel, with a dazed look of unbelief and growing enlightenment; he was not the first person to hear it as a Jewish name, on the model of Goldwater. "B-r-o-a-d," I began, automatically, but then I stopped. I disdained to spell it out for him; the victory was his. "One of the chosen, eh?" his brief grimace seemed to commiserate. For the last time, and in the final fullness of understanding, the hawk eye patrolled the green dress, the duster, and the earrings; the narrow flue of his nostril contracted as he curtly turned away. The train commenced to move.

My Confession

Fall, 1953

EVERY AGE HAS A keyhole to which its eye is pasted. Spicy court-memoirs, the lives of gallant ladies, recollections of an ex-nun, a monk's confession, an atheist's repentance, true-to-life accounts of prostitution and bastardy gave our ancestors a penny peep into the forbidden room. In our own day, this type of sensational fact-fiction is being produced largely by ex-Communists. Public curiosity shows an almost prurient avidity for the details of political defloration, and the memoirs of ex-Communists have an odd resemblance to the confessions of a white slave. Two shuddering climaxes, two rendezvous with destiny, form the poles between which these narratives vibrate: the first describes the occasion when the subject was seduced by Communism; the second shows him wresting himself from the demon embrace. Variations on the form are possible. Senator McCarthy, for example, in his book, *McCarthyism, the Fight for America*, uses a tense series of flashbacks to dramatize his encounter with Communism: the country lies passive in Communism's clasp; he is given a tryst with destiny in the lonely Arizona hills, where, surrounded by "real Americans without any synthetic sheen," he attains the decision that will send him down the long marble corridors to the Senate Caucus Room to bare the shameful commerce.

The diapason of choice plays, like movie music, round today's apostle to the Gentiles: Whittaker Chambers on a park bench and, in a reprise, awake all night at a dark window, facing the void. These people, unlike ordinary beings, are shown the true course during a lightning storm of revelation, on the road to Damascus. And their decisions are lonely decisions, silhouetted against a background of public incomprehension and hostility.

I object. I have read the reminiscences of Mr. Chambers and Miss Bentley. I too have had a share in the political movements of our day, and my experience cries out against their experience. It is not the facts I balk at—I have never been an espionage agent—but the studio atmosphere of sublimity and purpose that enfolds the facts and the chief actor. When Whittaker Chambers is mounted on his tractor, or Elizabeth Bentley, alone, is meditating her decision in a white New England church, I have the sense that they are on location and that, at any moment, the director will call "Cut." It has never been like that for me; events have never waited, like extras, while I toiled to make up my mind between good and evil. In fact, I have never known these mental convulsions, which appear quite strange to me when I read about them, even when I do not question the author's sincerity.

Is it really so difficult to tell a good action from a bad one? I think one usually knows right away or a moment afterward, in a horrid flash of regret. And when one genuinely hesitates—or at least it is so in my case—it is never about anything of importance, but about perplexing trivial things, such as whether to have fish or meat for dinner, or whether to take the bus or subway to reach a certain destination, or whether to wear the beige or the green. The "great" decisions—those I can look back on pensively and say, "That was a turning-point"—have been made without my awareness. Too late to do anything about it, I discover that I have chosen. And this is particularly striking when the choice has been political or historic. For me, in fact, the mark of the historic is the nonchalance with which it picks up an individual and deposits him in a trend, like a house playfully moved by a tornado. My own experience with Communism prompts me to relate it, just because it had this inadvertence that seems to me lacking in the true confessions of reformed Communists. Like Stendhal's hero, who took part in something confused and disarrayed and insignificant that he later learned was the Battle of Waterloo, I joined the anti-Communist movement without meaning to and only found out afterward, through others, the meaning or "name" assigned to what I had done. This occurred in the late fall of 1936.

Three years before, I had graduated from college—Vassar, the same college Elizabeth Bentley had gone to—without having suffered any fracture of my political beliefs or moral frame. All through college, my official political philosophy was royalism; though I was not much interested in politics, it irritated me to be told that "you could not turn the clock back." But I did not see much prospect for kingship in the United States (unless you imported one, like the Swedes), and, *faute de mieux*, I awarded my sympathies to the Democratic Party, which I tried to look on as the party of the Southern patriciate. At the same time, I had an aversion to Republicans—an instinctive feeling that had been with me since I was a child of eight pedaling my wagon up and down our cement driveway and howling "Hurray for Cox" at the Republican neighbors who passed by. I disliked businessmen and business attitudes partly, I think, because I came from a professional (though Republican) family and had picked up a disdain for businessmen as being beneath us, in education and general culture. And the anti-Catholic prejudice against Al Smith during the 1928 election, the tinkling amusement at Mrs. Smith's vulgarity, democratized me a little in spite of myself: I was won by Smith's plebeian charm, the big coarse nose, and rubbery politician's smile.

But this same distrust of uniformity made me shrink, in 1932, from the sloppily dressed Socialist girls at college who paraded for Norman Thomas and tirelessly argued over "Cokes"; their eager fellowship and scrawled placards and heavy personalities bored me—there was something, to my mind, deeply athletic about this socialism. It was a kind of political hockey played by big, gaunt, dyspeptic girls in pants. It startled me a little, therefore, to learn that in an election poll taken of the faculty, several of my favorite teachers had voted for Thomas; in them, the socialist faith appeared rather charming, I decided—a gracious and attractive oddity, like the English Ovals they gave you when you came for tea. That was the winter Hitler was coming to power and, hearing of the anti-Jewish atrocities, I had a flurry of political indignation. I wrote a prose-poem that dealt, in a mixed-up way, with the Polish Corridor and the Jews. This poem was so unlike me that I did not know whether to be proud of it or ashamed of it when I saw it in a college magazine. At this period, we were interested in surrealism and automatic writing, and the poem had a certain renown because it had come out of my interior without much sense or order, just the way automatic writing was supposed to do. But there my political development stopped.

The depression was closer to home; in New York I used to see apple-sellers on the street corners, and, now and then, a bread line, but I had a very thin awareness of mass poverty. The depression was too close to home to awaken anything but curiosity and wonder—the feelings of a child confronted with a death in the family. I was conscious of the suicides of stockbrokers and businessmen, and of the fact that some of my friends had to go on scholarships and had their dress allowances curtailed, while their mothers gaily turned to doing their own cooking. To most of us at Vassar, I think, the depression was chiefly an upper-class phenomenon.

My real interests were literary. In a paper for my English Renaissance seminar, I noted a resemblance between the Elizabethan puritan pundits and the school of Marxist criticism that was beginning to pontificate about proletarian literature in the *New Masses*. I disliked the modern fanatics, cold, envious little clerics, equally with the insufferable and ridiculous Gabriel Harvey—Cambridge pedant and friend of Spenser—who tried to introduce the rules of Latin quantity into English verse and vilified a true poet who had died young, in squalor and misery. I really hated absolutism and officiousness of any kind (I preferred my kings martyred) and was pleased to be able to recognize a Zeal-of-the-Land-Busy in proletarian dress. And it was through a novel that I first learned, in my senior year, about the Sacco-Vanzetti case. The discovery that two innocent men had been executed only a few years back while I, oblivious, was in boarding school, gave me a disturbing shock. The case was still so near that I was tantalized by a feeling that it was not too late to do something—try still another avenue, if Governor Fuller and the Supreme Court obdurately would not be moved. An unrectified case of injustice has a terrible way of lingering, restlessly, in the social atmosphere like an unfinished equation. I went on to the Mooney case, which vexed not only my sense of equity but my sense of plausibility—how was it possible for the prosecution to lie so, in broad daylight, with the whole world watching?

When in May, 1933, however, before graduation, I went down to apply for a job at the old *New Republic* offices, I was not drawn there by the magazine's editorial policy—I hardly knew what it was—but because the book-review section seemed to me to possess a certain elegance and independence of thought that would be hospitable to a critical spirit like me. And I was badly taken aback when the book-review editor, to whom I had been shunted—there was no job—puffed his pipe and remarked that he would give me a review if I could show him that I was either a genius or starving. "I'm not starving," I said quickly; I knew I was not a genius and I was not pleased by the suggestion that I would be taking bread from other people's mouths. I did not think this a fair criterion and in a moment I said so. In reply, he put down his pipe, shrugged, reached out for the material I had brought with me, and half-promised, after an assaying glance, to send me a book. My notice finally appeared; it was not very good, but I did not know that and was elated. Soon I was reviewing novels and biographies for both the *New Republic* and the *Nation* and preening myself on the connection. Yet, whenever I entered the *New Republic*'s waiting room, I was seized with a feeling of nervous guilt toward the shirtsleeved editors upstairs and their busy social conscience, and, above all, toward the shabby young men who were waiting too and who had, my bones told me, a better claim than I to the book I hoped to take away with me. They looked poor, pinched, scholarly, and supercilious, and I did not know which of these qualities made me, with my clicking high heels and fall "ensemble," seem more out of place.

I cannot remember the moment when I ceased to air my old royalist convictions and stuffed them away in an inner closet as you do a dress or an ornament that you perceive strikes the wrong note. It was probably at the time when I first became aware of Communists as a distinct entity. I had known about them, certainly, in college, but it was not until I came to New York that I began to have certain people, celebrities, pointed out to me as Communists and to turn my head to look at them, wonderingly. I had no wish to be one of them, but the fact that they were there—an unreckoned factor—made my own political opinions take on a protective coloration. This process was accelerated by my marriage—a week after graduation—to an actor and playwright who was in some ways very much like me. He was the son of a Minnesota normal school administrator who had been the scapegoat in an academic scandal that had turned him out of his job and reduced him, for a time, when my husband was nine or ten, to selling artificial limbs and encyclopedia sets from door to door. My husband still brooded over his father's misfortune, like Hamlet or a character in Ibsen, and this had given his nature a sardonic twist that inclined him to behave like a paradox—to follow the mode and despise it, live in a Beekman Place apartment while lacking the money to buy groceries, play bridge with society couples and poker with the stage electricians, dress in the English style and carry a walking stick while wearing a red necktie.

He was an odd-looking man, prematurely bald, with a tense, arresting figure, a broken nose, a Standard English accent, and wry, circumflexed eyebrows. There was something about him both baleful and quizzical; whenever he stepped on the stage he had the ironic air of a symbol. This curious appearance of his disqualified him for most Broadway roles; he was too young for character parts and too bald for juveniles. Yet just this disturbing ambiguity—a Communist painter friend did a drawing of him that brought out a resemblance to Lenin—suited the portentous and equivocal atmosphere of left-wing drama. He smiled dryly at Marxist terminology, but there was social anger in him. During the years we were married, the only work he found was in productions of "social" significance. He played for the Theatre Union in *The Sailors of Cattaro*, about a mutiny in the Austrian fleet, and in *Black Pit*, about coal miners; the following year, he was in *Winterset* and Archibald MacLeish's *Panic*—the part of a blind man in both cases. He wrote revue sketches and unproduced plays, in a mocking, despairing, but none the less radical vein; he directed the book of a musical called *Americana* that featured the song, "Brother, Can You Spare a Dime?" I suppose there was something in him of both the victim and the leader, an undertone of totalitarianism; he was very much interested in the mythic qualities of leadership and talked briskly about a Farmer-Labor party in his stage English accent. Notions of the superman and the genius flickered across his thoughts. But this led him, as it happened, away from politics, into sheer personal vitalism, and it was only in plays that he entered "at the head of a mob." In personal life he was very winning, but that is beside the point here.

The point is that we both, through our professional connections, began to take part in a left-wing life, to which we felt superior, which we laughed at, but which nevertheless was influencing us without our being aware of it. If the composition of the body changes every seven years, the composition of our minds during the seven years changed, so that though our thoughts looked the same to us, inside we had been altered, like an old car which has had part after part replaced in it under the hood.

We wore our rue with a difference; we should never have considered joining the Communist Party. We were not even fellow-travelers; we did not sign petitions or join "front" groups. We were not fools, after all, and were no more deceived by the League against War and Fascism, say, than by a Chinatown bus with a carload of shills aboard. It was part of our metropolitan sophistication to know the truth about Communist fronts. We accepted the need for social reform, but we declined to draw the "logical" inference that the Communists wanted us to draw from this. We argued with the comrades backstage in the dressing rooms and at literary cocktail parties; I was attacked by a writer in the *New Masses*. We knew about Lovestoneites and Trotskyites, even while we were ignorant of the labor theory of value, the law of uneven development, the theory of permanent revolution *vs.* socialism in one country, and so on. "Lovestone is a Lovestoneite!" John wrote in wax on his dressing-room mirror, and on his door in the old Civic Repertory he put up a sign: "Through these portals pass some of the most beautiful tractors in the Ukraine."

The comrades shrugged and laughed, a little unwillingly. They knew we were not hostile but merely unserious, politically. The comrades who knew us best used to assure us that our sophistication was just an armor; underneath, we must care for the same things they did. They were mistaken, I am afraid. Speaking for myself, I cannot remember a single broad altruistic emotion visiting me during that period—the kind of emotion the simpler comrades, with their shining eyes and exalted faces, seemed to have in copious secretion. And yet it was true: we were not hostile. We marched in May Day parades, just for the fun of it, and sang, "Hold the Fort, for We Are Coming," and *"Bandiera Rossa,"* and "The Internationale," though we always bellowed "The *Socialist* International shall be the human race," instead of "The International Soviet," to pique the Communists in our squad. We took part in evening clothes in a consumers' walkout at the Waldorf to support a waiters' strike—the Communists had nothing to do with this—and we grew very excited (we did have negative feelings) when another young literary independent was arrested and booked. During a strike at a department store, John joined the sympathetic picketing and saw two of his fellow actors carried off in the Black Maria; they missed a matinee and set off a controversy about what was the *first* responsibility of a Communist playing in a proletarian drama. We went once or twice to a class for actors in Marxism, just to see what was up; we went to a debate on Freud and/or Marx, to a debate on the execution of the hundred and four White Guards following Kirov's assassination.

Most ex-Communists nowadays, when they write their autobiographies or testify before Congressional committees, are at pains to point out that their actions were very, very bad and their motives very, very good. I would say the reverse of myself, though without the intensives. I see no reason to disavow my actions, which were perfectly all right, but my motives give me a little embarrassment, and just because I cannot disavow them: that fevered, contentious, trivial show-off in the May Day parade is still recognizably me.

We went to dances at Webster Hall and took our uptown friends. We went to parties to raise money for the sharecroppers, for the Theatre Union, for the *New Masses*. These parties generally took place in a borrowed apartment, often a sculptor's or commercial artist's studio; you paid for your drinks, which were dispensed at a long, wet table; the liquor was dreadful; the glasses were small, and there was never enough ice. Long-haired men in turtle-necked sweaters marched into the room in processions and threw their overcoats on the floor, against the wall, and sat on them; they were only artists and bit-actors, but they gave these affairs a look of gangsterish menace, as if the room were guarded by the goons of the future. On couches with wrinkled slipcovers, little spiky-haired girls, like spiders, dressed in peasant blouses and carapaced with Mexican jewelry, made voracious passes at baby-faced juveniles; it was said that they "did it for the Party," as a recruiting effort. Vague, soft-faced old women with dust mops of whitish hair wandered benevolently about seeking a listener; on a sofa against a wall, like a deity, sat a bearded scion of an old Boston family, stiff as a post. All of us, generally, became very drunk; the atmosphere was horribly sordid, with cigarette burns on tables, spilled drinks, ashes everywhere, people passed out on the bed with the coats or necking, you could not be sure which. Nobody cared what happened because there was no host or hostess. The fact that a moneyed person had been simple enough to lend the apartment seemed to make the guests want to desecrate it, to show that they were exercising not a privilege but a right.

Obviously, I must have hated these parties, but I went to them, partly because I was ashamed of my own squeamishness, and partly because I had a curiosity about the Communist men I used to see there, not the actors or writers, but the higher-ups, impresarios and theoreticians—dark, smooth-haired owls with large white lugubrious faces and glasses. The were the spiritual directors of the Communist cultural celebrities and they moved about at these parties like so many monks or abbés in a worldly salon. I had always liked to argue with the clergy, and I used to argue with these men, who had the air, as they stood with folded arms, of listening not to a disagreement but to a confession. Whenever I became tight, I would bring up (oh, *vino veritas*) the Czar and his family. I did not see why they all had had to be killed—the Czar himself, yes, perhaps, and the Czarina, but not the young girls and the children. I knew the answer, of course (the young Czarevitch or one of his sisters might have served as a rallying point for the counter-revolutionary forces), but still I gazed hopefully into these docents' faces, seeking a trace of scruple or compassion. But I saw only a marmoreal astuteness. The question was of bourgeois origin, they said with finality.

The next morning I was always bitterly ashamed. I had let these omniscient men see the real me underneath, and the other me squirmed and gritted her teeth and muttered, Never, never, *never* again. And yet they had not convinced me—there was the paradox. The superiority I felt to the Communists I knew had, for me at any rate, good grounding; it was based on their lack of humor, their fanaticism, and the slow drip of cant that thickened their utterance like a nasal catarrh. *And yet* I was tremendously impressed by them. They made me feel petty and shallow; they had, shall I say, a daily ugliness in their life that made my pretty life tawdry. I think all of us who moved in that ambience must have felt something of the kind, even while we laughed at them. When John and I, for instance, would say of a certain actor, "He is a Party member," our voices always contained a note of respect. This respect might be mixed with pity, as when we saw some blue-eyed young profile, fresh from his fraternity and his C average, join up because a sleazy girl had persuaded him. The literary Communists I sincerely despised because I was able to judge the quality of the work they published and see their dishonesty and contradictions; even so, when I beheld them in person, at a Webster Hall dance, I was troubled and felt perhaps I had wronged them—perhaps there was something in them that my vision could not perceive, as some eyes cannot perceive color.

People sometimes say that they envied the Communists because they were so "sure." In my case, this was not exactly it; I was sure, too, intellectually speaking, as far as I went. That is, I had a clear mind and was reasonably honest, while many of the Communists I knew were pathetically fogged up. In any case, my soul was not particularly hot for certainties.

And yet in another way I did envy the Communists, or, to be more accurate, wonder whether I ought to envy them. I could not, I saw, be a Communist because I was not "made that way." Hence, to be a Communist was to possess a sort of privilege. And this privilege, like all privileges, appeared to be a source of power. Any form of idiocy or aberration can confer this distinction on its owner, at least in our age, which aspires to a "total" experience; in the thirties it was the Communists who seemed fearsomely to be the happy few, not because they had peace or certitude but because they were a mutation—a mutation that threatened, in the words of their own anthem, to become the human race.

There was something arcane in every Communist, and the larger this area was the more we respected him. That was why the literary Communists, who operated in the open, doing the hatchet work on artists' reputations, were held in such relatively low esteem. An underground worker rated highest with us; next were the theoreticians and oracles; next were the activists, who mostly worked, we heard, on the waterfront. Last came the rank and file, whose work consisted of making speeches, distributing leaflets, attending Party and faction meetings, joining front organizations, marching in parades and demonstrations. These people we dismissed as uninteresting not so much because their work was routine but because the greater part of it was visible. In the same way, among individual comrades, we looked up to those who were close-lipped and stern about their beliefs and we disparaged the more voluble members—the forensic little actors who tried to harangue us in the dressing rooms. The idea of a double life was what impressed us: the more talkative comrades seemed to have only one life, like us; but even they, we had to remind ourselves, had a secret annex to their personality, which was signified by their Party name. It is hard not to respect somebody who has an alias.

Of fellow-travelers, we had a very low opinion. People who were not willing to "go the whole way" filled us with impatient disdain. The only fellow-travelers who merited our notice were those of whom it was said: the Party prefers that they remain on the outside. I think some fellow-travelers circulated such stories about themselves deliberately, in order to appear more interesting. There was another type of fellow-traveler who let it be known that they stayed out of the Party because of some tiny doctrinal difference with Marxism. This tiny difference magnified them enormously in their own eyes and allowed them to bear gladly the accusation of cowardice. I knew one such person very well—a spruce, ingratiating swain, the heir to a large fortune—and I think it was not cowardice but a kind of pietistic vanity. He felt he cut more of a figure if he seemed to be doing the Party's dirty work gratuitously, without compulsion, like an oblate.

In making these distinctions (which were the very distinctions the Party made), I had no idea, of course, that I was allowing myself to be influenced by the Party in the field where I was most open to suasion—the field of social snobbery. Yet in fact I was being deterred from forming any political opinions of my own, lest I find I was that despised article, a "mere" socialist or watery liberal, in the same way that a young snob coming to college and seeing who the "right" people are will strive to make no friends rather than be caught with the wrong ones.

For me, the Communist Party was *the* party, and even though I did not join it, I prided myself on knowing that it was the pinnacle. It is only now that I see the social component in my attitude. At the time, I simply supposed that I was being clear-sighted and logical. I used to do research and typing for a disgruntled middle-aged man who was a freak for that day—an anti-Communist Marxist—and I was bewildered by his anti-Party bias. While we were drinking hot tea, Russian style, from glasses during the intervals of our work, I would try to show him his mistake. "Don't you think it's rather futile," I expostulated, "to criticize the Party the way you do, from the outside? After all, it's the *only* working-class Party, and if *I* were a Marxist I would join it and try to reform it." Snorting, he would raise his small deep-set blue eyes and stare at me and then try patiently to show me that there was no democracy in the Party. I listened disbelievingly. It seemed to me that it would just be a question of converting first one comrade and then another to your point of view till gradually you had achieved a majority. And when my employer assured me that they would throw you out if you tried that, my twenty-three-year-old wisdom cocked an eyebrow. I thought I knew what was the trouble: he was a pathologically lazy man and his growling criticisms of the Party were simply a form of malingering, like the aches and pains he used to manufacture to avoid working on an article. A real revolutionary who was not afraid of exertion would get into the Party and fight.

The curious idea that being critical of the Party was a compelling reason for joining it must have been in the air, for the same argument was brought to bear on me in the summer of 1936—the summer my husband and I separated and that I came closest to the gravitational pull of the Communist world. Just before I went off to Reno, there was a week in June when I stayed in Southampton with the young man I was planning to marry and a little Communist organizer in an old summer house furnished with rattan and wicker and Chinese matting and mother-of-pearl and paper fans. We had come there for a purpose. The little organizer had just been assigned a car—a battered old Ford roadster that had been turned over to the Party for the use of some poor organizer; it may have been the very car that figured in the Hiss case. My fiancé, who had known him for years, perhaps from the peace movement, was going to teach him to drive. We were all at a pause in our lives. The following week our friend was supposed to take the car to California and do propaganda work among the migrant fruit-pickers; I was to go to Reno; my fiancé, a vivacious young bachelor, was to conquer his habits of idleness and buckle down to a serious job. Those seven days, therefore, had a special, still quality, like the days of a novena you make in your childhood; a part of each of them was set aside for the Party's task. It was early in June; the musty house that belonged to my fiancé's parents still had the winter-smell of mice and old wood and rust and mildew. The summer colony had not yet arrived; the red flag, meaning that it was dangerous to swim, flew daily on the beach; the roads were nearly empty. Every afternoon we would take the old car, canvas flapping, to a deserted stretch of straight road in the dunes, where the neophyte could take the wheel.

He was a large-browed, dwarfish man in his late thirties, with a deep widow's peak, a bristly short mustache, and a furry western accent—rather simple, open-natured, and cheerful, the sort of person who might have been a small-town salesman or itinerant newspaperman. There was an energetic, hopeful innocence about him that was not confined to his political convictions—he could *not* learn to drive. Every day the same thing happened; he would settle his frail yet stocky figure trustingly in the driver's seat, grip the wheel, step on the starter, and lose control of the car, which would shoot ahead in first or backward in reverse for a few perilous feet till my fiancé turned off the ignition; Ansel always mistook the gas for the brake and forgot to steer while he was shifting gears.

It was clear that he would never be able to pass the driver's test at the county seat. In the evenings, to make up to him for his oncoming disappointment (we smiled when he said he could start without a license), we encouraged him to talk about the Party and tried to take an intelligent interest. We would sit by the lamp and drink and ask questions, while he smoked his short pipe and from time to time took a long draught from his highball, like a man alone musing in a chair.

And finally one night, in the semi-dark, he knocked out his pipe and said to me: "You're very critical of the Party. Why don't you join it?" A thrill went through me, but I laughed, as when somebody has proposed to you and you are not sure whether they are serious. "I don't think I'd make very good material." "You're wrong," he said gravely. "You're just the kind of person the Party needs. You're young and idealistic and independent." I broke in: "I thought independence was just what the Party didn't want." "The Party needs criticism," he said. "But it needs it from the inside. If people like you who agree with its main objectives would come in and criticize, we wouldn't be so narrow and sectarian." "You admit the Party is narrow?" exclaimed my fiancé. "Sure, I admit it," said Ansel, grinning. "But it's partly the fault of people like Mary who won't come in and broaden us." And he confided that he himself made many of the same criticisms I did, but he made them from within the Party, and so could get himself listened to. "The big problem of the American Party," said Ansel, puffing at his pipe, "is the smallness of the membership. People say we're ruled from Moscow; I've never seen any sign of it. But let's suppose it's true, for the sake of argument. This just means that the American Party isn't big enough yet to stand on its own feet. A big, indigenous party couldn't be ruled from Moscow. The will of the members would have to rule it, just as their dues and contributions would support it." "That's where I come in, I suppose?" I said, teasing. "That's where you come in," he calmly agreed. He turned to my fiancé. "Not you," he said. "You won't have the time to give to it. But for Mary I think it would be an interesting experiment."

An interesting experiment... I let the thought wander through my mind. The subject recurred several times, by the lamplight, though with no particular urgency. Ansel, I thought (and still think), was speaking sincerely and partly in my own interest, almost as a spectator, as if he would be diverted to see how I worked out in the Party. All this gave me quite a new sense of Communism and of myself too; I had never looked upon my character in such a favorable light. And as a beneficiary of Ansel's charity, I felt somewhat ashamed of the very doubt it raised: the suspicion that he might be blind to the real facts of inner Party life. I could admire where I could not follow, and, studying Ansel, I decided that I admired the Communists and would probably be one, if I were the person he thought me. Which I was afraid I was not. For me, such a wry conclusion is always uplifting, and I had the feeling that I mounted in understanding when Sunday morning came and I watched Ansel pack his sturdy suitcase and his briefcase full of leaflets into the old roadster. He had never yet driven more than a few yards by himself, and we stood on the front steps to await what was going to happen: he would not be able to get out of the driveway, and we would have to put him on the train and return the car to the Party when we came back to New York. As we watched, the car began to move; it picked up speed and grated into second, holding to the middle of the road as it turned out of the driveway. It hesitated and went into third: Ansel was driving! Through the back window we saw his figure hunched over the wheel; the road dipped and he vanished. We had witnessed a miracle, and we turned back into the house, frightened. All day we sat waiting for the call that would tell us there had been an accident, but the day passed without a sound, and by nightfall we accepted the phenomenon and pictured the little car on the highway, traveling steadily west in one indefatigable thrust, not daring to stop for gas or refreshment, lest the will of the driver falter.

This parting glimpse of Ansel through the car's back window was, as it turned out, ultimate. Politically speaking, we reached a watershed that summer. The first Moscow trial took place in August. I knew nothing of this event because I was in Reno and did not see the New York papers. Nor did I know that the Party line had veered to the right and that all the fellow-travelers would be voting, not for Browder as I was now prepared to do (if only I remembered to register), but for Roosevelt. Isolated from these developments in the mountain altitudes, I was blossoming, like a lone winter rose overlooked by the frost, into a revolutionary thinker of the pure, uncompromising strain. The detached particles of the past three years' experience suddenly "made sense," and I saw myself as a radical.

"Book Bites Mary," wrote back a surprised literary editor when

I sent him, from Reno, a radiant review of a novel about the Paris Commune that ended with the heroine sitting down to read the *Communist Manifesto*. In Seattle, when I came to stay with my grandparents, I found a strike on and instantly wired the *Nation* to ask if I could cover it. Every night I was off to the Labor Temple or a longshoreman's hall while my grandparents took comfort from the fact that I seemed to be against Roosevelt, the Democrats, and the Czars of the A. F. of L.—they did not quite grasp my explanation, that I was criticizing "from the left."

Right here, I come up against a puzzle: why didn't I take the *next step*? But it is only a puzzle if one thinks of me not as a concrete entity but as a term in a logical operation: you agree with the Communist Party; *ergo*, you join it. I reasoned that way but I did not behave so. There was something in me that capriciously resisted being a term in logic, and the very fact that I cannot elicit any specific reason why I did not join the Party shows that I was never really contemplating it, though I can still hear my own voice, raised very authoritatively at a cafeteria table at the Central Park Zoo, pointing out to a group of young intellectuals that if we were serious we would join the Communists.

This was in September and I was back in New York. The Spanish Civil War had begun. The pay-as-you-go parties were now all for the Loyalists, and young men were volunteering to go and fight in Spain. I read the paper every morning with tears of exaltation in my eyes, and my sympathies rained equally on Communists, Socialists, Anarchists, and the brave Catholic Basques. My heart was tense and swollen with popular-front solidarity. I applauded the Lincoln Battalion, protested non-intervention, hurried into Wanamaker's to look for cotton-lace stockings: I was boycotting silk on account of Japan in China. I was careful to smoke only union-made cigarettes; the white package with Sir Walter Raleigh's portrait came proudly out of my pocketbook to rebuke Chesterfields and Luckies.

It was a period of intense happiness; the news from the battle-front was often encouraging and the practice of virtue was surprisingly easy. I moved into a one-room apartment on a crooked street in Greenwich Village and exulted in being poor and alone. I had a part-time job and read manuscripts for a publisher; the very riskiness of my situation was zestful—I had decided not to get married. The first month or so was scarifyingly lonely, but I survived this, and, starting early in November, I began to feel the first stirrings of popularity. A new set of people, rather smart and moneyed, young Communists with a little "name," progressive hosts and modernist hostesses, had discovered me. The fact that I was poor and lived in such a funny little apartment increased the interest felt: I was passed from hand to hand, as a novelty, like Gulliver among the Brobdingnagians. During those first days in November, I was chiefly conscious of what a wonderful time I was starting to have. All this while, I had remained ignorant of the fissure that was opening. Nobody, I think, had told me of the trial of Zinoviev and Kamenev—the trial of the sixteen—or of the new trial that was being prepared in Moscow, the trial of Pyatakov and Radek.

Then, one afternoon in November, I was taken to a cocktail party, in honor of Art Young, the old *Masses* cartoonist, whose book, *The Best of Art Young*, was being published that day. It was the first publisher's party I had ever been to, and my immediate sensation was one of disappointment: nearly all these people were strangers and, to me, quite unattractive. Art Young, a white-haired little kewpie, sitting in a corner, was pointed out to me, and I turned a respectful gaze on him, though I had no clear idea who he was or how he had distinguished himself. I presumed he was a veteran Communist, like a number of the stalwarts in the room, survivors of the old *Masses* and the *Liberator*. Their names were whispered to me and I nodded; this seemed to be a commemorative occasion, and the young men hovered in groups around the old men, as if to catch a word for posterity. On the outskirts of certain groups I noticed a few poorly dressed young men, bolder spirits, nervously flexing their lips, framing sentences that would propel them into the conversational center, like actors with a single line to speak.

The solemnity of these proceedings made me feel terribly ill at ease. It was some time before I became aware that it was not just me who was nervous: the whole room was under a constraint. Some groups were avoiding other groups, and now and then an arrow of sarcasm would wing like a sniper's bullet from one conversation to another.

I was standing, rather bleakly, by the refreshment table, when a question was thrust at me: did I think Trotsky was entitled to a hearing? It was a novelist friend of mine, dimple-faced, shaggy-headed, earnest, with a whole train of people, like a deputation, behind him. Trotsky? I glanced for help at a sour little man I had been talking with, but he merely shrugged. My friend made a beckoning gesture and a circle closed in. What had Trotsky done? Alas, I had to ask. A tumult of voices proffered explanations. My friend raised a hand for silence. Leaning on the table, he supplied the background, speaking very slowly, in his dragging, disconsolate voice, like a schoolteacher wearied of his subject. Trotsky, it appeared, had been accused of fostering a counter-revolutionary plot in the Soviet Union—organizing terrorist centers and conspiring with the Gestapo to murder the Soviet leaders. Sixteen old Bolsheviks had confessed and implicated him. It had been in the press since August.

I blushed; everybody seemed to be looking at me strangely. I made a violent effort to take in what had been said. The enormity of the charge dazed me, and I supposed that some sort of poll was being taken and that I was being asked to pronounce on whether Trotsky was guilty or innocent. I could tell from my friend's low, even, melancholy tone that he regarded the charges as derisory. "What do you want me to say?" I protested. "I don't know anything about it." "Trotsky denies the charges," patiently intoned my friend. "He declares it's a GPU fabrication. Do you think he's entitled to a hearing?" My mind cleared. "Why, of course." I laughed—were there people who would say that Trotsky was *not* entitled to a hearing? But my friend's voice tolled a rebuke to this levity. "She says Trotsky is entitled to his day in court."

The sour little man beside me made a peculiar, sucking noise. "You disagree?" I demanded, wonderingly. "I'm smart," he retorted. "I don't let anybody ask me. You notice, he doesn't ask me?" "Shut up, George," said my novelist friend impatiently. "I'm asking *her*. One thing more, Mary," he continued gravely. "Do you believe that Trotsky should have the right of asylum?" The right of asylum! I looked for someone to share my amusement—were we in ancient Greece or the Middle Ages? I was sure the U.S. government would be delighted to harbor such a distinguished foreigner. But nobody smiled back. Everybody watched dispassionately, as for form's sake I assented to the phrasing: yes, Trotsky, in my opinion, was entitled to the right of asylum.

I went home with the serene feeling that all these people were slightly crazy. *Right of asylum, his day in court!*—in a few hours I had forgotten the whole thing.

Four days later I tore open an envelope addressed to me by something that called itself "Committee for the Defense of Leon Trotsky," and idly scanned the contents. "We demand for Leon Trotsky the right of a fair hearing and the right of asylum." Who were these demanders, I wondered, and, glancing down the letterhead, I discovered my own name. I sat down on my unmade studio couch, shaking. How dared they help themselves to my signature? This was the kind of thing the Communists were always being accused of pulling; apparently, Trotsky's admirers had gone to the same school. I had paid so little heed to the incident at the party that a connection was slow to establish itself. Reading over the list of signers, I recognized "names" that had been present there and remembered my novelist-friend going from person to person, methodically polling...

How were they feeling, I wondered, when they opened their mail this morning? My own feelings were crisp. In two minutes I had decided to withdraw my name and write a note of protest. Trotsky had a right to a hearing, but I had a right to my signature. For even if there had been a legitimate misunderstanding (it occurred to me that perhaps I had been the only person there not to see the import of my answers), nothing I had said committed me to Trotsky's *defense*.

The "decision" was made, but according to my habit I procrastinated. The severe letter I proposed to write got put off till the next day and then the next. Probably I was not eager to offend somebody who had been a good friend to me. Nevertheless, the letter would undoubtedly have been written, had I been left to myself. But within the next forty-eight hours the phone calls began. People whom I had not seen for months or whom I knew very slightly telephoned to advise me to get off the newly formed Committee. These calls were not precisely threatening. Indeed, the caller often sounded terribly weak and awkward, as if he did not like the mission he had been assigned. But they were peculiar. For one thing, they usually came after nightfall and sometimes quite late, when I was already in bed. Another thing, there was no real effort at persuasion: the caller stated his purpose in standardized phrases, usually plaintive in tone (the Committee was the tool of reaction, and all liberal people should dissociate themselves from its activities, which were an unwarranted intervention in the domestic affairs of the Soviet Union), and then hung up, almost immediately, before I had a proper chance to answer. Odd too—the voices were not those of my Communist friends but of the merest acquaintances. These people who admonished me to "think about it" were not people whose individual opinions could have had any weight with me. And when I did think about it, this very fact took on an ominous and yet to me absurd character: I was not being appealed to personally but impersonally warned.

Behind these phone calls there was a sense of the Party wheeling its forces into would-be disciplined formations, like a fleet or an army maneuvering. This, I later found, was true: a systematic telephone campaign was going on to dislodge members from the Committee. The phone calls generally came after dark and sometimes (especially when the recipient was elderly) in the small hours of the morning. The more prominent signers got anonymous messages and threats.

And in the morning papers and the columns of the liberal magazines I saw the results. During the first week, name after name fell off the Committee's letterhead. Prominent liberals and literary figures issued statements deploring their mistake. And a number of people protested that their names had been used without permission…

There, but for the grace of God, went I, I whispered, awestruck, to myself, hugging my guilty knowledge. Only Heaven—I plainly saw—by making me dilatory had preserved me from joining this sorry band. Here was the occasion when I should have been wrestling with my conscience or standing, floodlit, at the crossroads of choice. But in fact I was only aware that I had had a providential escape. I had been saved from having to decide about the Committee; *I* did not decide it—the Communists with their pressure tactics took the matter out of my hands. We all have an instinct that makes us side with the weak, if we do not stop to reason about it, the instinct that makes a householder shield a wounded fugitive without first conducting an inquiry into the rights and wrongs of his case. Such "decisions" are simple reflexes; they do not require courage; if they did, there would be fewer of them. When I saw what was happening, I rebounded to the defense of the Committee without a single hesitation—it was nobody's business, I felt, how I happened to be on it, and if anybody had asked me, I should have lied without a scruple.

Of course, I did not foresee the far-reaching consequences of my act—how it would change my life. I had no notion that I was now an anti-Communist, where before I had been either indifferent or pro-Communist. I did, however, soon recognize that I was in a rather awkward predicament—not a moral quandary but a social one. I knew nothing about the cause I had espoused; I had never read a word of Lenin or Trotsky, nothing of Marx but the *Communist Manifesto*, nothing of Soviet history; the very names of the old Bolsheviks who had confessed were strange and almost barbarous in my ears. As for Trotsky, the only thing that made me think that he might be innocent was the odd behavior of the Communists and the fellow-traveling liberals, who seemed to be infuriated at the idea of a free inquiry. All around me, in the fashionable Stalinist circles I was now frequenting, I began to meet with suppressed excitement and just-withheld disapproval. Jeweled lady-authors turned white and shook their bracelets angrily when I came into a soirée; rising young men in publishing or advertising tightened their neckties dubiously when I urged them to examine the case for themselves; out dancing in a night club, tall, collegiate young Party members would press me to their shirt-bosoms and tell me not to be silly, honey.

And since I seemed to meet more Stalinists every day, I saw that I was going to have to get some arguments with which to defend myself. It was not enough, apparently, to say you were for a fair hearing; you had to rebut the entire case of the prosecution to get anybody to incline an ear in your direction. I began to read, head-long, the literature on the case—the pamphlets issued by Trotsky's adherents, the verbatim report of the second trial published by the Soviet Union, the "bourgeois" press, the Communist press, the radical press. To my astonishment (for I had scarcely dared think it), the trials did indeed seem to be a monstrous frame-up. The defendant, Pyatakov, flew to Oslo to "conspire" with Trotsky during a winter when, according to the authorities, no planes landed at the Oslo airfield; the defendant, Holtzmann, met Trotsky's son, Sedov, in 1936, at the Hotel Bristol in Copenhagen, which had burned down in 1912; the witness, Romm, met Trotsky in Paris at a time when numerous depositions testified that he had been in Royan, among clouds of witnesses, or on the way there from the south of France.

These were only the most glaring discrepancies—the ones that got in the newspapers. Everywhere you touched the case something crumbled. The carelessness of the case's manufacture was to me its most terrifying aspect; the slovenly disregard for credibility defied credence, in its turn. How did they dare? I think I was more shaken by finding that I was on the right side than I would have been the other way round. And yet, except for a very few people, nobody seemed to mind whether the Hotel Bristol had burned down or not, whether a real plane had landed, whether Trotsky's life and writings were congruent with the picture given of him in the trials. When confronted with the facts of the case, people's minds sheered off from it like jelly from a spoon.

Anybody who has ever tried to rectify an injustice or set a record straight comes to feel that he is going mad. And from a social point of view, he *is* crazy, for he is trying to undo something that is finished, to unravel the social fabric. That is why my liberal friends looked so grave and solemn when I would press them to come to a meeting and listen to a presentation of the facts—for them this was a Decision, too awful to be considered lightly. The Moscow trials were a historical fact and those of us who tried to undo them were uneasily felt to be crackpots, who were trying to turn the clock back. And of course the less we were listened to, the more insistent and earnest we became, even while we realized we were doing our cause harm. It is impossible to take a moderate tone under such conditions. If I admitted, though, to being a little bit hipped on the subject of Trotsky, I could sometimes gain an indulgent if flickering attention—the kind of attention that stipulates, "She's a bit off but let's hear her story." And now and then, by sheer chance, one of my hearers would be arrested by some stray point in my narrative; the disparaging smile would slowly fade from his features, leaving a look of blank consternation. He would go off and investigate for himself, and in a few days, when we met again, he would be a crackpot too.

Most of us who became anti-Communists at the time of the trials were drawn in, like me, by accident and almost unwillingly. Looking back, as on a love affair, a man could say that if he had not had lunch in a certain restaurant on a certain day, he might not have been led to ponder the facts of the Moscow trials. Or not then at any rate. And had he pondered them at a later date, other considerations would have entered and his conversion would have had a different style. On the whole, those of us who became anti-Communists during that year, 1936–37, have remained liberals—a thing that is less true of people of our generation who were converted earlier or later. A certain doubt of orthodoxy and independence of mass opinion was riveted into our anti-Communism by the heat of that period. As soon as I make this statement, exceptions leap into my mind, but I think as a generalization it will stand. Those who became anti-Communist earlier fell into two classes: the experts and those to whom any socialist ideal was repugnant. Those whose eyes where opened later, by the Nazi-Soviet pact, or still later, by God knows what, were left bruised and full of self-hatred or self-commiseration, because they had palliated so much and truckled to a power-center; to them, Communism's chief sin seems to be that it deceived *them*, and their public atonement takes on both a vindicating and a vindictive character.

We were luckier. Our anti-Communism came to us neither as the fruit of a special wisdom nor as a humiliating awakening from a prolonged deception, but as a natural event, the product of chance and propinquity. One thing followed another, and the will had little to say about it. For my part, during that year, I realized, with a certain wistfulness, that it was too late for me to become any kind of Marxist. Marxism, I saw, from the learned young men I listened to at Committee meetings, was something you had to take up young, like ballet dancing.

So, I did not try to be a Marxist or a Trotskyite, though for the first time I read a little in the Marxist canon. But I got the name of being a Trotskyite, which meant, in the end, that I saw less of the conventional Stalinists I had been mingling with and less of conventional people generally. (My definition of a conventional person was quite broad: it included anyone who could hear of the Moscow trials and maintain an unruffled serenity.) This, then, was a break or a rupture, not very noticeable at first, that gradually widened and widened, without any conscious effort on my part, sometimes to my regret. This estrangement was not marked by any definite stages; it was a matter of tiny choices. Shortly after the Moscow trials, for instance, I changed from the *Herald Tribune* to the *Times*; soon I had stopped doing crossword puzzles, playing bridge, reading detective stories and popular novels. I did not "give up" these things; they departed from me, as it were, on tiptoe, seeing that my thoughts were elsewhere.

To change from the *Herald Tribune* to the *Times*, is not, I am aware, as serious a step as breaking with international Communism when you have been its agent; and it occurs to me that Mr. Chambers and Miss Bentley might well protest the comparison, pointing out that they were profoundly dedicated people, while I was a mere trifler, that their decisions partook of the sublime, where mine descended to the ridiculous—as Mr. Chambers says, he was ready to give his life for his beliefs. Fortunately (though I could argue the point, for we all give our lives for our beliefs, piecemeal or whole), I have a surprise witness to call for my side, who did literally die for his political views.

I am referring to Trotsky, the small, frail, pertinacious old man who wore whiskers, wrinkles, glasses, shock of grizzled hair, like a gleeful disguise for the erect young student, the dangerous revolutionary within him. Nothing could be more alien to the convulsed and tormented moonscapes of the true confessions of ex-Communists than Trotsky's populous, matter-of-fact recollections set out in *My Life*. I have just been rereading this volume, and though I no longer subscribe to its views, which have certainly an authoritarian and doctrinaire cast that troubles me today, nevertheless I experience a sense of recognition here that I cannot find in the pages of our own repentant "revolutionaries." The old man remained unregenerate; he never admitted that he had sinned. That is probably why nobody seems to care for, or feel apologetic to, his memory. It is an interesting point—and relevant, I think, to my story—that many people today actually have the impression that Trotsky died a natural death.

In a certain sense, this is perfectly true. I do not mean that he lived by violence and therefore might reasonably be expected to die by violence. He was a man of words primarily, a pamphleteer and orator. He was armed, as he said, with a pen and peppered his enemies with a fusillade of articles. Hear the concluding passages of his autobiography: "Since my exile, I have more than once read musings in the newspapers on the subject of the 'tragedy' that has befallen me. I know no *personal* tragedy. I know the change of two chapters of revolution. One American paper which published an article of mine accompanied it with a profound note to the effect that in spite of the blows the author had suffered, he had, as evidenced by his article, preserved his clarity of reason. I can only express my astonishment at the Philistine attempt to establish a connection between the power of reasoning and a government post, between mental balance and the present situation. I do not know, and never have known, of any such connection. In prison, with a book or pen in my hand, I experienced the same sense of deep satisfaction that I did at mass-meetings of the revolution. I felt the mechanics of power as an inescapable burden, rather than as a spiritual satisfaction."

This was not a man of violence. Nevertheless, one can say that he died a natural death—a death that was in keeping with the open manner of his life. There was nothing arcane in Trotsky; that was his charm. Like an ordinary person he was hospitably open to hazard and accident. In his autobiography, he cannot date the moment when he became a socialist.

One factor in his losing out in the power-struggle at the time of Lenin's death was his delay in getting the telegram that should have called him home from the Caucasus, where he was convalescent, to appear at Lenin's funeral—*had* he got the telegram, the outcome perhaps would have been different. Or again, perhaps not. It may be that the whims of chance are really the importunities of design. But if there is a Design, it aims, in real lives, like the reader's or mine or Trotsky's, to look natural and fortuitous; that is how it gets us into its web.

Trotsky himself, looking at his life in retrospect, was struck, as most of us are on such occasions, by the role chance had played in it. He tells how one day, during Lenin's last illness, he went duck-shooting with an old hunter in a canoe on the River Dubna, walked through a bog in felt boots—only a hundred steps—and contracted influenza. This was the reason he was ordered to Sukhu for the cure, missed Lenin's funeral, and had to stay in bed during the struggle for primacy that raged that autumn and winter. "I cannot help noting," he says, "how obligingly the accidental helps the historical law. Broadly speaking, the entire historical process is a refraction of historical law through the accidental. In the language of biology, one might say that the historical law is realized through the natural selection of accidents." And with a touch of quizzical gaiety he sums up the problem as a Marxian: "One can foresee the consequences of a revolution or a war, but it is impossible to foresee the consequences of an autumn shooting-trip for wild ducks." This shrug before the unforeseen implies an acceptance of consequences that is a far cry from penance and prophecy. Such, it concedes, is life. *Bravo*, old sport, I say, even though the hall is empty.

Letter from Portugal

February, 1955

"THE HAPPIEST MONTH OF my life—an idyll," said a German-refugee publisher in New York, kissing his fingertips to Portugal, when he heard that my husband and I were coming here last winter. "You probably think we have a dictatorship. Ho, ho, ho!" roared Portugal's vice-chieftain of propaganda, when I went to see him in his office on our third day in Lisbon. I had to confess that this was what we Americans had been given to understand—"a benevolent dictatorship," I hurriedly qualified, this being the formula that had been current among the passengers on the *Vulcania* as the ship glided up the Tagus. We were expecting an idyll and apprehending a dictatorship. These two notions had fused, for the time being, in a resolve not to be insular: democracy was not necessarily suited to *all* countries, we assured each other, gripping our travel books. "Salazar is a very good man, very wise for his people," said an old Portuguese-American, brown-skinned as an Arab, who was identifying the approaching sights of pink-and-white Lisbon for us from the deck. "He must be *wonderful,*" sighed a lady in a tricorne, who came from Manchester, Vermont. The old man went on to relate eagerly, in broken English, how terrible conditions had been in Portugal in 1928, when António de Oliveira Salazar, born a poor peasant, left his post in Economics at the University of Coimbra to serve his country, first as Minister of Finance and then as Premier, saving, always saving, till the national debt was paid; and how he had sacrificed his personal life to the Estado Novo—never married, lived very simply and austerely, stayed up late at night, working, always working. "What's that?" I kept asking, pointing to orange-roofed white buildings, gleaming new, that were spread out on the green hills of Lisbon's suburbs. "Housing project," the old man invariably answered, simply and proudly. This was the first thing I found out about the Estado Novo; whenever you point to anything, the answer is "Housing project." After a few days, I learned to frame the question the other way around. "Housing project?" I would cautiously inquire. "*Sim, Senhora.*"

Most visitors to Portugal have come here to see something old, but the Portuguese are full of zeal to show you something new—Economic Homes, syndicate apartments, the *auto-estrada*, the airport, the stadium, the modernistic shrine of Our Lady of Fátima, that twentieth-century vision who came to warn against Communism. And in Lisbon signs of progress are not far to seek. Walking through the streets the first evening, I felt as though I had made an appointment in Samarra. The shop-windows glittered with radios, pressure cookers, electric mixers, automobile hubcaps, washing machines, gas ranges, soda-water siphons, mechanical ice-boxes, grills, electric razors, soap flakes, plastics, hot-water bottles. In the delicacy shops, Tootsie Rolls and Ritz crackers rested on beds of red velvet, like holy images. There was a din of horns honking. Everybody, at first glance, appeared to have a new car; it was several days before I realized that what I had been noticing, actually, was that every car was new. In the Rossio, the yellow principal square, the coffee-houses, which look like New York cafeterias, were dense with men in overcoats, reading the newspaper and having their shoes shined. Outside, electric signs were advertising TWA and Philips electrical products. Movie palaces, playing French and American films, disgorged crowds into the teashops of the Avenida da Liberdade. From the open doors of taverns near the waterfront you could hear the radio playing the *fado*. The liquor-store windows were full of Haig & Haig. In the center of the pale-green Praça de Comércio—the famous Black Horse Square, on the harbor—there was a parking lot. And everywhere, in every quarter, there were windows and windows of shoes for sale. Lisbon, as every tourist knows, has a law forbidding the people to go barefoot; the shoe, I perceived, was a talisman of Portuguese progress, the fulfillment of a prophecy, a miracle, like the wonder-working relics in the churches, meant to be venerated through glass. I had never seen so many shoes displayed anywhere: oxfords, brogues, sandals, loafers, slippers, mules, pumps, play shoes, beach shoes, baby shoes—all in the latest American-style models, perforated, fringed, crêpe- or wedge-soled.

This "little America" aspect of Lisbon contrasts rather naïvely with the rest of Portugal, like a figure out of drawing in a primitive painting. Yet just this naïveté comes to seem, after a time, typically Portuguese. This small country, with its variety of climates and mixture of racial strains, is an assiduous copyist, mimic, and borrower. Any sizable Portuguese town looks like a superstitious bride's finery—something old, something new, something borrowed, and something blue. Portugal has its "little Versailles," in the pink palace of Queluz (with a miniature Dutch canal added); its Balmoral, in the Scottish-baronial Pena Palace. It has its "little Switzerland," in the merry northern province of the Minho; its bit of Africa, in the southern Algarve. The Miguelite wars were a small-scale version of the Carlist wars in Spain; the present government's politics were borrowed from Charles Maurras, the originator of "integral nationalism." Portugal got its characteristic *azulejos* (painted tiles) from the Arabs and then subjected them to a Dutch influence. Its painters copied the Flemish, and its furniture makers the English and the French. "*Style renaissance française, travail portugais... Style anglais, travail portugais,*" drone the guides as they conduct you through the palaces. "They can copy anything," say the resident foreigners, speaking of the "little" dressmakers and the shoemakers. "But you must be sure to give them a model." This appears to have been true of nearly all the crafts throughout Portuguese history. Even the Manueline architecture, done in the Age of Discoveries and uniquely Portuguese, with its stone ropes and knots and anchors, seems not so much a true architectural style as an innocent imitation of real life, too literally conceived. It is only in the far north, in the Minho and the "lost" province of Trás-os-Montes (Beyond the Mountains), that you find a pure architecture—the Portuguese baroque, done in granite and severe white plaster, and decorated with gold—that is not like anything else in the world.

This persistent copying of foreign models, this literal translation from one medium to another, produces an effect of monkey humor—a slight absurdity that at its best is charming, like a child's recitation, and at its worst grotesque. The Portuguese genius, in fact, ranges between the charming and the grotesque: on the one hand, a miniature barnyard exquisitely worked in marzipan, a statue of Saint Anthony wearing a British officer's sash, pink-faced baroque angels in buskins and powdered periwigs, Saint Anne sitting in a Queen Anne chair; on the other, the horrors of late Manueline realism, the gross "cute" ceramics of lifelike cabbages and wrinkled spinach leaves, the votive offerings in the shrines and chapels, where one sees arms, legs, and ears painstakingly executed in mortuary greenish-white wax.

Lisbon itself is almost wholly charming—a model city of nearly a million people and an incalculable number of dogs. These multitudinous dogs—in muzzles, as prescribed by law—are forever underfoot, like stray bits of torn fur scattered on the streets; they are and must always have been one of the charms and absurdities of Lisbon. (The rational French, under Junot, during Napoleon's occupation, killed ten thousand of them.) The Portuguese love animals. In the country, the donkeys and oxen look better nourished, often, than their owners. In Lisbon, pet shops abound, full of lovebirds, parrots, parakeets, hens, and puppies, and along the narrow slum streets, hung with clean, bright washing, bird cages swing in the sun. Every day is washday in Lisbon. The Portuguese are famous for their cleanliness; no matter where you go, in city or suburb or country, you see laundry festooning the scene—spread out on cactus plants, flapping in back yards, hanging from windows. The smallest, muddiest rivulet has its band of women pounding clothes on flat rocks. "You can eat off their floors," the foreigners say, and this is very nearly true. But I have been in Portuguese restaurants where I would rather eat off the floor than off the plate before me. The Portuguese are very erratic and confound generalization.

But the cleanness of Lisbon *is* dazzling. In January, the steep stone streets are washed several times daily by sudden tropical showers, and Nature is assisted by street-cleaners with brooms made of twigs. The Portuguese have a green thumb. Lisbon, in winter, is brilliant with orange calendulas, blooming everywhere, together with geraniums and succulents; oranges and lemons dangle from trees in the walled gardens like bright Christmas balls, the oranges matching the orange sails of the little fishing boats on the blue Tagus. The seasons at this time of year are all awry. Autumn is present in the calendulas and oranges; spring in the first wicker baskets of camellias that come down from the nearby mountains to the florist shops; summer lingers in a few exhausted petunias; winter—last January, at least—came for a day in a fall of snow, which brought the population, marveling, out into the streets to touch it. As the new year gets under way, everything is growing, all at once; even the old tile roofs have windfall crops of grass and yellow mustard, which, if you look down from a window, over the rooftops to the Tagus, make the whole city seem fertile—a sort of semitropical paradise that combines the exuberance of the south, with the huge palms in the public squares, the oranges and the monumental statuary, and the neatness and precision of the north, seen in the absence of dirt and litter, the perfectly kept public gardens and belvederes, the black-and-white mosaic patterns (ships and ropes and anchors) of the sidewalks, and the bright tiles of so many house fronts, painted in green-and-white diamonds or pink roses or solid Dutch blues and yellows. Lisbon is a city built on hills, like San Francisco, and it is full of beautiful prospects, of which every advantage has been taken. It is designed, so to speak, for a strolling tourist, at sunset, to ensconce himself in a belvedere and gaze out over the Tagus, down to the pink-and-white dome of the Basilica of Estrela, or across a ravine of buff and pink and gold buildings to the old fortress of São Jorge.

Lisbon is a planned city. It sprang from the despotic imagination of the Marquis of Pombal, who rebuilt it in the eighteenth century,

after the great earthquake. It was planned, I should think, for pleasure and efficient administration, and this is what makes it seem
like a toy city. It is full of ingenious contrivances—underpasses and
cable cars and a tall outdoor elevator tower that has a view and
a restaurant on top of it. The ferryboats chugging back and forth
across the harbor, the little blue train that sets forth, on time, for
Estoril, half an hour away, and the yellow open streetcars all seem
part of the toy mechanism; the very fragrance of fresh coffee that
drifts like a golden haze over the city seems to have come from a
doll's electric stove. The eighteenth-century taste for curios and for
a ruin, rightly placed, still animates the twentieth-century administrators. Lisbon has recently created one of the wonders of the
world—the Estufa Fria, which is a sort of reverse hothouse, a large,
shady terrarium for trees and plants that like coolness and moisture.
Full of grottoes, streams, and bridges in a green, subaqueous light, it
is in the height of early romantic feeling, a cultivated jungle popular
with lovers and with French governesses on holiday. Lisbon also
has a romantic ruin—an old Carmelite convent, just off the Chiado,
the fashionable shopping street.

Above the cathedral there is an old quarter, called the Alfama,
that escaped the earthquake and preserves the sights and smells
of the Middle Ages. The Lisbonese are proud of the Alfama, which
resembles the worst pages of Victor Hugo. Rags, smells, and ema-
ciation teem here; the narrow, cobbled streets, where the leaning
houses almost meet overhead, are dirty and full of verminous-look-
ing dogs; every orange in the stalls has been felt a hundred times
by skinny hands; there are cripples, and one-eyed men, and every
species of deformity. Yet the Portuguese are eager to show the
Alfama, as a bit of local color. The tourist is directed to visit it at
night to hear the *fado* sung in the taverns, and is assured that it is
perfectly safe; you will never get a knife in your back nowadays
in the Alfama, they say, though before Salazar you risked your life
in broad daylight every day, right on the Avenida. Before Salazar,
they say, a rich man never went out without wondering whether he
would come home.

I wondered myself, I must confess, the Sunday morning we picked our way through the Alfama after Mass at the cathedral. I was afraid, and at the same time repelled by the vivid poverty. But everybody assured me that the people in the Alfama were a special breed, that they *liked* their way of life and would not live respectably if you made them. In fact, the government had considered cleaning up the district in the course of a slum-clearance program and had been compelled to desist, hastily, by the outcry of the populace. In the Estado Novo there is a whole repertory of such tales—of slum dwellers who refuse to be moved from their hovels, of men who refuse to work. "Is there unemployment?" I asked the propaganda man. There was seasonal unemployment in agriculture, he said, but no real unemployment—any man who wanted to could get work. "But what about the people in the Alfama?" I inquired. He shrugged and replied, "They don't want. A few work; others don't want." And to illustrate the government's plight he told me a "personal experience"—of a well-dressed man who asked him for money one day in a café, saying that he could not get work, and how he, the government official, promised the man a job but the man failed to turn up for the appointment, and how again he saw the man begging and beckoned him over to his table and again got a hard-luck story and again promised him work, and again discovered him begging. The plot of the story was familiar; I had heard it on occasion in my own country. No doubt these experiences really do befall people who, as it were, act as lightning rods for them; it is a case of serendipity.

"Still," I murmured, when the propaganda man had finished, "many of the people look very poor." "Oh, Alfama!" he said genially, and started to explain again that the Alfama was an institution. "Not the Alfama," I interrupted. "Other places." I had not intended to bedevil the propaganda chieftain, a big, dark, rubicund, jolly fat man, pronounced by foreigners to be more civilized and indulgent than his predecessors. But without my wishing it, it began to happen. The Portuguese, as I have since learned, are very sensitive, and certain words offend them; one of these words is "poor." "Portugal is a poor country," they will begin by telling you, with an air of self-deprecation. But they do not like *you* to say it. "Poor?" they will reply, as the propaganda man did now, contemplating the word with a kind of majestic wonder, as if it were susceptible of many different meanings. "Where did you see poor people?" The answer was, nearly everywhere, but I simply named the Rua de São Bento, a main street in a working-class quarter. There I had seen half-naked children, and women, like shapeless rummage bundles, buttoned into two or three torn sweaters, their feet tied up in rags and stuffed into men's shoes of odd pairs, or into gaping old felt bedroom slippers; some of the younger women wore once-fancy mules on raw, chapped, bare feet. I tried to describe this. When I had finished, he leaned back in his chair, lit a cigarette, and gave a long, tolerant laugh. "You don't understand," he said. "These women are very saving. They have good clothes, but they don't wear them. They keep them for Sunday or a special occasion. If you meet them on Sunday or a holiday, you will see they have a nice dress, nice shoes, pocket-book, stockings. You would not know them for the same person. Our women are not like yours; they save, save, save. You cannot get them out of it."

I smiled dubiously. The strange thing was that I had not been especially conscious of poverty in Lisbon until I spoke of it in the propaganda man's office. In this bureaucratic setting, all the sorry sights I had beheld, almost without seeing them, came out as if they had been recorded on a photographic plate that was only now immersed in a solution. Not to see, in fact, is a part of the Portuguese idyll, a sort of trick of the dazzling light and brilliant weather. It is easy for the foreigner in Lisbon, bewitched by the fruit and flowers and the myriad cakes and cheeses and sausages in the glittering shopwindows, to miss the signs of poverty or to assimilate them to the picturesque. Oporto is different. There, gray misery is very evident; the Oporto equivalent of the Alfama is a scene of such purulent horror that the tourist flees, with his handkerchief to his nose, under the gaze of the mustached Mmes. Defarges along the riverbank. But Oporto, a dirty, foggy industrial city and the classic hotbed of Portuguese radicalism and rebellion, is under a cloud, both literally and figuratively, and nothing has been done to make it charming or colorful—while Lisbon has been beautified by government fiat. Visitors see the pink and pistachio and buff and yellow washes of the houses gleaming in the Lisbon sun and take this as evidence of individual prosperity and initiative, whereas the fact is that Lisbon houseowners are compelled by law to repaint every five years, and in the government-subsidized housing projects the range of colors is prescribed by the authorities.

The visitor's first impression is that the people of Lisbon are extraordinarily well dressed, on the whole; outside the Alfama and some of the poorer working-class sections, practically every man you see, not counting the lottery-ticket sellers and the street-cleaners and the policemen and the laborers repairing the streets, is wearing a business suit, a clean shirt, and a necktie. It is a little time before you get to realize that the suit on the man next to you in the streetcar is terribly frayed and patched and mended, the surface of the shoes worn and cracked, the briefcase ragged and made of simulated leather, and the hand holding it seamed and cracked, too, like red leatherette. The laundry garlanding the streets is so fetching at first glance that you do not notice that many of the articles hung out are, literally, shreds and tatters of garments—scarecrow shirts and underwear. And there is something about Lisbon, not only the government's enterprise but the pride and politeness of the people, that makes you, politely, not want to notice.

Portugal has a misleading reputation for being an inexpensive country to live in. From our point of view, food and wine and rent and laundry and tobacco *are* cheap. There are a number of hotels and *pensãos* where you can get a room and three meals, with wine, for two dollars and forty-five cents a day, plus a ten-percent service charge, plus, in most places, a three-percent tax if you are a tourist. At a restaurant, you can have an excellent meal—a shrimp omelet to start, then a golden *bacalhau* (dried cod, done with egg yolks, black olives, sauté potatoes, and onions), a tender beefsteak, a salad, white-mountain or *Azeitão* cheese, a superb peeled and sugared orange, and black coffee—for a dollar and seventy-five cents, which includes a bottle of good wine. (This is the ideal meal; you can eat less and pay less, or you can eat a worse meal and pay more in a luxury restaurant.) Taxis and trolleys are cheap by our standards, and buses and trains very reasonable. In general, any product or service that has human labor as its chief component is not at all costly. But if you want to buy something imported (a pressure cooker, an electric stove, a radio) or something made in a modern factory, it is often quite expensive by any standards. Cars are very expensive, and gasoline costs around seventy cents a gallon. Kleenex is about seventy-five cents a small box. I had to buy a one-piece bathing suit with a skirt, as decreed by the authorities, to take to the Algarve coast; this, quite ugly and made of inferior wool in a Portuguese factory, cost twelve dollars. If, however, I had had the suit made up by a seamstress, in cotton, it would have cost five dollars, or even less. My husband had a pair of shoes made for him by a shoemaker in Potimão; they squeak, like all Portuguese shoes, but they cost only eight dollars and fifty cents. A factory-made shoe of comparable quality but ugly design costs ten dollars.

Thus even the most slow-witted foreigner begins to wonder, as I did, who buys the things in the Chiado—the refrigerators and electric mixers and washing machines. A maid's monthly salary, one learns, is from two hundred to four hundred escudos, or from seven to fourteen dollars, plus room and board. Construction workers get about twenty escudos (seventy cents) a day take-home pay, with no pay for days when rain halts work; workers in the sardine canneries get about the same, and are frequently laid off for a day or more, depending upon the catch of fish. "How do they live on it?" foreigners ask one another. The answer is that nobody seems to know. Most economic questions dissolve into mystery in Portugal. The Portuguese themselves, except those in the poorer classes, have no curiosity about such matters. "Who buys the things in the Chiado?" In the early days of my stay in Portugal, this question harried me. In a country where labor was the cheapest of all commodities, who was buying the labor-saving devices? And who was munching the Tootsie Rolls? Not the *marquesas*, surely, gliding by, with eyes like black diamonds, in their Rolls-Royces. After a while, I gave up asking these questions, as most Americans do who stay on here, because I never got a satisfactory answer. "Foreigners," some Portuguese say, vaguely, and some think it may be the parvenus—the people who made money on Portuguese wolfram during the war. ("Wolfram" is one of those ready answers, along with "Housing project," that come like responses in a litany. "Wolfram?" you learn to ask, pointing to a fur piece or a stream of traffic on the *auto-estrada,* and your companion nods.) After my curiosity had shrunk, from constant thwarting, I finally met an actual consumer—a high government official, who had given his wife a pressure cooker, which she had used, or had her cook use, once or twice, to see how it worked; it was evidently a toy.

Certainly there is new money in Portugal. They did well on wolfram, and on refugees, during the war. The Oppositionists say that many of these gains found their way into the pockets of the government bureaucrats, and that these bureaucrats continue to profit, through bribery, on every business transaction. A surprising thing about Portugal, which is admired as a model state by laissez-faire conservatives abroad, is that it does not have a free economy. Prices, wages, and the profit margin are mostly fixed by law. "Why, it's Communism!" lamented an American who is in the chemical business here. He also had a low opinion of the Caixa de Previdência, the Portuguese social-security system, which exacts from the employer an amount equal to fifteen per cent of the worker's wages, adds to it two per cent from the worker, and invests the whole in a fund for sickness, disability, old age, widows' pensions, and burial allowances; there is no unemployment insurance. The chemicals man was objecting not so much to the tax itself as to what he called the "Socialist" use the government was making of the Caixa de Previdência fund—investing it in public housing, which competes with private industry. "It's the economic principle behind it that's all wrong!" he said excitedly, adding that there had been scandals in the administration of the funds.

But this man is a foreigner. Portuguese businessmen do not

worry about principle; they look at the facts. Except for the two-per-cent levy on wages, there is no income tax in Portugal. The rich do not forget that they were saved, as they say, from anarchy; it is Salazar or worse, they declare. "You never had it better," the government tells them, in effect, and doubtless this is true. If the margin of profit is fixed (as it is even for the small retailer; the customer can send in a complaint if he is overcharged in a shop), most wages are fixed, also. Strikes are forbidden; agitators are run out of the syndicates, which might be described as government company unions; Communists are outlawed. It is true that there is a heavy duty on imports, which is tantamount to a tax on the rich—the only people who can afford cars and French neckties and foreign gadgets, Chesterfields and Yardley's—but to some this has marked social advantages, for it preserves class distinctions. A Chesterfield cigarette is a badge of class; the Portuguese make a queer, characteristic little grimace—the lower lip thrust out in pouting dismay—when they see a foreigner smoking one of the domestic Dianas or Suaves. The same with gin; the English in residence drink Portuguese gin, but the Portuguese middle class serves Gordon's. Coca-Cola is not permitted to enter the country—for moral aesthetic reasons, I was given to understand by the propaganda man, although I have since heard that the Coca-Cola case was "mishandled"; pressure was applied too heavily and at the wrong spot. At any rate, other foreign companies that compete with Portuguese manufacturers have been able to come to terms with the government; Lux, for instance, made in Portugal and not very sudsy, can be bought, at considerable cost, by ladies with nylons to wash.

A number of taxes assume the form of licenses. Cigarette lighters are licensed. Cars, naturally, are licensed, and so are bicycles and dogs; every parrot, croaking in its cage, is licensed; every donkey toiling up a mountain road. There is the three-per-cent tourism tax, which is taken from the tourist in most hotels and *pensãos* and in luxury restaurants. And there are hosts of regulations, conducive to a disciplined atmosphere. You have to have a permit to buy a typewriter ribbon. Hotel rates are regulated, and the hotel and

boardinghouse keepers are required to serve a third of a litre of
wine (the *vinho da casa*) with every lunch or dinner. Road menders—poor men who work from sunrise to sundown for a tiny wage
as part of the Portuguese P.W.A.—salute every passing car; it is a
rule, one is told. Every newspaper must be approved, daily, by the
censor. Political parties are proscribed, except Salazar's National
Union, which calls itself not a party but an "organ" of the people.
Workers' syndicates are bound "to abstain from all ideological
discussions and to concentrate on the defense of the material and
moral interests of their members, on the technical improvement
of their trade, and on the creation of the frame of mind necessary
for social peace." Factories with more than twenty employees must
conduct adult-education courses for the illiterate. Every landowner
is assessed for the number of hands his property can theoretically
employ, and in periods of agricultural crisis or general unemployment he is required to take on workers up to that capacity. The
assessments, I have heard, are often unjust, and fall hardest on the
small landowner, who cannot afford to bribe the proper officials.
For such a landowner, they put mechanization out of the question;
there is no point in buying a tractor if you are obliged to employ
extra field hands, whose labor you must contrive a use for.

This is corporativism; everybody, except the housewives, is
organized, or "integrated," in some fashion, even the priests. To be
expelled from a syndicate means literal outlawry for a worker; if
anybody is to hire him, he must change his name or get his record
expunged. Agricultural workers are incorporated into Houses of
the People, which are syndicates of a sort; employers are incorporated into *gremios*, or guilds; lawyers, doctors, engineers, and
other professional people are incorporated into *ordens*, or societies.
Youth is mobilized into the Mocidade Portuguesa—a semi-military
youth movement—but membership in it is not compulsory. There
are five kinds of police—municipal and national—plus a National
Guard, a Fiscal Guard, and the volunteer Portuguese Legion. "Two
persons, one policeman" is the sardonic comment of the lower-class
Portuguese on the omnipresent police, who are also referred to as

"Salazar's friends." The size of the Regular Army is under a security blanket at present, although there can be no real secrecy, since the figures are known to NATO, and it is typical of Portugal that nobody can explain why this regulation was imposed. "Perhaps the Army is afraid the Russians will find out," one Portuguese suggested to me hopefully. In any case, there are sour-looking soldiers and their barracks everywhere, most noticeably in the provincial towns. Many of the big convents, from which Christ's volunteers were driven out half a century ago, now house Army conscripts.

But all such hardships and annoyances do not worry government officials or the well-to-do Portuguese and foreigners living in villas in the resort towns of Sintra, Estoril, and Paria da Rocha. "I adore Salazar" is the cry of the English lady-in-exile, with a blue chiffon scarf at her throat. "*Dictature? Pas du tout. C'est ridicule,*" the chief male dancer of the Portuguese ballet said to me. This young man adored Salazar, too, while holding *les choses portugaises* in a certain wry contempt. He read only French books, and disliked port and the *fado* and cooking with oil. This is typical of the sophisticated Portuguese. "Manueline—it's simply futurism, the *parvenu* art of commerce," I was told by a Portuguese art historian who was also in the cotton business. People of standing complain about the servants, about the food, about the Portuguese character, but not about the corporate state. The more vexed such critics are with the Portuguese people, the more they applaud the strong hand the government takes with them. Most of the few kind words I have heard about the Portuguese character have come from Oppositionists—people who have been in prison or are living on the edge of disaster. There are many exiles in Portugal, including some famous kings and pretenders, and the Portuguese of the upper classes have developed an air of living in exile themselves; there is a tendency among them to look upon the people of the lower classes as natives, in the colonial sense of the term—to berate them, bewail them, smile over their idiosyncrasies, boast of their devotion.

And, indeed, there is something at once maddening and endearing about the Portuguese people—"*le peuple portugais, le vrai*

peuple," as the upper classes and the intelligentsia call them, to distinguish them from the middle classes, whom all the other classes
unite in abominating. This maddening quality—a sort of bizarre
inefficiency, lumpishness, and illogicality—is encountered chiefly
in the men and overgrown boys, the *rapazes* of the hotels and shops
and boarding houses. The women and children are angels, most
people agree. But the word "*rapaz*," meaning "boy," comes for the
foreigner to be a word of horror, combining, in the Anglo-Saxon
mind, the worst features of "rascal" and "rapscallion" and evoking
a picture of a tepid, scowling, scurfy, lazy, lying youth who cannot
get anything right and who will soon grow into a man with the
same characteristics—his sole source of drowsy interest his football
club. (There are charming boys and men, too, of course—sensitive,
courteous, but somewhat frail and pensive, as though their virtues
had attenuated them.) The Spanish call the Portuguese "*estúpido*,"
and the Portuguese men say it of one another, furiously, leaning out
of their cars to bellow it at a pedestrian, at a policeman, at another
driver: "*Estúpido, estúpido, estúpido!*"

"*Fantástico!*" our intelligent young Portuguese driver kept saying,
with a grin, whenever we struck on some instance of illogicality
during a ten-day trip through the north. "Fontaschtic," he would
sigh. It was his favorite word, in Portuguese and English, the sign
that he had become an onlooker, like the foreigners he drove.
"Fontaschtic," we would agree, as the road menders stopped work
to salute. This fantastically, or freakishness, as of a piebald horse
or a flower curiously streaked, runs irrepressibly through the
Portuguese character. Doubtless it is partly the result of the con-
junction of an illiterate peasant people and modern machinery.
(Critics, biologically minded, trace it to hereditary syphilis, brought
back during the Age of Discoveries, and there are certainly many
freaks of nature in Portugal—hunchbacks and mustached women,
recalling the Middle Ages. In the course of our ten days in the north,
we saw three women bearded like prophets.) What is strange about
Portugal, on the whole, is the unevenness of its development. The
terraced farms in the mountains, with their rock walls like rows of

teeth, are masterpieces of masonry; a plowed field in Portugal is more beautiful than a garden elsewhere. Many of the mechanical contrivances one sees are extremely inventive. Yet there are eerie zigzags and contradictions. For instance, practically all of Portugal is electrified, including the most primitive villages, but the lights are always going out, even in the big hotels, often several times in an evening, and the boy who goes to fix them does not understand electricity. Though this happens with almost predictable regularity, nobody thinks to provide candles. Only once in my three months' stay here have candles been on hand when the fuses blew, and that was in a hotel run by an Englishman. In Praia da Rocha, the lights went out every Sunday morning all over the town; it was explained that the authorities were "washing" the electricity. In the same town, at the principal hotel, which was filled with foreigners of all nationalities, there was nobody on the staff who spoke any language other than Portuguese, and there was no railway timetable; an adventurous old Swiss gentleman with a beard, who spoke eight languages and had once made an ascent in a balloon over Moscow, nearly lost his reason trying to discover how to get a train to nearby Loulé. An Englishman at the hotel was dying from a heart condition; the ambulance taking him to Lisbon ran out of gas on a hill, the hand brake did not work, and the two orderlies stood by as the vehicle, with the stretcher in it, slipped jerkily back down to level ground.

On the comical side, there is the turkey walk from Estoril. Once every fortnight or so, the turkeys for the Lisbon market are walked in from there by a turkeyherd; driving along the *auto-estrada*, you can sometimes see them—the turkeyherd sleeping under a tree with his flock beside him. It is a fifteen-mile walk, and the turkey is a tough, seasoned veteran by the time you look him in the eye, still alive and ready to be poked, in the Lisbon market.

Most Americans shun Lisbon and huddle together in a sort of stockade in Estoril, which is an ugly little beach resort, with a casino, and houses painted blue and cream, like so many filling stations. The American wives in Estoril hate Portugal and complain that there is nothing to do here. There is some justice in the charge.

Lisbon has a delightful rococo opera house in which a German and an Italian company appeared last season, but the National Theatre did one play for dreary months on end—a Portuguese adaptation of a Spanish or Italian comedy laid in England in 1850. The movies are rather wearying, with many intermissions, and a great deal of cutting by the censor; when "The Seven Deadly Sins," a French picture, opened in Lisbon, only four deadly sins were left in it. There is very little artistic life—though not for lack or "intellectuals," as a man in the government wryly explained to me. Foreign books, chiefly, are read by the avant-garde—Sartre and Camus and Baudelaire and Rimbaud and Tolstoy. The most recent Portuguese literary renaissance was in the nineteenth century. Portuguese painting continues in its derivative course; last spring, in a tiny gallery, there was an abstract show for which all the local painters obligingly became abstractionists.

In time, most of the resident foreigners become disaffected and moody. Some take to drink, driven loco by the Portuguese peculiarities. As in the tropics, trifles begin to get on their nerves. I, for instance, cannot bear the way the Portuguese answer the telephone. "Não está," they usually growl, and hang up. You can never tell whether the person you have asked for is out or whether you have the wrong number. One American girl, whose husband is here on business, has become obsessed by the Portuguese men's habit of spitting. I told her one day that I had heard that some Oppositionists had been tortured. "What did they do to them?" she asked sharply. "Prevent them from spitting?" All winter, the Portuguese nose runs; most of the children one sees on the street have colds. The men seldom use handkerchiefs, except in the highest reaches of society. The American girl told me the other day that she nearly burst into tears of affection when she saw a very poor, ragged old man on the cable car get out a handkerchief and blow his nose. She gave him ten escudos.

It is the beggars who rasp the nerves of most foreigners—the shawled women with babies in their arms, and the old men, and the children whining, "Gimme an escudo, Mister." The English tell you never to give to children; it gets them into bad habits. But it is hard to resist the children, either because they are so pretty or, on the contrary, because they are so wretched-looking, with cold, thin, raw legs, and running noses and sores. In the Algarve, the children have caught on to the English moral disapproval of begging, and offer to sell you things instead—necklaces of sea shells, and small shell dangles meant to be worn on the lapel. One little boy, on the beach, tried to sell my husband his homework.

Whether you give or not, the beggars will not leave you alone. As soon as a foreigner goes outdoors, he is surrounded, as if by a swarm of mosquitoes, and he begins to grow angry at the Portuguese. "There are plenty of rich people in Portugal!" cried an exacerbated old lady from Iowa in a hotel in the north. "Why don't they take care of their own poor?" This indignant question echoes through the hotels and *pensãos*. The old American ladies and retired couples who arrive in Portugal—from upstate New York, largely, and the Middle West—are not especially well-to-do; they come because they have read in a magazine that Portugal is cheap. And the rich in Portugal are said to be the richest in Europe. As you watch them in the hotels—silent, like sharks, endlessly masticating, with their medicines before them—you form a new conception of what cold selfishness can be. Strangely, it is not the peasants on their donkeys, with their umbrellas, or the white-collar workers in the cafés, with their newspapers, or the working-class women, with their baskets on their heads, who look foreign to American eyes; it is the moneyed classes who appear to be of a different breed. The lowering, heavy darkness of the moneyed classes seems to be as much a state of mind or soul as a physical appearance. The thick skin, the somnolent, heavy-lidded gaze are perhaps a kind of protection against fellow-feeling. The difference between rich and poor is so extreme in Portugal that it seems to have formed a carapace over the rich, making them torpid and incurious. A gentle Portuguese lady, herself engaged in charity, explained to me, rather apologetically, that there is very little charity in Portugal. "It is not that they are bad," she said of the wealthy. "They simply do not think. They have never been trained to think. In America and England, at Christmas, your children are taught to make packages and send toys to poor children. Here they are not taught things like that."

The Caixa de Previdência is the fruit of official thought on the subject of the underprivileged; so are Economic Homes, and the various limited-rent housing projects, and the National Federation for Joy in Work, which is a workers' vacation plan. Among the official class, there is a good deal of social consciousness. There are breezy young bureaucrats—half playboy, half hard-driving worker—who remind you of enlightened young businessmen in America. They are "selling" Portugal to the tourist trade and fighting for appropriations to build hotels and clean up slums. There are other officials of a different type—stodgy, sincere, devoted, of lower social origins, fathers of growing families, who make you think of the Soviet officials of the early thirties, before the great trials and the purges. This is a government of "new men." Portugal is called a Fascist state by the Oppositionists, but the term seems a little out-of-date, for Fascism as we knew it expired with Hitler and Mussolini. General Franco's regime already appears superannuated beside the Estado Novo. The quality of Portugal is modern. It is a semi-totalitarian state, with certain positive aspects. It is possible for an official here to believe in the value of his work, to think that he is furthering the cause of progress as it is generally understood in the world by combatting illiteracy, improving health and hygiene, building dams and roads, rehousing the underprivileged, reforming the school curriculum (less "book learning," more training in citizenship; less "strictly intellectual culture," more physical education).

Except for the question of dictatorship, on which they are stiff and sensitive, many of the officials I have met here (and this is a troubling fact) do not differ greatly in their views from many progressive American school superintendents. The functionaries of Salazar talk like practical idealists; they have no patience with "sentimentality." Salazar's own rhetoric belongs to an older school: "Although with delays, with possible wanderings from detail which the difficult times explain, we still stride along the same road, with our spirit faithful to the everlasting truth… For every arm a hoe, for every family a home, for every mouth its bread." Yet even Salazar, in his most exalted vein, engages in the bureaucratic self-criticism that is characteristic of the modern totalitarian state. He complains that corporativism is slowing down, that the people are relaxing, and urges the pursuit of "our corporative crusade"; he bewails the "lack of indoctrination of the Portuguese people." This self-criticism is prevalent in the ranks of the franker officials all along the line, among whom it wears the mask of tolerance. One thing they tolerate is the Opposition, which, as they point out, was allowed to run candidates during the most recent election, in 1953—the first "free" election since the military coup in 1926. This election had a little of the flavor of a Soviet election. The Oppositionists were permitted to run candidates, but they were not permitted to organize as political parties. Their newspaper, the *Republica*, was allowed more freedom than previously, but it was still under censorship; it could "criticize but not defame," as my propaganda informant put it. The campaign was a rather improvised affair; without funds, without organization, the old parliamentarians and Socialists who had been in jail or exile off and on were restored to life in a state of slight confusion, somewhat like old Dr. Manette in *A Tale of Two Cities*. In many districts, they were not able to arrange a slate of candidates. Nevertheless, they did very well, considering; in the districts where they had candidates they polled up to twenty-five per cent of the vote. Indeed, in a country in which the government was in a position (to say the least) to take economic reprisals against every citizen through his syndicate or *gremio* or *orden*, in which mass arrests and long detentions on mere suspicion were a thing of the very recent past (1948 is the latest I have heard of), this was remarkable. But it was also sad for the veteran parliamentarians and Socialists, since it represented probably a better showing than they would ever again be able to make in their lifetimes. Since the election, the censorship has tightened again. The real standard of living, say the Oppositionists, is lower than it has ever been: the rich have been getting richer throughout Salazar's regime and the poor steadily poorer, in real wages, despite housing projects and social benefits. Moreover, they point out, the intensification of the corporativist program makes the state steadily more powerful: two bureaucracies—the ordinary state servants and the functionaries of the corporative society—have the people in double harness. And the Oppositionist leaders themselves, a handful of persons—notably Dr. Francisco Cunha Leal, engineer and former professor at Coimbra; Dr. António Sérgio, humanist, critic, and educational theorist; and Dr. Egas Moniz, neurologist and Nobel Prize winner—are in their sixties, seventies, and eighties. For Dr. Sérgio, a charming old man with an engraving of Kant in his study, it is a cross that the government does not trouble to arrest him anymore but confines itself to persecuting his associates in various petty ways.

"Ah, António Sérgio!" said the press chief of Salazar's National Union, smiling broadly. "He is a little pink. We let these people talk unless they go too far." This official was a live wire, in his early thirties, who had been to America and conferred with John L. Lewis. He was proud to tell me that he knew very well the difference between a Communist and an old-style socialist intellectual. The Communists were jailed, of course, whenever the government could catch them, but even in dealing with *them*, he declared, the state showed moderation; the most dangerous Communists got only five years. Were we in America any more tolerant? he demanded. I replied that in the Algarve I had heard of some people being arrested as Communists who were simply attending a funeral service for an old parliamentarian. Yes, that had happened, he acknowledged, but it had been a mistake, and such mistakes were rare. In the case I mentioned, the innocent bystanders had been released after two days' interrogation, and the more suspicious ones had been held for only a month and a half. The press chief spoke with a cocky frankness of what he called the small mistakes and shortcomings of the government. If he could have his way, he said, he would push the social-security program much further and take the equivalent of twenty-five per cent of each worker's wage from the employer for the Caixa de Previdência. And he would break up the big estates in the Alentejo—the great central dust bowl of Portugal. He aired these daring views coolly, rather like an insouciant young Marxist; he belonged, evidently, to the left, or "Bolshevik," wing of Salazar's National Union. For some reason—a kind of delicacy, I suppose—I never mentioned Salazar during our conversation. But as the press chief was guiding me out through a conference room hung with pictures of dignitaries, he suddenly whirled around and, with a violent jab of his short arm, pointed to a photograph of Salazar. "Do you know who that is?" he shouted, in a completely new voice, as though an angry public-address system had been switched on. "Dr. António de Oliveira *Salazar!*"

Here, apparently, was a case of political dual personality, a special mutation of our period. Another example was provided by a bilious-looking official of the Casa dos Pescadores who, with his colleague (officials here often come in pairs, like FBI men), was explaining to me matter-of-factly how corporativism works in fish. All at once, abruptly interrupting his colleague, he leaned over, fastened his yellowed eyeballs on me, and said, in a soft, menacing purr, "Have you ever heard of a man called *Salazar?*" In Portugal, Salazar's name, like God's, is usually spoken in a special manner—not exactly fearful, but dutiful, as if the voice were in a Sunday suit. There are dozens of stories about him, illustrating his economical habits, his modesty, his late and lonely vigils, his reluctance to wield power; they all sound apocryphal, like the stories that used to be told about Stalin. Some of them have a sort of gingerly humor—one, for instance, that I heard from a Portuguese chauffeur who drives for some English friends of mine. According to this story, Salazar, while driving in his Packard, encountered a Volkswagen on the road, got out, and asked its driver what it was. "It is the People's Car," said the driver, translating the German name into Portuguese. "And what is that?" he continued, pointing to Salazar's Packard. "That," said Salazar, "is *my* car," and he got in and drove away.

Mister Rodriguez of Lisbon

August, 1955

ONE RARELY SEES NOWADAYS a completely happy person, but that
was how Mr. Rodriguez struck me, like a sunburst. He believed
tremendously in his work; this was evident from the outset. He
leaped up from his desk to meet me—a stoutish, ruddy-cheeked
man, about thirty-five years old, with black, wavy hair, a round
potato nose, very clean hands, and linen snowy as an alb. Outside,
on the tessellated pavement, a car was waiting, with a driver, furnished through the Ministry of Information, to take us on a tour of
housing projects in the Lisbon area. Mr. Rodriguez searched in his
desk and found me a speech he had delivered to an international
conference of housing experts, describing the achievements his
department had made. He was the director of "Economic Homes,"
one of the "new men" of the Salazar régime, a former schoolteacher
who had married a social worker.

Yes, he said proudly: Portugal had social workers as well as
super-highways, social security, adult education, housing projects,
rent controls, price controls, modern psychiatry, football, workers'
vacation plans, and a reformed school curriculum based on citizenship and vocational training, rather than on book learning. "Just
like America." I nodded, wanly. It was not the first time the resemblance had been called to my attention. Portugal, though a small,
poor country, as her officials assured me, had nearly everything
America had, plus social discipline.

The Portuguese were children, so their leaders said. Mr.
Rodriguez did not express this thought in words, but his whole

being radiated a chaste paternal glow. He was, as he told me immediately, the father of a growing family, the head of an office family
of engineers and social workers and secretaries, and the patriarch
of 10,084 "Economic Homes," occupied, according to his estimate,
by 40,336 persons. Health and philoprogenitiveness burst from
him, together with vital statistics, as he sped me about his offices,
joyously introducing me to his staff and citing their qualifications.
Three bashful young women social workers, wearing little merit
stars in their dark suit-lapels, lined up before him, like convent
pupils, to hear their names pronounced and tell, in Portuguese,
what they did. The secretaries and "typewriters" sat demurely at
their desks or hurried to open the files at Mr. Rodriguez' bidding.
At the head of the office class, in Mr. Rodriguez' doorway, stood a
beaming engineer who had propagated thirteen children.

Thanks to the charts and figures which had been showered on
me by the Ministry of Information, I understood the principle of
"Economic Homes," and I had observed, for myself, the blocks of
new housing scattered throughout Portugal. There were housing
projects everywhere, for the fishermen, the sardine workers, the
miners; in the slums, bulldozers were at work; in the remotest
mountains, developments were springing up, complete with elec-
trification, new streets, church, school, and recreation center. The
wise philosophy of Salazar, as the official texts explained, embodied
itself characteristically in the medium of housing, the *casa* being
the symbol of family life and political stability. "For every family a
home, for each arm, a hoe, for every mouth, its bread." There were
Prefabs, "Limited Rent Housing," "Free Housing"—all subsidized
or controlled by the government.

But "Economic Homes," I learned, were the backbone of the
building program. They differed from the other types of housing in
that the rent, scaled to the occupants' wages, was paid as amortiza-
tion over a twenty-five year period, so that at the end of this period,
the tenant owned his *casa*. The houses were divided into four
classes, according to occupation: unskilled; skilled; white-collar;
and professional (college graduate or equivalent). The four classes,

in turn, were divided into types, according to the size of the family and the sex of the children: no children; one child; two children of the same sex; two children of opposite sex; three children, and so on, the requirement being that no more than two children should share a room, and that these two must be of the same sex.

This scholastic precision, as of dogmatic theology, dazzled my mind, and I found it hard to distinguish "Economic Homes" from "Economic Rent"—a branch of "Limited Rent," which was also divided and subdivided into multiple categories. Mr. Rodriguez explained the vast difference as he bustled me into the car. "Economic Rent" consisted of large apartment houses, built by workers' syndicates or by other corporative organizations or by private enterprise. Such housing projects, he understood, existed everywhere, while the *Casas Economicas*, combining individual ownership with state control and giving to each worker his separate house and garden, were typically Portuguese.

I then confessed that I found it hard not to confuse "Free Housing" (for the totally indigent) with "Free Rent Housing" (luxury apartments outside government control). And I mixed them both up with the *Casas do Povo* ("Houses of the People"), which had nothing to do with housing but were centers for agricultural workers. Mr. Rodriguez laughed. For a foreigner, he said, I had mastered the distinction well. He was relieved, he acknowledged, to find I had done my homework; this would leave us time to talk.

Time oppressed Mr. Rodriguez; the shortage of it was his only vexation. As he sat beside me in the back seat of the car, in his dark suit, with his black hair leaping into a vibrant pompadour, he gave the impression of a solid package of restless energy, like a quantum. He sat with arms folded and rump perched on the edge of the seat; one eye rested on the driver, to make sure he was taking the shortest route; the other, so to speak, roamed out the window; noting points of touristic interest that we were going too fast to see.

He began to tell me about himself, conscientiously, as we sped along, like a man dictating a memo while having his shoes shined. He came from Miranda-do-Douro, in Tras-os-Montes, far off in the north, near the Spanish border; his wife—a nice contrast—came from Silves, in the southern Algarve. He had been to America, as a representative of his teachers' syndicate; he showed me a photograph of himself in a group of teachers at the summer school of a Midwestern American college. He was still active in his teachers' syndicate, though housing kept him very busy and he had other obligations, as husband, citizen, father, and faithful son of the Church. Meetings, always meetings, he said happily. "Just like America." He had felt very much at home in America, he confided, and in his office he used American methods, treating his subordinates democratically and working harder than any of them, to show what he expected. He tried to keep up his English; at home, on his bookshelves, I would see, there were volumes he had brought back: St. Augustine, in the Modern Library, and Mortimer Adler's *How to Read a Book*.

As he spoke, he kept interrupting himself, looking at his watch, leaning forward and abruptly directing the driver this way and that, whenever a new idea crossed his active mind. "*Em frente*," "*Direito*," "*Esquerda*"—Mr. Rodriguez' interests far transcended the boundaries of his field, and the car shot about like a ball in a pinball machine, forward, left, right, under his dynamic impetus. During the course of our tour, we saw not only "Economic Homes," Mr. Rodriguez' own domain, but Prefabs, Free Housing, Limited Rent Housing, and Free Rent Housing ("You cannot tell the difference?" he inquired proudly). Crisscrossing Lisbon at a wild pace several times during the afternoon, we also saw the *auto-estrada*, the airdrome, outside and in, the new science laboratories, the new belvedere of Santa Clara, and the new church, metallically modern, of Our Lady of Fatima, where Mr. Rodriguez knelt down and rapidly said a prayer.

Thinking of the chauffeur, waiting outside, I too sent up a prayer—of thanks, for once, that we were not in a democratic country. As a democratic person, I was already feeling apologetic toward the chauffeur, who was not Mr. Rodriguez' employee but had been assigned to me through the Bureau of Tourism. But what could I do? Mr. Rodriguez had assumed command, and the driver,

I told myself, was probably used to obeying. Under a dictatorship, Mr. Rodriguez would not be expected to give his reasons.

For my own part, I was a little sorry that Mr. Rodriguez' interests pertained so strictly to the new. When I glimpsed a pink palace, once, and turned my eyes hopefully toward him, he took no notice of my curiosity.

"Pretty," I murmured, hinting.

"*Em frente*," said Mr. Rodriguez sternly ("Straight ahead"), as the driver started to slow down. For a moment, looking at his profile, with its stubby, turned-up nose and glowing round cheek, I thought of a Soviet official. And like so many revolutionaries, he was a puritan; he had turned over a "new" leaf. At one point, hearing that I too had been educated in the classics, he proposed that we should speak Latin together, but set aside the idea, stalwartly, as belonging to the "former" Mr. Rodriguez.

It was mid-afternoon when we drove into the first block of *Casas Economicas* in the Madre de Deus district. I had asked to see Class A and Class B, unskilled and skilled—the lowest categories. As we drove along the new streets, laid out on a rectangular plan, Mr. Rodriguez emphasized that these were not houses but homes. The owner-tenants were screened by the young social workers I had met in his office, to make sure they were the right kind of people. The rents were fixed in each category not to exceed one-sixth of the family's total earnings, and fifteen per cent of this rent went to cover insurance premiums for death, disability, and sickness, also for fire insurance.

What if a worker loses his job? I asked. The social workers would find him one, Mr. Rodriguez replied. And if he died, even if he had just moved in, the house would belong to his widow, without further payments. Still, I said, there must be some occasions when the worker-tenant could not keep up the installments and the house would revert to the state. Very seldom, said Mr. Rodriguez. The screening was very thorough. "If we suspect a man is unstable, we do not give him the house." Once in a while, of course, human nature being what it was, a tenant might begin to drink or go crazy, but again the social worker would step in and have him treated by psychiatry.

It sounded very good, I observed. But what if the owner-tenant's wife was a slatternly housekeeper and they let the place run down? The government, he answered, had thought of that too. Each block of houses was supervised by a Fiscal officer, who lived in the end house, where he could keep an eye on things. But generally there were no problems. The Portuguese were naturally neat, and since the *casa* belonged to the worker, he had a special interest in keeping it in good condition. Many improved their houses, working after hours. There, for example—his eye traveled down a street commendingly—was a garage an owner-tenant had built himself.

A feeling of surprise came over me as I turned to look at the garage, draped in bougainvillea. I knew what a car cost and I knew what workers were paid. A building worker, in a good month, might get $23.40, minus taxes and social security deductions. The cook (skilled) in my *pensão* got $7 a month. What, I murmured, was the rent in these Class A houses? He was not sure; each case was different—about a hundred and thirty escudos, $4.55. (He was wrong; as I later learned, the Class A rents in this district were about two hundred escudos—$7.)

This was not too bad, I reflected; some workers could afford to live here, especially with the gardens yielding fruit and vegetables; according to Mr. Rodriguez, many of the tenants kept chickens and rabbits also. And if all your insurance were paid and there were no heating bills to think of, in this temperate climate, and the state sent the doctor when you were sick? The houses, in pale pastels with orange-tile roofs, looked pleasant from the outside; the streets were clean and sunny and the children were riding tricycles up and down the pavement. If the interiors lived up to the outside, the worker's lot here would compare quite favorably to America, with its dreary television aerials and canned spaghetti dinners. I still wondered about the garage, but it occurred to me that the owner might be a taxi-driver.

Our own car had stopped, in front of the Fiscal's house. Mr.

Rodriguez jumped out and knocked at the door. There was no answer. An expression of annoyance crossed Mr. Rodriguez' face. He jotted down a note in his notebook, and we drove along slowly, trying to choose a house.

A uniformed maid, with a child hiding behind her skirts, answered the door of the house we finally selected.

"Class A?" I queried, feeling that there must be a mistake.

"Class A," said Mr. Rodriguez, firmly, piloting me forward. I glanced at the young chauffeur for confirmation.

"Class A," he nodded, grinning, and folding his arms proudly, in imitation of Mr. Rodriguez, before the picture of (unskilled) working-class prosperity that presented itself framed in the doorway. The mistress of the house was out, but the maid consented to show the house to us when Mr. Rodriguez revealed his identity. She was eager, indeed, to show it, hurrying ahead of us to plump a cushion here or straighten a hanging there. I tried to conceal my astonishment. The house was furnished in the height of Portuguese bourgeois taste. There was a huge crystal chandelier in the small boxlike living room; there were carved cabinets, heavy embossed draperies, a wall-to-wall armoire in the Chinese style, Oriental-type rugs, floppy velvet dolls, lace antimacassars on dark, overstuffed chairs. The dining room and the upstairs were furnished with the same abandon; the only room that could be called economic was the maid's room, which had nothing in it but a bed, a cheap chest of drawers, and the toys of the son of the house.

"*Bonita*," I echoed the maid's soft comment, as we moved from room to room, Mr. Rodriguez stopping to demonstrate that the house had everything the charts distributed by the Information Ministry promised: modern bath, modern kitchen, room for the child, room, as he put it, "where the couple sleeps," flower garden in front, vegetable garden in back. There was, however—in the chart—no maid's room in Class A, Type 2 (one child). The house we were in, from its layout, was in fact Class A, Type 3 (two children of opposite sexes). I did not call this to Mr. Rodriguez' attention, and if he noticed it, he gave no sign.

"They have fixed it up, I think," he said instead to me, uncomfortably, passing his hand through his pompadour, as we came out into the street.

I could have told Mr. Rodriguez not to worry, that this too was "just like America." We too had housing projects designed for the poor and pre-empted by grafters who got in through pull. But instead, rather meanly, I said nothing, and we went on to a house across the street—another Class A, which belonged, said Mr. Rodriguez, to a railway worker. This one was more modest. The crystal chandelier ("*muinte caro*") was smaller, and there were fewer rugs and carved cabinets. There was no maid, and the housewife kept apologizing for the state of the rooms, though in fact they were very clean and redolent of furniture wax. Here again (poor Mr. Rodriguez!), we were invited to inspect the quality of all the appointments: the mirrors and the china and the chiffon-covered boudoir lamps.

"*Bonita*," I said, "*Muinte bonita.*" I knew what this house reminded me of—the Massachusetts home of an Italian liquor-store dealer who was reputed to be a millionaire by his humble Portuguese-American neighbors. There was the same smell of wax and there were the same iridescent taffetas and holy pictures in gilt frames and sets of matched colored glasses. The chief difference was that the Massachusetts wine merchant had a radio that lit up with a colored sign, "Four Roses," when you turned it on. In his backyard, the liquor-store Croesus had a fig tree. Here there was a goat in the backyard, and a pair of rabbits in a hutch. We lingered on the back steps, talking to the flustered housewife, who apologized, laughingly, for the goat.

Out on the street again, Mr. Rodriguez mopped his brow and looked up and down the rows of houses in perplexity. "Let's try to find one that isn't fixed up," I suggested, feeling sorry for him, since he was a nice man, a sincere progressive, too, according to his lights. I *liked* Mr. Rodriguez, and I could not make out whether he was surprised by what we were finding or merely taken aback at seeing it suddenly from a foreigner's point of view. The driver was grinning, and I could not make out what he was thinking, either. When I caught sight of a shoemaker's sign hanging from a door, Mr. Rodriguez gladdened.

"Class B," he said—the skilled working class—and on his behalf I was honestly hoping to find a poor shoemaker inside, at his last, with a parrot and potted herbs. But the shoemaker was not at home, and there were no signs of his trade. The housewife let us in and told us that her husband worked at one of the big hospitals, making shoes. This house, curiously enough, was inferior to the others structurally, though it was in a higher category on paper. It had less light; the kitchen was smaller and the bath not so up-to-date. (I cannot explain this; neither could Mr. Rodriguez, though he admitted the difference when pressed.) The rooms still had the original cheap lighting fixtures. The divans were older; the decoration had homemade touches—in the couple's room, besides the usual Madonnas, there was a framed colored photo of Queen Elizabeth, in her Coronation dress, cut out of a magazine. But in the dining room, luxury reappeared, in the form of an enormous dark polished sideboard, covered with a lace cloth, like an altar, and laden with a display of bottles—wines, brandies, ports.

"These people drink, I am afraid," murmured Mr. Rodriguez, discreetly closing the door.

As we left, the woman next door, who had been watching us and gossiping with the driver, invited us to see her *casa*, which was much the same as the shoemaker's—another Class B.

"You want to look at more?" inquired the driver, when we came out onto the sidewalk again. I glanced at Mr. Rodriguez and hesitated. A sort of tact prevented me from asking the indelicate question pulsing through my mind: "Are there *any* poor people in these houses?"

There was no shortage of poor people, certainly, in Portugal; their absence, in fact, from this district was its most remarkable feature. I *missed* the familiar signs of poverty, both ugly and picturesque: the tattered laundry on the clotheslines, the birds in their cages, the orange horse meat in the stalls, the beggars and ragged children, the women in shawls and shapeless sweaters, the men in thin suits, like paper, the flower sellers, the reek of wine from the taverns, the mongrel dogs, the smell of codfish, the baskets of eels and fresh bread. But I dared not intimate this to Mr. Rodriguez, whose round face wore a troubled, anxious expression, as if he were conscious suddenly of a lack in his Creation, like God, when he made Eden, and forgot to put in woman.

Instead, I told the driver no, thank you. If they were all like this, I said, I had seen enough to get the idea. We got into the car and drove off. The houses were very nice, I said repeatedly, to comfort Mr. Rodriguez—very clean, very clean. And I did not bother to speculate, even inwardly, as to how these owner-tenants had qualified for their homes: had they concealed their assets or were they devoted members of Salazar's National Union or did they have a cousin or a godfather in Mr. Rodriguez' office? Looking sidewise at Mr. Rodriguez, I could not believe that he was corrupt, in any of the ordinary ways. For one thing, he looked much too uncomfortable, like a person who feels criticized and does not know where to begin his defense.

The problem, evidently, was turning over in his mind, for he came, all at once, out of a fit of abstraction and directed the driver to turn back and take us along the edge of this Madre de Deus section, where, on the outskirts of the *Casas Economicas*, on razed ground, a few leaning hovels were still standing.

"It was all like that—a slum—before we built the houses," he said excitedly.

"Terrible," I agreed. And he made the driver take us around the circuit a second time, to compare before and after. I inquired what had happened to the inhabitants whose houses had been torn down, to create the Economic Homes. On this point, Mr. Rodriguez was vague, but he was certain they had been taken care of. Some might be in Free Housing, for the indigent, and some in the Prefabs in the Tin District, some in Limited Rent, and some, maybe, in *Casas Economicas*. Again, I held my peace, mindful of the New York slum dwellers who had been dispossessed to create Stuyvesant Town and

Peter Cooper Village. What Mr. Rodriguez didn't know wouldn't hurt him, I decided patriotically.

After this, we saw Prefabs (temporary housing). These were authentic working-class houses, very charmingly done, with strings of bright laundry, bird cages, potted geraniums, and large families in the doorways, watching us as we drove by and shading their eyes against the late afternoon sun. I liked these much better than the *Casas Economicas*, but I did not want to hurt Mr. Rodriguez' feelings by saying so. On his side, he assured me that these Prefabs were only a makeshift; the tenants who made good here would be moved into *Casas Economicas*, the others into Limited Rent. In time, the whole district would be torn down, but progress was a question of stages. We paused here only briefly; he was in a hurry to be on. From the car, we looked at two more districts of Economic Homes.

"They are all alike," said Mr. Rodriguez, "but some are more fixed up. You do not wish to go in?" I shook my head. I was satisfied, I said, that they were all very nice. We were hastening on, I realized, to the climax of our tour: Mr. Rodriguez' own home, Class D, Type 3—college graduate, two or more children of different sexes.

His wife, his young sister-in-law, who was a "typewriter" in his office, his children, and a maid were all waiting to receive us and show us in shy trepidation their *casa* and family life. Their house was large and sunny, more restrained in its decorative appointments than any we had yet seen. It had a splendid modern kitchen, two baths, bedrooms for the children and the parents, a comfortable book-lined study for Mr. Rodriguez, and a small bare room for the maid. I had to inspect everything—the ribboned baby in its bassinet, the toilets and the laundry facilities, whose workings the father of the home energetically demonstrated; the whole family gathered round while Mr. Rodriguez turned on the shower in the main bath to show that the water was hot. "Feel," urged Mrs. Rodriguez, a pretty, gentle little girl with big dark eyes, and we all put in our hands and felt.

As we came down the polished stairs, Mr. Rodriguez hurried ahead and flung open the door to the dining room, which I had not yet been shown. He revealed a table spread with a lace table-cloth and cups and plates and saucers and heaped with fruits and cakes. This, it seemed, was in my honor; I was expected to stay for tea. There were olives and ham and sausages; salted almonds from the Algarve; five kinds of cakes from Silves, Mrs. Rodriquez' home; frilly little sponge cakes, like daffodils, from Lisbon; a special cake from Evora, in the Alentejo; sweets made of figs and almonds, four kinds, from the Algarve; and finally a decorated birthday cake that had been made the day before to honor one of the family. Mr. Rodriguez took an appraising look at this banquet and at once ordered the maid to make sandwiches. The sandwiches came in; Mr. Rodriguez examined them critically; he feared the bread was cut too thick. Tea was poured, and Mr. Rodriguez sent out to the kitchen for a fresh round white mountain cheese.

Everything was homemade, Mr. Rodriguez attested—in the kitchens of cousins or aunts or friends. And I had to partake of it all, especially the candies and cakes from Silves, because I had been there and walked in the grass-carpeted old Moorish fortress and dropped stones into the great cistern that was used in the famous siege when the Portuguese were fighting the Arabs.

"She has been there!" Mr. Rodriguez assured the two shy sisters, and we talked happily of Silves in English, French, and Portuguese. Mr. Rodriguez proudly demonstrated that Mrs. Rodriguez spoke French. When I had sampled everything on the table, paper nap-kins were brought to make up a package of cakes and sweets for my husband, because he too had been in Silves and climbed on the red parapets of the castle, looking out over almond and mimosa and figs and kumquats to the blue mountains of Monchique. "Tell him they are from Silves," said Mrs. Rodriguez softly.

Mr. Rodriguez went to the sideboard and poured port, two kinds, into liqueur glasses. They all—the sisters, the maid, and the older children—watched while I drank under Mr. Rodriguez' supervi-sion, as they had watched when he demonstrated the miracle of the hot shower bath.

"Drink," said Mr. Rodriguez, fetching another bottle from the sideboard. Rather troubled, I tasted the liqueur—something regional, from the Upper Douro, with a flavor like Drambuie—that he poured into a fresh glass. It was nearly eight o'clock, and I was worried about the driver, waiting all this time outside. Even if it *was* a dictatorship, there were, I felt, limits.

At last, they let me leave the table to go into the study and telephone my husband, who had been expecting me at our *pensão* for the past two hours. While I was waiting for the boardinghouse to answer, I saw Mr. Rodriguez open the front door and curtly beckon the chauffeur in.

"Eat," commanded Mr. Rodriguez, in Portuguese, directing the young man to the now-empty dining room, where the table lay strewn with crumpled napkins and the debris and crumbs of our feast. The driver, cap in hand, declined, and I secretly applauded his spunk, even though I feared he was hungry. Mr. Rodriguez shrugged, the picture of offended beneficence. Nevertheless, we all said goodbye very warmly. Mr. Rodriguez presented me with the marital calling card of himself and Lucinda Maria Duarte Estrelo. "You will not forget us?" he said, glancing at his watch, for he was off to a teachers' syndicate meeting. I promised that I would not.

The chauffeur did not forget him either. The next week he took us—my husband and me—on a ten-day trip through the north, to see baroque churches with painted ceilings and eighteenth-century palaces and Roman remains. All along the way, outside once-Phoenician fishing villages or walled medieval towns, in the savage recesses of dark mountains where the inhabitants lived in granite huts without windows or chimneys and where wolves were said to roam, we kept seeing or, rather, spotting blocks of bright new orange-roofed white houses deposited on the countryside, like Mr. Rodriguez' calling-card.

"*Casas Economicas,*" the driver would sigh. "Mr. Rodriguez. '*Direito,*' '*Esquerda,*' '*Em frente.*'" And his laugh, like a wild dog's bark, would echo sardonically across the emerald ravines.

Naming Names
The Arthur Miller Case

Spring, 1957
WHEN AUTHUR MILLER, AUTHOR of *Death of a Salesman,* was
indicted for contempt of Congress this February, the American
liberal public was not aroused. The Civil Liberties Union in New
York has about thirty such cases in its files; none of them, including
the Miller case, has awakened much interest. This may be attributed
to apathy ("People feel that this subject has had it," Mr. Miller says)
or, in this particular instance, to a sense that nothing bad can really
happen to the husband of Marilyn Monroe. Mr. Miller, if con-
victed, is liable to a year in prison and a fine of $1,000. But these
are maximums; they represent a potential of punishment which
the government, even if it convicts the playwright, may shrink
from imposing under the circumstances. Meanwhile, another case,
parallel with Mr. Miller's, that of a trade union organizer named
Watkins, is before the Supreme Court; if the Watkins conviction
should be reversed, the Miller case might be dropped altogether.
And even if the Watkins decision were upheld, the Miller case
might still be won, since it presents small points of difference, and
even if the Miller case were lost in the lower courts, appeals would
follow. In short, assuming the very worst, a long time would have
to pass before Mr. Miller would be behind bars; the slow workings
of American justice make such a prospect seem unreal and, considering the persons, positively fantastic. Off the screen, it is hard to
summon up a vision of Miss Monroe talking to Mr. Miller (wearing
convict garb) across a prison partition while stony guards look on.

We have seen this scene too often in the movies to accept it in real life; the plot, too, is familiar; the husband is doing time for having refused to inform on his buddies. Mr. Miller's last play, *A View from the Bridge*, was about an informer.

Yet this is precisely the issue which the courts will consider: the refusal to play the informer before a Congressional Committee. Called before the House Un-American Activities Committee last June, Mr. Miller declined to name the names of persons he had seen at Communist-sponsored meetings, although he testified freely about his own past association with Communist-front groups. He was not the first witness to find himself impaled on a dilemma, that is, to be willing to talk about himself and unwilling to talk about others. But he was almost the only prominent figure heard by the Committee who did not either tell all or take refuge in the Fifth Amendment, which protects a witness against self-incrimination. Against the ritual reply droned out so often during these past years—"I decline to answer on the ground that it might tend to incriminate me"—Mr. Miller's forthrightness struck a note of decided nonconformity.

Regardless of the legalities, in the eyes of the public, every witness who invoked the Fifth Amendment appeared to be guilty, and this fact was traded on by Senator McCarthy and other Congressional investigators, who delighted in confronting America with a parade of witnesses who, one after another, invoked the Fifth Amendment and were handed down from the witness stand with an air of crisp satisfaction, just as though they had confessed to a long bill of dark particulars. Some of these witnesses, like Mr. Miller, had never been Communists; others had broken, years before, with the Party. But to the ordinary newspaper reader, every witness who used the Fifth Amendment was as a dyed-in-the-wool member of what was felt to be a Communist conspiracy to keep the truth from him personally. The right to know took on the character of a basic democratic right which was being trampled upon by these silent witnesses with impunity. It was the public's right to know and Congress' right to ask

that Mr. Miller challenged on June 21, in his testimony before the
Un-American Activities Committee. Or, to be more exact, he conceded the Committee's right to ask him any questions about himself
(a right I am not sure the Committee really possessed), but denied
its right to extract from him, under threat of contempt proceedings, the names of other people he had known in the Communist
movement. As the transcript of the hearing shows, he spoke at
length (though frequently interrupted) about the motives that had
impelled him to take an interest in Communist groups, and what
he called the "mood" that kept him in the Communist orbit up to
1948. He remained polite and informative, despite a good deal of
badgering and repeated attempts to trap him in merely verbal contradictions. But when it came to giving names he balked, and this
balking, in the view of his questioners, amounted to a limitation on
Congress' power to investigate. The contempt citation against him
was voted eventually by the House of Representatives—373 to 9.

Congress' power to investigate had already been somewhat limited by the courts. Witnesses, the courts have decided, cannot be
called before a Congressional committee, except to testify on matters involving legislation. Mr. Miller was called, officially, as a witness in a study of passports; a numbered bill on passports had been
put in the hopper by Representative Francis Walter, the chairman
of the Un-American Activities Committee, and Mr. Miller was told,
at the outset: "We're investigating passports." The first questions put
him dealt closely with his passport history—the passport that had
been given him in 1947, and the question of what oath he had sworn
then (like everyone else, he had sworn to uphold the Constitution
of the United States), the passport that had been refused him in
1954 (when he had been invited to go to Brussels for a performance
of *The Crucible*), the passport he had applied for four and a half
weeks prior to the hearing and on which he had still received no
reply (in the end, he was given a passport, for six months only, to go
to England and join Miss Monroe and see *A View from the Bridge*).
These questions could be thought to have some remote bearing on
legislation: his experiences with the passport bureau of the State

Department might, in an ideal state of affairs, have prompted some remedial law-making, to curb the high-handed behavior of passport officials. But the Committee soon departed from the theme of passports to interrogate Mr. Miller about his past. They wanted to know whether he had opposed the Smith Act, which makes it a crime to teach or advocate the overthrow of the government by force and violence; whether he had signed various protests and petitions; what his attitude had been toward Ezra Pound; how he felt about Elia Kazan, once a director of his plays, who had testified before a committee and named names (had there not, in fact, been a "break" between them?), whether he had not attacked the Un-American Activities Committee itself and satirized Congressmen in a skit.

What emerged from this dogged questioning was the fact, which no one denied, that Arthur Miller in the past had some affiliation with Communists and had been critical of some legislators and legislation. This was not and is not a crime, though the tone of the questioning implied that it was; at one point, the chairman, Mr. Walters, had to step in to announce to Mr. Miller, with an air of largesse, that to disagree with the Smith Act was his right as a citizen (some of the other questioners seemed not to be aware of this). Moreover, everything that emerged from the testimony was previously known to the Committee and to the public as well, for the whole matter had been aired in the newspapers; it was a newspaper campaign against Mr. Miller, perhaps, that had first drawn the Committee's attention to him, even before his wedding plans were known—he had been called an improper person to write a documentary film on juvenile delinquency. Long before this, he had been blacklisted by Hollywood and by television. In short, no fresh information was gained from the hearing, except possibly by Mr. Miller, who had forgotten the names of some organizations he had sponsored.

The Committee indeed showed a keen reluctance to taking in any new material. Mr. Miller was eager to talk about his present views, and the Committee kept turning him a deaf ear. They wanted to hear about the past—that is, they wanted him to repeat, under interrogation, facts they already knew. Mr. Miller, for instance, wished to say that he had changed his mind about Ezra Pound, toward whom he now felt less anger than he had just after the war; but the Committee was bent only on reading him aloud what he had written about Pound *then*: "You confirm that you wrote that about this anti-Communist writer?" "At the present time..." Mr. Miller kept proffering throughout the hearing, but the Committee was not interested in what he thought or might say "at the present time," though once he made them sit up and take notice when he announced that he not only *had* been against the Smith Act but that he was against the Smith Act now. "Right now? Right this minute?" his questioner exclaimed, taken aback. "Right this minute," Mr. Miller replied. This led to a long, meandering discussion in which stirrings of curiosity were evident among the legislators. "Would you approve of someone writing a *poem* advocating the overthrow of the government?" asked one Congressman, in wonder. Mr. Miller answered that he would or that at least he would not disapprove of it, and the curiosity slowly flickered out, as though the witness were a phenomenon too weird to command more than a passing interest. It wakened again, briefly, at the very end of the hearing, when one Congressman, more sympathetic to Mr. Miller than the majority, asked him with what appeared to be genuine solicitude, "Why do you write so morbidly, so sadly?" And then, offering something positive: "Why don't you use that magnificent talent of yours in the cause of anti-Communism?"

Meanwhile, they had asked him to identify two persons as having been present at certain meetings, years before. Mr. Miller was not asked to supply their names; the Committee, of course, already knew them. All the Committee wanted was for Mr. Miller to agree that two persons, whom they themselves named for him, had been present at those meetings. This was the climax of the hearing. Ever since a subpoena had been served on him in Reno, Nevada, while he was getting a divorce, the Committee had been trying to find out whether Mr. Miller was going to be "cooperative." The investigator who served him with the subpoena invited him to have a little talk. "I think I could be helpful to you," he suggested, mentioning other writers and actors whom he had been "helpful" to under the same circumstances. "A lot of them," he observed, "have become my very good friends." He started sounding out Mr. Miller by asking him, as if idly: "What do you think of Lee Cobb? He's a great guy, don't you think?" Lee Cobb, who had had the leading part in *Death of a Salesman*, had testified before the Committee, naming names. Mr. Miller agreed that Lee Cobb was a great guy, which seemed to the investigator to promise that Mr. Miller might be cooperative, after all. "You know," he volunteered, "you surprise me. I expected you to be rougher." But until Mr. Miller was three-quarters through his testimony before the Committee itself, nobody, except his lawyers, knew how he was going to answer when the crucial question was put, and, for his part, Mr. Miller actually imagined that he might get away without having the question put at all.

This was a hopeful delusion. It is clear from his testimony that Mr. Miller and his questioners were utterly at cross purposes. He supposed, to judge from his attitude, that these Congressmen he was facing were authentically seeking knowledge and he sought earnestly to explain his views to them, rather in the manner of an author discussing his work at a writers' forum. He brought in Socrates and the Spanish Civil War and how it had felt to be a Jew in Brooklyn witnessing anti-Semitism during the early Hitler years. To the Congressmen, all this was a matter of total indifference. For them, the whole hearing hinged on a single point: was the witness willing to name others or not? That was the litmus test. Mr. Miller kept trying to explain to them what kind of man he was, but the Congressmen knew that they would learn what kind of man he was, very simply, when he let them know whether he would play the informer or not. And, in a sense, they were right. This really was the issue, and all the rest was cat-and-mouse play.

In the phrase, *play the informer*, lies the curious and twisted significance of these hearings. For the Committee's purpose, it was not necessary that Mr. Miller *be* an informer; he was merely being asked to *act* like one, to define himself as the kind of person who would interpose no obstacle between them and their right to know. The two persons he was required to identify as Communists (for that was what the questions amounted to) had already been named as Communists by other witnesses, dozens of other witnesses, no doubt. That was how the Committee had their names. The Committee was not seeking information from Mr. Miller; it was applying a loyalty test. And for Mr. Miller it was not in reality a question of betraying specific people (who had already been denounced, so that his testimony could hardly have done them further harm), but of accepting the *principle* of betrayal as a norm of good citizenship. As a leading playwright with a wide audience, he was being asked to set an example of civic obedience; not Mr. Miller but the Committee was to judge whether the disclosure of those names served any useful purpose. And if it did not serve a useful purpose, if evidently no harm could come from it, then he would seem to be straining at a gnat. He alleged conscientious scruples in defending his refusal, but the whole purport of such hearings is to reduce the private conscience to a niggling absurdity.

The Vita Activa

Teaching, for the wisest Teaching of the ancients, was only a
form of prompting. Socrates' pupils, who sought to know what was
love, what was justice, what was beauty, and so on, were shown
by the philosopher that they already knew the answers to these
questions, though they did not know they knew them, just as the
slave boy in the *Meno* "knew" a theorem in geometry, though he
did not know he knew it until Socrates, by patient prompting and
by drawing a series of squares on the ground, showed him that he
did, before an audience. Knowledge, as Socrates demonstrated
with the slave boy, who had never been taught mathematics and yet
was found to know Pythagoras' golden theorem (the forty-seventh
proposition of the first book of Euclid), is simply recollection, or
re-putting together. There are no new truths, but only truths that
have not been recognized by those who have perceived them without noticing. A truth is something that everybody can be shown to
know and to have known, as people say, all along.

This old theory of truth as the common property of mankind or,
one might say, as a vast Lost Property Office full of articles that can
be reclaimed if anyone wants to take the trouble is at the basis of
Hannah Arendt's inquiries in her new book, *The Human Condition*,
a long essay on the life of action. The author is a graduate of
Heidelberg and a pupil of the existential philosophers Jaspers and
Heidegger, who calls herself, unassumingly, a historian; the history she collects and analyzes, however, is of a special kind—the
history of ideas, but not only philosophers' ideas; common ideas,

too, stock ideas, ideas reflected in behavior and worn by use to the point that they are no longer recognized as ideas at all, just as the bourgeois gentleman in Molière was unaware that he was speaking prose.

Miss Arendt's earlier book, *The Origins of Totalitarianism*, was a piece of scholarship so novel and so unexpected in its findings that it was read like a detective story by those who first laid hands on it; *The Human Condition*, which is about man's active life as a member of his species in its habitat, the earth, has the same faculty of surprising, then awakening suspense, and finally coming to appear clear as daylight to the initially puzzled reader. The combination of tremendous intellectual power with great common sense makes Miss Arendt's insights into history and politics seem both amazing and obvious;) "Elementary, my dear Watson," the author disclaims, which is true, but only in a way—elementary to Sherlock but not to Watson.

The human condition is the old *vita activa* as opposed to the *vita contemplativa* of the philosophers. Miss Arendt sees it as divided into three spheres—labor, work, and action, action denoting politics or all the words and deeds of the public realm, where men inter*act* with each other. The clue to this novel division, which at first baffles the reader as to its import, lies, where it would in a detective story, in one of those innocent-seeming facts that are so much taken for granted that no one has thought to query them: the "elementary" fact that in most European languages there are, as in English, two words, etymologically distinct, for what would appear to be the same activity—"labor" and "work."

Aren't labor and work synonymous? Or Almost? Isn't labor merely hard work? That is what most people would say, or assume without saying. And yet there are the two words—very old words, too, as though the human race had long ago felt a great gulf of distinction between the two activities, a distinction now forgotten and confused but preserved, nonetheless, stubbornly. In Greek, there are *ponein* and *ergazesthai*. In Latin there are *laborare* and *facere* or *fabricari*. In French, there are *travailler* and *ouvrer* (now rather

obsolete as a verb but retaining its root in the noun *œuvre*). In
German, there are *arbeiten* and *werken* (*werken* again being somewhat obsolete as a verb but retaining its root in the noun *Werk*). In
Italian, three verbs—*travagliare, lavorare,* and *operare*—are in use,
together with their nouns. In all these languages, the word for labor
carries with it connotations of pain and heaviness; it means hard,
grinding, repetitive toil, and in all these languages except Italian,
which has a special word, *doglie,* the word for labor is also the word
for the pains of childbirth. *Travail* and *travaglio* come from an old
Latin word, *tripalium,* which was a kind of torture. A man is condemned to "hard labor," not to "hard work." You speak of "sweated
labor," "child labor," and so on, when you wish to show work in its
most inhuman aspect, and you speak of "labor-saving" devices, not
"work-saving" devices. Cleaning the Augean stables was one of the
labors of Hercules. The English philosopher Locke speaks of "the
labour of our body and the work of our hands."

The more these verbal differences are examined, the more evident it becomes that humanity (or Western humanity) has always
distinguished between the two activities and that one is not just
a more intense or laborious form of the other. The exceptions in
English idiom ("housework," "day's work," "workhouse") usually
reveal themselves as euphemisms or as survivals, or as a mixture of
the two: the "housework" of a lady in the Middle Ages, at the loom
or distaff, was true work, while the scrubbing, cleaning, cooking,
and laundering of the household serfs was labor. Indeed, the labor
of keeping house is labor in its most naked state, for labor is toil that
never finishes, toil that has to be begun again the moment it is completed, toil that is destroyed and consumed by the life process. (It is
significant that the discoveries of *The Human Condition* were made
by a woman, for housework, honorifically so called, is one of the
few forms of unadulterated, primitive labor besides agriculture that
still exist in advanced countries and will continue to exist forever,
even if the kitchen becomes a communal kitchen and the nursery
a crèche.) The essence of labor is its repetitiveness, its monotonous,
rhythmic, cyclical character, well expressed in the washing of dishes,

which will only get dirty again, or of children's laundry. The laboring man or woman is the equivalent of a tame animal in servitude to biology and the seasons; labor, as Miss Arendt puts it, following Marx, is man's metabolism with nature, and man, as a member of a species, is an *animal laborans*. The doom of labor, pronounced on our first parents at the time of the Expulsion from the Garden, is a life sentence of cyclical repetition, in which the earth itself shares, condemned to endless rotation and yet to eternal fixity; that is, to a routine.

The routine quality of labor is one of its distinguishing marks; the other is its consumptibility. Labor is concerned with maintenance, whether it is the maintenance of the subway or the sewer system or a tilled field or a home or life itself; it is that basic exertion required of the human race by necessity for the sake of animal survival. It can be done alone or in unison, in silence or accompanied by chants (mistakenly called "work songs"), but its essential character is mute and solitary, even if it is done in a chain gang, for each member of a labor squad is only an arm or a "hand," as he is called in the farm country, and possesses no individuality, only a measurable amount of labor power, which can be descried as if on a graph in the action of the hoe or the fall of the pickaxe.

Labor is work that leaves no trace behind it when it is finished, or if it does, as in the case of the tilled field, this product of human activity requires still more labor, incessant, tireless labor, to maintain its identity as a "work" of man. (The confusion in Italian between the various nouns and verbs for "labor," "work," and "worker" is perhaps due to the fact that in Italy agriculture is almost a craft, and, indeed, all labor, even of the most menial kind, approximates there to craftsmanship; in Italy, darning or putting on patches becomes, absurdly, a sort of work of art.)

The earth itself and the biological process tend to devour labor as a hungry person devours a loaf of bread. The products of labor, such as the loaf of bread, are characterized, like the hero Achilles, by being born to a short life. Ordained by stark necessity ("the staff of life"), they must be consumed at once or they deteriorate. Thus

a kind of urgency surrounds both their appearance and their dis-
appearance in the world. They have no durability. The products of
labor are designed to be used, like the products of work, yet the use
they are put to destroys them at once, as with the loaf of bread or,
more pathetically, with the frosted, tiered wedding cake. (The old
joke about the man who ordered from a bakery shop a cake made
in the shape of the letter "S" and, when asked whether he wanted it
in a box, said, "No, thanks; I'll eat it here," illustrates, to the point
of pain, the wasted work or craftsmanship that may go into a labor
product.) A work product, on the contrary, such as a table, which
is also designed to be used, is not destroyed or consumed in the
process. A table or a chair is devoured not by use—only by misuse;
its life expectancy may be ten years, twenty, several hundred for an
"antique," which use may be said to have improved. A table, moreover, does not spoil, like a loaf of bread or an apple, if not used; nor
does a pair of shoes put away in a closet for a year. When taken
down, they may be out of style, but they are still "good," as people
say; that is, wearable by someone.

The products of work belong not to the daily biological process
of birth and death, decay and renewal but to the man-made world,
the world of things with which man has surrounded himself and
which define him as human, as *homo faber*, man the maker and creator. This world of artifacts is characterized by durability. A bird's
nest, generally, is "good" only for a year, but a house, properly cared
for, may last for centuries. Even a pair of shoes, given decent care,
will last several years before the friction of use consumes them. The
fact that shoes, too, do finally wear out means not that they were
intended to be used up but, rather, that they, like everything else
in the exposed realm of nature, are subject to decay and attrition—
even "imperishable" stone. All work products—shoes or tables or
marble temples—affirm solidity and permanence and make man
feel at home in nature; they, in fact, taken together, constitute his
earthly residence, his "frame," as people demonstrate when they
carry a few possessions about with them, bright shawls and bowls

and cigarette boxes, to make a hotel room or a sublet apartment "seem like home."

A work product is created not out of the furious urgency of necessity but in relative leisure and in conformance with a mental picture of a table or a pair of shoes that the fabricator holds up to himself as a model. The craftsman or fabricator, classically, works alone, though he may use apprentices for the less important parts of the task, and in the Middle Ages he often worked in public, demonstrating his art or skill in the great fairs or carnivals or simply in the market place. Labor, in the ancient world, was felt to be shameful because it showed man driven by necessity, a slave of his needs or the needs of others, and the laboring activity was kept hidden in the privacy of the household, like illness and bodily "needs," but work as a process was displayed in the market. The exhibits of glass-blowing and lace-making in Venice and of leathercraft and straw-weaving in Florence are a survival of this. The worker or craftsman, like a sword swallower or juggler, exhibits his skill in the open market, where he offers its product for sale.

Finally, through politics, men reveal not their skill or their products but themselves in their words and actions, held up to admiration or contempt in the free open space of the agora or forum—a tradition still maintained in the open-air "forums" of Union Square and Hyde Park. The desire to achieve glory and everlasting remembrance through conspicuous deeds and words has shrunk, however, in modern times, to the right to "blow off steam"—the most evanescent thing there is.

In such a comparison (though this one is not in fact made in her book), the purpose of Miss Arendt's skillful distinctions suddenly becomes clear, like the glass blower's vase drawn from the furnace: she has been talking all along, really, about the present world; it has been taking shape before our eyes and now "makes sense." Those ancient categories of labor, work, and action have served as a kind of memory-jogger and a measure of what has happened. Progress has effected not a steady march but a bewildering transformation. The supplanting of tools by machinery has reached its logical conclusion in automation; the discoveries of physics and chemistry have interfered with the life process (artificial insemination) and with inanimate nature, while the vast growth of the social, steadily encroaching on both private and public life, has produced the eerie phenomenon of mass society, which rules everybody anonymously, just as bureaucracy, the rule of no one, has become the modern form of despotism. And all this has happened, or so it feels, "since yesterday."

A commonplace of parlor conversation, everywhere, in all countries, these days, is the lament for vanished "standards of workmanship," "pride in work." etc., and this commonplace is fatuous only because it is inadequate to express the real situation, which is, as Miss Arendt demonstrates with a terrible cogency, that there are no workers, unless you count artists, left in the modern world— only laborers. Industrial unions have replaced craft unions, and the "worker" in modern industry is only a labor unit. The assembly-line technique, the "division of labor" has turned work into labor; that is, into monotonous, rhythmic, repetitive toil, whose products, because of their very abundance, are no longer work products but consumer products born to a short life, like the loaf of bread. Automobiles, refrigerators, tables, chairs, shoes, houses are manufactured with a built-in obsolescence; a car or a house in a development is treated as disposable, as if it were a Kleenex or a paper napkin or a disposable diaper. Mass-produced, manufactured articles are made not to last or to express durability or guarantee permanence and stability but to be "used up" and junked as quickly as possible, and advertising agencies seek to create a demand for these products that will have all the uncontrollable urgency of a "demand" of nature. Mechanized factory labor of today has only one object, which is a cyclical one: to provide the laborer with the buying power to consume the products of his labor and thereby to keep the factory wheels turning, as though the factory were the mill of nature or of the gods' necessity, grinding on forever.

Labor and consumption, as Miss Arendt points out, are only two stages of the same thing, and a laboring society such as our own is a pure consumer society, in which everything is done to "make a living." The conspicuous production of the market economy has given way to conspicuous consumption, well expressed by the businessman's expense account, in which he takes a big "slice" of his salary in the form of meat, drink, theatre tickets, and airplane rides. Saving, whether of string or money, is naturally discouraged, and property, which shelters privacy, is dissolved into wealth; i.e., into "spending money." The ideal of a laboring society is the ideal of empty leisure and unalloyed consumption—the image, in fact, of the original Garden from which man was expelled, where Nature herself labored and man only consumed; this image is summed up, for the modern laboring man, in the hammock, the Hawaiian sports shirt, and the trip to Florida.

This ideal, far from being a daydream, is on the verge of realization, for, with automation, as Miss Arendt puts it, machines have become a "second nature," and with electricity and atomic energy, nature's never-ending processes have been channeled into the human world. This means, however, that the human artifice itself, the man-made world of things, has been endangered, for the inherent destructiveness of nature has been let loose into the thin structure of fabrication, of tables, chairs, houses, and "immortal" works of art—the old homestead of *homo faber*, where the laboring animal, too, was protected from the elements. Meanwhile, with the launching of satellites, the basic premise of the human condition, man's bondage to the earth, has been abolished, and whatever the new creatures who will inhabit the universe of the future will be, they will be not men but some sort of space creature, such as the writers of science fiction and children's horror comics have tried to imagine. Finally, modern science, which is able to do things that can be made intelligible not in words but only in formulae, has, in a sense, abolished speech as vital communication between men, and this implies that the life of action, the matching of great words with great deeds, is finished.

The pessimism of these conclusions is stoic in the finest sense. Miss Arendt's essay explains what has happened and how it happened, without dismay or grievance. Nor does it offer any remedy. It only tells a story in noble language, matching its words with the action it describes. An epigraph to one of the chapters, from Isak Dinesen, declares, "All sorrows can be borne if you put them into a story or tell a story about them." The spirit of this maxim quickens a book that has in it a great deal more than a review can mention, for the author is full of determination to get everything in—remarks on love, friendship, and the nature of works of art, on statistics, hobbies, servants, means and ends, violence, and the ancient view of slavery, on suicide, common sense, science, and logic. It is as though she were hurriedly stuffing a trunk with all the valuables, trifles, and curios of human experience in the hope that something might survive. This hurry becomes excessive in the later sections, where technical questions of philosophy and science are packed in with too much density for the ordinary reader, but the fault is one of generosity. *The Human Condition* contains a little of everything, including the kitchen stove.

A review of The Human Condition, *by Hannah Arendt.*

II

WOMAN

Tyranny of the Orgasm

April, 1947

STATISTICS COMPILED BY DR. of the University of Indiana give the text for today's sermon preached by a journalist and a woman psychiatrist to the women of America. Using the Gallup Poll method, Dr. Kinsey discovered that from 50 to 85 per cent of American women college graduates had never experienced an orgasm. High school graduates had a better record; less than 20 per cent reported the same deficiency. The percentage continued to decline as schooling was less intensive, and among uneducated Negro women the incidence of orgasm was nearly 100 per cent. If frigidity is to be viewed as a national scandal on a par with political corruption and inadequate housing, the remedy at least seems obvious. The mother of little girls has only to present Dr. Kinsey's figures to the truant officer. Mr. Ferdinand Lundberg and Dr. Marynia F. Farnham, however, disclaiming such hasty inferences, arrive at the same result by a more devious route. Their book is an adjuration to American women to return to the home and leave men's pursuits to men. Their itinerary to his conclusion follows:

(A) Modern man is unhappy, more unhappy than he has ever been before. We know this from statistics on crime, divorce, alcoholism, juvenile delinquency, the falling birth rate. Other signs of his unhappiness are Communism, socialism, fascism, anarchism, feminism, war, and modern art.

(B) Unhappiness equals neurosis. The argument that the unhappiness apparent in such mass movements as socialism and Communism has an objective base in intolerable social conditions is readily disposed of. Material conditions have improved.

(C) Modern neurosis began with the discoveries of Copernicus. Science made man feel small by showing him that the earth was not the center of the universe. He retaliated with the assertion of his penis through the conquest of nature, the invention of machines, the industrial revolution.

(D) In the course of these compensatory activities, he unwittingly destroyed the home, replacing it with the factory as the center of his life.

(E) The devaluation of the home made woman lose her function and her sense of self-importance.

(F) Woman, to recover her prestige, began to compete with man in his own domain, to work outside the home, vote, get educated, fornicate, and neglect her children. She did all this because she grudged her husband his penis, her own vagina, with the collapse of the home, having lost its *cachet*.

(G) But woman's biological nature demands reproduction and nurture of her. It punished her for not having children, for undervaluing the home and the feminine activities (nursing, dishwashing, sewing, furniture-polishing, cooking, tutoring), by refusing her the orgasm.

(H) Statistics show that the educated (ego-striving, competitive) woman has fewer children than the uneducated woman, besides being more frigid.

(I) Woman can recapture the orgasm by accepting her biological destiny. She must have at least three children and renounce her ego-striving activities in higher education and career-seeking, except in very special instances, such as that of the female doctor. She must also renounce sexual freedom—for her always self-defeating; she should preferably be a virgin when she marries.

(J) If she fails to exemplify this rule, she will be neurotic and almost invariably frigid. Her one or two children will be socially undesirable problem-cases, phallo-narcissists like Byron, compulsive bachelor system-builders like Leibnitz or Newton, or passive-feminine males with gentle, affectionate dispositions.

(K) Naturally, however, childbearing cannot be recommended for all, but only for the "fit." About two-thirds of American women are unfit. The "fit" demonstrate their fitness by producing three children. That is, childbearing is recommended for women who bear children. For the protection of these children, spinsters should be barred from our schools, teaching posts being reserved for married women with at least one child. Bachelors should be punitively taxed.

(L) Psychotherapy is recommended for the unfit. It is expensive.

Before entering into a discussion of its contents, it must be acknowledged that this book has the crude beauties of a cartoon. The mechanical view of psychology has never been so broadly rendered. Other pictures of women vanish before a vision of The Lost Sex as a broken-down sedan with Mr. Lundberg and Dr. Farnham in mechanics' overalls peering under the hood. The frigid wife in the other twin bed will never look the same again to the husband with the psychiatric know-how. Private parts become "parts" to be sent to the psychoanalytic repair shop for reconditioning. The terminology of love and of medicine is replaced by the jargon of the factory and the garage: there is no more talk of *passion* or of *healing*, but only of *functioning* and *adjustment*. Mass production methods (statistics) yield an average woman who is tested by a bureau of standards that expects uniform "performance"—the regular production of orgasm and the regular production of children. Erraticism or failure condemns her to the junkyard of society, like an airplane grounded by the Federal Aviation Authority. The American scene takes on a new, technological desolation. This junkyard is the national eyesore, a vast dump disfiguring the suburbs of the well-regulated community, presided over by the truly feminine mother and the fully genitalized male.

To the idealized machine that is the "feminine" American woman, the husband plays a subordinate but respected part. He is converted into its servant or its tender, and to qualify him for this position, his whole life must be a character reference open to the investigation of experts. The "fully masculine male" must marry, make money, work regularly and prolifically, sustain an erection for the "normal" length of time, somewhere under half an hour. He must enjoy good health, show no feminine traits of character and have "a masterful ego-structure"; at the same time, he must not quarrel with society—radical affiliations, here as in industry, will get him dismissed as a troublemaker. Intellectual and esthetic accomplishments are not denied him, provided he is a family man, steady, with good habits, sleep-in. The author's own description of the candidate for distinction follows:

"The libidinal life of authentic genius, working with a strong, completely integrated and masterful ego-structure, is fully realized in every way... The more prolific the work output of a given man, the more uniform it is in excellence and originality, the more ease there is in producing it and the higher it stands in the estimation of top workers in the field, the more likely it is to be the work of a physically healthy man. Such a man is more likely than not to be leading a sober life, married and with several children. His material establishment is apt to be better than moderately satisfactory. He never has lived in a garret. He has never had serious money difficulties, but has always been able to meet the world successfully on its own terms."

The only successful entrants mentioned by the authors are J. S. Bach and two mathematicians. Failures to qualify include Bacon, Spinoza, Schopenhauer, Rousseau, Nietzsche, Hume, Hegel, Descartes, Marx, Diderot, Napoleon, Hitler, Shelley, Keats, Coleridge, and Pascal, "much of whose work must be considered socially demoralizing." This list might be fortified by the names of Plato, Beethoven, Da Vinci, Dostoevsky, Dante, Kant, and of virtually any other great men that occur to the reader's mind. Its comparative length suggests that the problem is really one for the medieval schoolmen: that is, if by the abortion of a single Spinoza, Bacon, Descartes, et cetera, every housewife in Iowa could have an orgasm, should it be done? Fortunately, the question is indeed a scholastic one. In the practical sphere, the authors have as yet no means of enforcing the new puritanism, the puritanism of the orgasm; bachelors may, in the authors' phrase, be "suspicious" characters, and the authors may call for state-subsidized psychotherapy, but, legislators being backward, the new psychoanalytic police force has yet to be put in uniform. In the intellectual sphere, the Lundberg-Farnham argument remains purely contentious. No jot of evidence is brought forward to support the crucial proposition, that the large family and the orgasm are interdependent. College women as a group may have fewer children and be more frigid than the population as a whole, but is the college woman with three children less frigid than her classmate with none? Certainly, in the middle class, children are often the wife's excuse for terminating *amour* with her husband: don't, dear, you'll wake the baby. And the unsexed career woman may be frigid with men and amorous with women—is the Lesbian orgasm not certified by these authorities? Frigidity is a more peculiar and puzzling phenomenon than these authors admit. According to another study made by Dr. Kinsey, which has been cited to me in conversation, the female animals do not have orgasm; it is the exclusive property of the human female, who is presumed to have learned it from men. If this is so, then the biological argument is absurd, and frigidity becomes, not a hidden scandal to be exploited by sensational journalists, but a condition into which the human female rather easily, perhaps, relapses. If psychoanalysis has a cure for it, as these authors intimate, this must be the best-kept medical secret of modern times; Mr. Lundberg and Dr. Farnham, at least, are discreet enough not to introduce any evidence into the sanctuary of the assertion.

Here, as in other connections, the phrase, "clinical experience shows," relieves the authors of the necessity of proof. This phrase serves the same purpose as the photograph of the bearded doctor in the white gown extensively used in advertisements of beauty creams, reducing nostrums, and toothpaste before the passage of the Food and Drug Act. "Clinical experience," moreover, has an infinite elasticity. It shows, for example, that every child masturbates; for the patient who tells a different story, amnesia is "understood" and his failure to remember masturbating constitutes proof that he did.

In the same way, clinical experience can show that a man who has intercourse several times a day is "orgastically" impotent.

For the disingenuousness of this kind of reasoning that uses its own hypothesis as proof, that appeals always to the authority of "facts" and allows itself at the same time an anarchy of interpretation, *Modern Woman, The Lost Sex* offers an unforgettable illustration. This disingenuousness, mastering contradictions, has become indifferent to them—these authors will say *anything*. Their hardened character is well exemplified by a comparison between the book jacket and pages 220 and 221 of the text. Inside, the authors are exposing the "suggestive" innuendo of contemporary advertising and pointing particularly to the use made of "illustrations of ecstatic young models half-swooning in the moonlight." Outside, on the dust-cover, is a drawing of a young model naked in the moonlight. She does not appear to be swooning but blushing. She is hiding her eyes.

A review of Modern Woman, The Lost Sex, *by Ferdinand Lundberg and Marynia F. Farnham.*

Up the Ladder from *Charm* to *Vogue*

July-August, 1950
"WILL YOU WEAR A star in your hair at night…or a little embroidered black veiling hat?…Will you wear a close little choker of pearls or a medal on a long narrow velvet ribbon?…Will you serve a lunch, in the garden, of *prosciutto* and melon and a wonderful green salad…or sit in the St. Regis' pale-pink roof and eat *truite bleue*?"…

It is the "Make Up Your Mind" issue: *Vogue*'s editresses are gently pressing the reader, in the vise of these velvet alternatives, to choose the looks that will "add up" to *her* look, the thing that is hers alone. "Will you make the point of your room a witty screen of drawings cadged from your artist friends…or spend your all on a magnificent carpet of flowers that decorates and almost furnishes the room itself?"

Twenty years ago, when *Vogue* was on the sewing-room table of nearly every respectable upper-middle-class American house, these sapphic overtures to the subscriber, this flattery, these shared securities of *prosciutto* and *wonderful* and *witty* had no place in fashion's realm. *Vogue*, in those days before *Mademoiselle* and *Glamour* and *Charm* and *Seventeen*, was an almost forbidding monitor enforcing the discipline of Paris. An iron conception of the mode governed its semimonthly rulings. Fashion was distinguished from dress; the woman of fashion, by definition, was a woman of a certain income whose clothes spoke the idiom of luxury and bon ton; there was no compromise with this principle. Furs, jewels, sumptuous materials, fine leathers, line, cut, atelier workmanship, were the very fabric of fashion; taste, indeed, was insisted on, but taste without money had a starved and middle-class pathos. The tastefully dressed little woman could not be a woman of style.

To its provincial subscribers *Vogue* of that epoch was cruel, rather in the manner of an upper servant. Its sole concession to their existence was a pattern department, *Vogue's Designs for Dressmaking*, the relic of an earlier period when no American woman bought clothes in a shop. And these patterns, hard to cut out as they were, fraught with tears for the amateur, who was safer with the trusty Butterick, had an economical and serviceable look that set them off from the designer fashions: even in the sketches they resembled maternity dresses.

As for the columns of etiquette, the bridal advice, the social notes from New York, Philadelphia, San Francisco—all these pointedly declined acquaintance with the woman-from-outside who was probably their principal devotee. Yet the magazine was read eagerly and without affront. Provincial women with moderate incomes poured over it to pick up "hints," carried it with them to the family dressmaker, copied, approximated, with a sense, almost, of pilferage. The fashion ideas they lifted made the pulse of the Singer race in nervous daring and defiance (What would *Vogue* say if it knew?).

This paradoxical relation between magazine and audience had a certain moral beauty, at least on the subscribers' side—the beauty of unrequited love and of unflinching service to an ideal that is arbitrary, unsociable, and rejecting, like Kierkegaard's God and Kafka's Castle. Lanvin, Paquin, Chanel, Worth, Vionnet, Alix—these stars of the Paris firmament were worshipped and charted in their courses by reverent worshippers who would come no closer to their deities than to copy, say, the characteristic fagoting that Vionnet used in her dress yoke or treasure a bottle of Chanel's Number Two on the bureau, next to father's or husband's photograph.

Like its competitor, *Harper's Bazaar*, and following the French dressmaking tradition, *Vogue* centered about the mature woman, the *femme du monde*, the sophisticated young matron with her clubs, her charities, and her cardcase. The jewels, the rich fabrics, the furs and plumes, the exquisite corseting, the jabots and fringe, implied a sexual as well as a material opulence, something preening, flavorsome, and well satisfied. For the *jeune fille* (so defined) there was a page or two of party frocks, cut usually along princess lines, in pastel taffetas, with round necks. In this Racinean world, where stepmother Phèdre and grandmother Athalie queened it, the actual habits of the American young girl, who smoked and wore lipstick, were excised from consideration. Reality was inferior to style.

Covertly, the assumptions of this period remain in force. Despite social change, fashion is still luxurious. It is possible to dress prettily on a working girl's or business wife's income, but to dress handsomely is another matter, requiring, as before, time, care, and money. Fashion is a craft, not an industrial, conception, exemplifying to perfection the labor theory of value. The toil of many hands is the *sine qua non* of fashion. The hand of the weaver, the cutter, the fitter, the needleworker must be seen in the finished product in a hundred little details, and fashion knowledge, professionally, consists in the recognition and appraisal of the *work* that has gone into a costume. In gores and gussets and seams, in the polish of leather and its softness, the signature of painstaking labor must be legible to the discerning, or the woman is not fashionably dressed. The hand-knit sweater is superior to the machine-knit, not because it is more perfect, but on the contrary because its slight imperfections reveal it to be *hand*-knit. The Oriental pearl is preferred to the fine cultured pearl because the marine labor of a dark diver secured it, a prize wrested from the depths, and the woman who wears Oriental pearls believes that they show variations in temperature or that they change color with her skin or get sick when they are put away in the safe—in short, that they are alive, whereas cultured pearls, mass-stimulated in mass beds of oysters, are not. This sense of the accrued labor of others as a complement to one's personality, as *tribute* in a double sense, is intrinsic to the fashionable imagination, which desires to *feel* that labor next to its skin, in the hidden stitching of its underwear—hence the passion for handmade lingerie even among women whose outer clothing comes off the budget rack.

In spite of these facts, which are known to most women, if only
in the form of a sudden anguish or hopelessness ("Why can't *I* look
like that?"), a rhetoric of fashion as democracy, as an inherent right
or manufacturer's guarantee, has swept over the style world and
created a new fashion public, a new fashion prose, and a whole hier-
archy of new fashion magazines. *Mademoiselle, Glamour, Charm*—
respectively "the magazine for smart young women," "for the girl
with the job," "the magazine for the BG (Business Girl)" offer to the
girl without means, the lonely heart, and the drudge, participation
in the events of fashion, a sense of belonging, en masse and yet
separately, individually, of being designed for, shopped for, read for,
predicted for, cherished. The attention and care and consideration
lavished on the woman of leisure by lady's maid, coiffeur, *vendeuse*,
bootmaker, jeweler, are now at the disposal of the masses through
the various Shophounds, Mlles. Wearybones, beauty editors, culture
advisers, male and female confidants. The impersonally conceived
Well-Dressed Woman of the old *Vogue* ("What the Well-Dressed
Woman Will Wear") is tutoyered, so to speak, as *You* ("Will you
wear a star in your hair?..."); and a tone of mixed homage and
familiarity: "For you who are young and pretty," "For you who have
more taste than money," gives the pronoun a custom air.

The idea of a custom approach to ready-made, popular-priced
merchandise was first developed by *Mademoiselle*, a Street and
Smith publication launched during the depression, which differed
from *Vogue* and the *Bazaar*, on the one hand, and from *McCall's*
and *Pictorial Review*, expressions of the housewife, on the other.
Before the depression, there had been, roughly speaking, only three
types of women's apparel: the custom dress, the better dress, and
the budget or basement dress. Out of the depression came the college shop and out of this the whole institutionalized fiction of the
"debutante" shop and the "young-timers'" floor. These departments,
which from the very outset were swarming with middle-aged
shoppers, introduced a new category of merchandise: the "young"
dress, followed by the "young" hat, the "young" shoe, the "young"
petticoat, and so on. The "young" dress was a budget dress with

status, an ephemeral sort of dress, very often—a dress that excited comment and did not stand up very well. Its popularity proved the existence of a new buying public of high school and college girls, secretaries and office workers, whose dress requirements were very different from those of the busy housewife or matron. What these buyers demanded, for obvious vocational reasons, was not a durable dress or a dress for special occasions, even, but the kind of dress that would provoke compliments from coworkers, fellow students, bosses—a dress that could be discarded after a few months or transformed by accessories into the simulation of a new dress. To this public, with its craving for popularity, its personality problems, and limited income, *Mademoiselle* addressed itself as "your" magazine, the magazine styled for *you*, individually.

Unlike the older magazines, whose editresses were matrons who wore (and still wear) their hats at their desks as though at a committee meeting at the Colony Club, *Mademoiselle* was staffed by young women of no social pretensions, college graduates and business types, live wires and prom queens, middle-class girls peppy or sultry, fond of fun and phonograph records. Its tone was gamely collegiate, a form of compliment perhaps, since its average reader, one would have guessed, was either beyond college or below it, a secretary or a high-school student. It printed fiction—generally concerned then with the problems of adolescence—job hints and news, beauty advice, and pages of popular-priced fashions photographed in Burpee-catalogued hues against glamorous backgrounds. Its models were windswept and cute.

Fashion as fun became *Mademoiselle*'s identifying byword, a natural corollary to the youth theme. *Fun* with food, *tricks* with spices, herbal *magic*, Hawaiian pineapple, Hawaiian ham, Hawaiian bathing trunks, Hollywood playclothes, cruise news, casserole cookery, Bar-B-Q sauce reflect the dream mentality of a civilization of office conscripts to whom the day off, the two weeks basking in the sun during February or August, represent not only youth but an effortless, will-less slack season (*slacks*, *loafers*, hostess *pajamas*), quite different from the dynamic good time of the 1920s.

In the *Mademoiselle* play world, everything is romp-diminutive or make-believe. The beau is a "cute brute," the husband a "sahib," or "himself," or "the little fellow." The ready-mix cake "turns out *terrific.*" Zircons are "almost indistinguishable from diamonds." "Little tricks of combination, flavor and garnishment help the bride and enchant the groom… who need never know!" Brides wearing thirty-five-dollar dresses are shown being toasted in champagne by ushers in ascots and striped trousers.

Work may be fun also. "I meet headline people on the Hill every day." Husband-and-wife *teams* do "the exciting things" together. And the work-fun of a reader-surrogate named Joan, *Mademoiselle*'s Everygirl, is to be continually photographed backstage at "exciting" events, "meeting summer halfway on a Caribbean island," meeting Maurice Evans in his dressing room, or gapily watching a chorus rehearsal. The word *meet*, in the sense of "coming into contact with or proximity of is a denotation of holiday achievement. Resort news is eternal, like hotel-folder sunshine.

The strain of keeping up this bright deception is marked by the grotesquerie of adverbs ("Serve piping hot with a dish of wildly hot mustard nearby"), by the repeated exclamation point, like a jerky, convulsive party smile, and by garish photographic effects. The typical *Mademoiselle* model with her adolescent, adenoidal face, snub nose, low forehead, and perpetually parted lips is immature in an almost painful fashion—on the plane, in the Parisian street, or the tropic hotel she appears out of place and ill at ease, and the photography which strives to "naturalize" her in exotic or expensive surroundings only isolates her still further. Against the marble columns or the balustrades, with fishing rod, sailboat, or native basket, she stands in a molar eternity, waving, gesticulating, like the figures in home movies of the vacation trip.

Another magazine, *Seventeen*, which from its recipes and correspondence column appears to be really directed to teenagers and their problems, strikes, by contrast with *Mademoiselle*, a grave and decorous note. Poorly gotten out and cheaply written, it has nevertheless an authentic small-town air; more than half its circulation is in towns under twenty-five thousand. It is not, strictly speaking, a fashion magazine (though it carries pages of fashions, gifts, and designs for knitting and dressmaking), but rather a home magazine on the order of *Woman's Home Companion*. How to make things at home, simple dishes to surprise the family with, games to play at parties, nonalcoholic punches for after skating, candies, popcorn balls, how to understand your parents, how to stop a family quarrel, movies of social import, the management of high school proms, stories about friendships with boys, crushes on teachers, a department of poems and stories written by teen-agers—all this imparts in a rather homiletic vein the daily lesson of growth and character-building.

Pleasures here are wholesome, groupy ("Get your gang together") projects, requiring everybody's cooperation. Thoughtfulness is the motto. The difficulty of being both good and popular, and the tension between the two aims (the great crux of choice for adolescence), are the staple matter of the fiction; every boy hero or girl heroine has a bitter pill to swallow in the ending. The same old-fashioned moral principles are brought to bear on fashion and cooking. The little cook in *Seventeen* is not encouraged, à la *Mademoiselle*, to think she can make "high drama" out of a Drake's Cake and a pudding mix; she starts her party biscuits or her cake with fresh eggs, fresh butter, and sifted flour. Her first grown-up jewelry is not an "important-looking" chunk of glass but a modest gold safety pin or, if she is lucky and has an uncle who can give it to her for graduation, a simple gold wrist watch.

And in *Seventeen*, surprisingly, the fashions, while inexpensive, have a more mundane look than *Mademoiselle*'s dresses, which tend to be junky—short-waisted, cute, with too many tucks, pleats, belts, and collars for the money. The *Seventeen* date dress is not very different from the "young fashions" in *Harper's Bazaar*. It has been chosen to give its wearer a little air of style and maturity, on the same principle that an actor playing a drunk tries, not to stagger, but to walk straight. The artifice of youth in the *Mademoiselle* fashions betrays the very thing it is meant to cover—cheapness—and the little short bobbing jackets and boleros and dirndls become a sort of class uniform of the office worker, an assent to permanent juniority as a form of second-class citizenship, on the drugstore stool.

In the upper fashion world, the notion of fashion as fun acquires a delicate savor. The *amusing*, the *witty*, the *delicious* ("a deliciously oversized stole") evoke a pastoral atmosphere, a Louis Seize scene where the queen is in the dairy and pauperdom is Arcadia. The whim, piquant or costly, defines the personality: try (*Harper's Bazaar*) having *everything* slip-covered in pale Irish linen, including the typewriter and the bird cage; and "just for the fun of it, black with one white glove." The idea of spending as thrift, lately coined by *Vogue*, implies the pastoral opposite of thrift as the gayest extravagance. "There is the good handbag. The pairs of good shoes... The wealth-to-spare look of rich and lean clothes together." A "timeless" gold cross made from old family stones, and seventy-dollar shoes are proposed under the heading "Economical Extravagances." "And upkeep, extravagantly good, is the ultimate economy. Examples: having your books with fine bindings oiled by an expert every year or having your wooden shoe-trees made to order... And purely for pleasure: flowers, silver, and the price of keeping it polished; an Afghan hound, the collection, from stamps to butterflies, to Coalport cabbages, that you, or we, skimp for rather than do without."

The fabrication here of a democratic snobbery, a snobbery for everyone, is *Vogue's* answer to the tumbrils of Truman. The trend of the times is resolutely reckoned with: today "the smaller collectors who have only one Giorgione" buy at Knoedler's Gallery, just as Mellon used to do. As John Jacob Astor III said, "A man who has a million dollars is as well off as if he were rich." (What a *delicious* sow's ear, my dear, where did you *get* it? The *small* collection, the *little* evening imply the intimate and the choice, as well as the tiniest pinch of necessity. *Little* hats, *little* furs, *tiny* waists—*Vogue* and the *Bazaar* are wriggling with them; in the old days hats were *small*. And as some images of size contract or cuddle ("Exciting too the tight skull of a hat with no hair showing"; "the sharp, small, polished head"), others stretch to wrap and protect: *enormous, huge, immense*—"a colossal muff," "vast" sleeves; how to have *enormous* eyes. By these semantic devices the reader is made to feel small, frail and valuable. The vocabulary has become extremely tactile and sensuous, the caress of fine fabrics and workmanship being replaced by the caress of prose.

The erotic element always present in fashion, the kiss of loving labor on the body, is now overtly expressed by language. Belts *hug* or *clasp*; necklines *plunge*; jerseys *bind*. The word *exciting* tingles everywhere. "An outrageous amount of S.A." is promised by a new makeup; a bow is a "shameless piece of flattery." A dress is no longer low-cut but *bare*. The diction is full of movement: "hair swept all to one side and just one enormous earring on the bare side." A waist rises from a skirt "like the stem of a flower." Images from sport and machinery (*team, spark*) give this murmurous romanticism a down-to-business, American twang and heighten the kinetic effect. "First a small shopping expedition…Then give your mind a good going-over, stiffen it with some well-starched prose; apply a gloss of poetry, two coats at least."

The bugaboo of getting in a rut, of letting your mind, your figure, or your wardrobe become habit-ridden and middle-aged, is conjured up with a terrible seriousness by all fashion magazines and most vividly of all by *Harper's Bazaar*, which sees culture as a vital agent in the general toning-up process, tries to observe unifying trends and to relate a revival of interest in Scott Fitzgerald to Carol Channing and the cloche hat, and is the victim of its own orderliness in collating a mode to a movement.

Literature and the arts, in the middle and upper fashion magazines, are offered as a tonic to the flabby personality, a tonic frequently scented with the musky odor of Tabu or My Sin. The fiction published by *Harper's Bazaar* (*Vogue* does not print stories), to be conned by suburban ladies under the drier, belongs almost exclusively to the mannerist or decadent school of American writing. Truman Capote, Edita Morris, Jane Bowles, Paul Bowles, Eudora

Welty, Jean Stafford, Carson McCullers—what these writers have
in common, beyond a lack of matter and a consequent leukemia
of treatment (taken by the *Bazaar* editors to be the very essence
of art), is a potpourri of *fleurs de mal*, a preoccupation with the
décor of sorrow, sexual aberration, insanity, and cruelty, a tasteful
arrangement of the bric-a-brac of pathology around the whatnot
of a central symbol. This fashionable genre of literary story is published in good faith by the *Bazaar*, with a positive glow, in fact, of
high-minded, disinterested evangelism. The editors, to do them
justice, are as honestly elated by the discovery of a new decadent
talent as by the announcement of a new silhouette, a new coiffure,
a new young designer.

For both *Vogue* and *Harper's Bazaar*, the regular discovery of
younger and younger authors, of newer and newer painters, is a
rather recent development and a concession to democratic principle. Society people do not read, and are not interested (ask a modern
dealer) in any painters later than the Impressionists. (The theatre
is the only branch of art much cared for by people of wealth; like
canasta, it does away with the bother of talk after dinner.) A society person who is enthusiastic about modern painting or Truman
Capote is already half a traitor to his class: It is middle-class people
who, quite mistakenly, imagine that a lively pursuit of the latest in
reading and painting will advance their status in the world. It is
for them and for their financial inferiors, students of interior deco-
rating or the dance, bookstore clerks, models, assistant buyers and
advertising copywriters, that photographs of Picasso drawing with
a ray of light, reproductions of paintings by De Kooning or Baziotes,
stories by Carson McCullers, Peggy Bennett, or Speed Lamkin have
moment. For all those engaged in competition for status, the surge
of a new name forward anywhere, in any field, in astrophysics
even, or medicine, is of intense personal reference and concern.
Any movement in the social body, any displacement, is felt at once
by every mobile member of the organism as relating to his own
case, and the inside knowledge of these distant events gives poise
and assurance—hence the relevance of the yearly awards given by

Mademoiselle and other fashion magazines for achievement in science, medicine, human relations, and the like.

A writer for *Mademoiselle* expresses the position of those on the lower rung of the ladder very clearly when she tells about how exciting it is to live in Washington, and adduces as an example the fact that her husband, Bob, once rode on a plane with the U.S. special representative to Israel and another time "bumped into Henry Wallace and General Vaughan coming out of the White House the day Wallace had his farewell row with the President." Here the sense of being close to important events (itself vicarious) passes from the husband to the author to the reader. It is three removes off. What she likes about a certain Washington couple, she continues, is "that they always have interesting people around them, kicking around interesting ideas." And of her friends, in general, "What really roots them to the spot is that the work they do has intrinsic, social meaning." The concluding phrase, with its queer use of the comma, suggests that the intrinsic and the social are distinct and antithetical properties. But from the context it is plain that work that has intrinsic, comma, social meaning is work that is close to the big, busy, important things.

What has happened, in the course of twenty years, is that culture and even political liberalism have been converted by the mass-fashion mind, with its competitive bias, into a sort of Beaux Arts Ball. "A literary and artistic renaissance is what they're talking about over coffee at the Francis Scott Key, Martinis at the Press Club... The Phillips Gallery... pace-sets with frequent shows of important contemporary artists, photographers... At Whyte's Bookshop and Gallery... the important draw is..." The idea that it's smart to be in step, to be liberal or *avant-garde*, is conveyed through the name-dropping of a Leo Lerman in *Mademoiselle*. To allude negligently to Kafka, Yeats, Proust, Stendhal, or St. John of the Cross in a tone of of-course-you-know-them is canonical procedure for *Mademoiselle* contributors, whatever the topic in hand, while the minor name here (Capote, Buechner, Tennessee Williams, Vidal) has the cachet of the little evening, the little hat, the little fur. The

conception of a mass initiate involves an assembly-line production
of minority objects of virtu, and is producing a new conformity
altogether dominated by the mode, in which late Beethoven, boo-
gie-woogie, the UN, Buechner, Capote, FEPC, and *The Cocktail
Party* are all equally important names to be spent. Contrary to
the practice in high society, the *recherché* is more prized than the
known great, and Shakespeare is a virtually worthless counter,
which Mrs. Astor never was.

The conspicuous mass display of the bibelots of a curio culture
is the promotional secret of *Flair*, the new Cowles magazine, with
its first-naming of the New Bohemians, "Carson," "Truman," and
"Tennessee," and its splashy collage of democrats and decadents—
Margaret Mead and Salvador Dali, Simone de Beauvoir and Mme.
Pompadour, Jean Genet and W. H. Auden, Thomas Jefferson and
Angus Wilson, Barbara Ward and Franco Spain, Leonor Fini and
the Middleburg Hunt, Cocteau and Mauriac. As an instrument of
mass snobbery, this remarkable magazine, dedicated simply to the
personal cult of its editress, to the fetishism of the flower (Fleur
Cowles, *Flair*, a single rose), outdistances all its competitors in the
audacity of its conception. It is a leap into the Orwellian future, a
magazine without contest or point of view beyond its proclamation of itself, one hundred and twenty pages of sheer presentation,
a journalistic mirage. The principle of the peep show or illusion
utilized in the cutouts, where the eye is led inward to a false perspective of depth, is the trick of the entire enterprise. The articles,
in fact, seem meant not to be read but inhaled like a whiff of scent
from the mystic rose at the center (flair, through Old French, from
fragrare, to emit an odor: an instinctive power of discriminating or
discerning). Nobody, one imagines, has read them, not even their
authors: grammatical sentences are arranged around a vanishing
point of meaning. Yet already, in the very first, quite androgyne
number, an ectoplasmic feminine *you* is materialized, to whom
a fashion editor's voice speaks in tones of assured divination:
"Fashion is Personal... Seven silhouettes chosen from wide possibil-
ities, not because they are extreme high fashion, but because they

are silhouettes you might claim…" There follow seven dresses in the current high fashion.

The cynicism and effrontery of this surpass anything previously tried out in journalism. And yet *Vogue* immediately fell into line with its own warm defense of the reader against fashion's tyranny. "Ignore the exquisite exaggerations of fashion drawings" when trying to determine the weight that is right for you; study yourself, know yourself, wear what is timelessly yours. Copy courageous Mrs. Carroll Carstairs, who wears the same beanies every year regardless of the milliners; or Pauline Potter, who carries the same custom-made suede handbag suspended from a jeweler's gold chain." To an experienced reader, this doctrine is merely a 1950 adaptation of the old adage about knowing your own type, a text that generally prefaces the suggestion that the reader should go out and spend a great deal of money on some item of quality merchandise. But beyond the attempt to push quality goods during a buying recession like the recent one, or to dodge responsibility for an unpopular mode (this year's sheaths and cloches are widely unbecoming), there appears to be some periodic feminine compulsion on the editresses' part to strike a suffragette attitude toward the merchants whose products are their livelihood, to ally themselves in a gush with their readers, who are seen temporarily as their "real" friends.

And as one descends to a lower level of the fashion structure, to *Glamour* (Condé Nast) and *Charm* (Street and Smith), one finds a more genuine solicitude for the reader and her problems. The pain of being a BG (Business Girl), the envy of superiors, self-consciousness, awkwardness, loneliness, sexual fears, timid friendliness to the Boss, endless evenings with the mirror and the tweezers, desperate Saturday social strivings ("Give a party and ask *everyone* you know"), the struggle to achieve any identity in the dead cubbyhole of office life, this mass misery, as of a perpetual humiliating menstrual period, is patently present to the editors, who strive against it with good advice, cheeriness, forced volubility, a psychiatric nurse's briskness, so that the reiterated "Be natural," "Be yourself," "Smile,"

"Your good points are you too" (*Mademoiselle*), have a therapeutic justification.

A characteristic running feature in *Glamour* and *Charm* is a newsy letter from the editors, date-lined London, Paris, New York, or Rome, a letter back home full of gossip and family jokes, the sort of letter one writes to a shut-in. The vicarious here is carried to its furthest extreme: the editors live out for the readers a junketing, busy life in which the readers, admittedly, will share only by mail—quite a different thing from the *Mademoiselle* Everygirl projection. The delegation of experience from reader to editor is channeled through a committee of typical (*Charm*) or outstanding (*Glamour*) business girls—the Charm Advisory Committee, the Glamour Career Counselors—selected from all over the country, who are polled from time to time on problems of special interest and who not only keep the editors in touch with the desires of the readers but pass on, through the editors, their own superior know-how to the lowest members of the caste.

A publication of Street and Smith, *Charm* has a more vulgar tone than *Glamour*, which belongs to the *Vogue* chain. Its circulation, considerably smaller than *Glamour*'s, larger than *Mademoiselle*'s, seems drawn preponderantly from the West and the South, backward fashion areas, while *Glamour*'s public is Eastern or urban, the differences being sharpest in the vicinity of New York, Philadelphia, Boston, and Los Angeles. *Glamour*'s dresses are more expensive than *Charm*'s. It is conscious of Paris, Italy, and London, and will illustrate, in the front of the magazine, the work of Italian craftsmen and French designers for their own sake, as objects of beauty and wonder. As in the old *Vogue*, the cultivation of taste, the development of a fashion sensibility which impersonally delights in the finely made and the rare, are, at least in part, the editorial purpose.

A letter from *Glamour*'s editor to the readers in last year's Christmas number, suggesting that the American girl lives too much on dreams and illusions and proposing impersonal goals, has the gently remonstrative seriousness of a young woman dean exhorting her alumnae. Maturity and dignity are valued. Photographs of secretaries of well-known persons, photographs of successful women who began as secretaries, a history of the secretarial profession emphasize the dignity of office work and gives it status through history and a tradition. Serenity in work ("Why I Like My Job"—a contest) and at home are stressed to the point where this itself becomes an aristocratic illusion: an article called "These Gracious Customs" showing the cocktail party with hunt-breakfast silver; the inevitable wedding pictures with champagne, striped trousers, and a butler. Yet the general attitude of *Glamour* is sensible, without much side, and in its own terms idealistic, the eye being directed less downward toward the immediate bargain counter than inward toward self-examination and outward toward the great cities and fine artisans of the world.

With Charm, on the other hand, the nadir of the personal is reached: the Business Girl is greeted at her lowest common denominator. The editor becomes "Your Ed," the fun-fabulous-wonderful-sensational shriek ("Learn to make one fabulous dish…Give your earrings a new locale…Carry an umbrella as a costume adjunct…DARE TO DO IT"), addressed to the insecure and the maladroit, echoes in a national hollowness of social failure and fear. A presumption of previous failure in the reader, failure with men, with friends, failure in schoolwork, is the foundation of the average feature: "This Little Girl Never Had Any Fun," "Stood Up."

A lead article on "Smiles" in the January issue points to the Roosevelt smile, the Mona Lisa smile, the Betty Grable smile, the Jolson smile, the Dietrich smile: "…people in the public eye have never underestimated the power of a smile: it's odd that *you* have so often overlooked it…Though smiling is nicer as a *spontaneous* thing, you might, just in the nature of an experiment, start smiling as a *conscious* thing. Smile at your family…your husband…your employer…your young man. Smile deliberately at some point in an argument…at a break in the conversation…Smile a while in front of your mirror." The article finishes characteristically with some hints about dentifrices and the art of toothbrushing. In another feature by the same author, the natural attractions of the bride-to-be are so despaired of that she is advised to apply a lip-coloring base before going to bed, spray the room with "fragrance," and even "steal" a sachet under the pillow.

A preoccupation with deodorants and "personal hygiene" becomes more and more noticeable as the economic scale is descended. Social failure is ascribed to a lack of "fastidiousness," a lower-middle-class fear that first reveals itself in *Mademoiselle*, where the likelihood of giving "offense" is associated with the male sex. "It's the rare man... who isn't considerably more attractive when he uses some [toilet water or cologne]." "A consistently fastidious, scrubby male is mighty nice to have around the house... If he doesn't mind tomorrow's garlic and you do, get him a bottle of the leaf-fresh mouth wash that *all* men love on first gargle. If he uses a deodorant—and more men could—keep his brand on hand. If he doesn't, put a squeeze-spray version where he'll see it—it will appeal to a man's mechanical instinct."

The bridal number of *Charm* carries a feature ("His and Hers") on bathroom etiquette, showing pictures of a man and woman gargling, shaving, creaming, brushing teeth, putting powder between the toes against athlete's foot, using a deodorant (male); the bathroom is called the *lavabo*. In the same number, a marriage article, "The Importance of Not Being Prudish," contains the following advice: "You'll also be a silly prude if you squeak like a mouse when he, thoughtlessly, walks into the bedroom without knocking and finds you standing in your bra and panties. Don't make like September Morn. Respecting your natural modesty, he'll probably say he's sorry, walk backward through the door... (He *should* have knocked...)." And another feature, "Beauty Steps to the Altar," includes two "Secret Steps"; crayons to color your gray hair give a "natural, plausible performance... And remember there are very good preparations that make a secret of scars and blemishes."

Thus, at the lowest fashion level, a most painful illusionism becomes the only recipe for success. Admiration and compliments provide momentarily the sense of well-being which, for the woman of fashion of the upper level, is an exhalation of the stuffs and stays that hold her superb and erect as in a vase of workmanship. For the reader of *Charm* it is her very self that is the artifact, an artifact which must be maintained, night and day, in the close quarters of marriage, brought to higher sparkle for party evenings with the gang ("Your quips were a tearing success; his gags killed 'em"), at the office, in the subway ("Smile"). The continued tribute to be extorted from others, which the *Charm* policy promises its untouchables, if only they will follow directions, is laid down as an American right, to be fought for, creamed for, depilated and massaged for—more than that, as duty, with ostracism threatened for slackers. Every woman, says *Glamour* categorically, can be fifty per cent more beautiful. It is the rigorous language of the factory in which new production goals are set yearly, which must not only be met but exceeded. "Mirror, mirror on the wall...?" begs the reader. "You," answers the editor, "if you did your exercises, were the prettiest girl in the Republic."

The Vassar Girl

May, 1951

LIKE ATHENA, GODDESS OF wisdom, Vassar College sprang in full battle dress from the head of a man. Incorporated at Poughkeepsie, New York, in 1861, the year of Lincoln's inauguration and the emancipation of the serfs in Russia, it was the first woman's college to be conceived as an idea, a manifesto, a declaration of rights, and a proclamation of equality.

It did not evolve, like Mount Holyoke, chartered in 1836, from a female seminary into a college; it came into being at one stroke, so to speak, equipped with a museum of natural history, a library, a main building modeled on the Tuileries, an observatory with a gigantic telescope, a collection of paintings and a course of study. This was to embrace, in the specifications of the Founder, "the English language and its Literature; other Modern Languages, the Ancient Classics, so far as may be demanded by the spirit of the times; the Mathematics, to such an extent as may be deemed advisable; all the branches of Natural Science...Anatomy, Physiology, and Hygiene...the elements of Political Economy; some knowledge of Federal and State Constitutions and Laws; Moral Science, particularly as bearing on the filial, conjugal, and parental relations; Aesthetics...Domestic Economy...last, and most important of all, the daily, systematic Reading and Study of the Holy Scriptures, as the only and all-sufficient Rule of Christian faith and practice..."

The promulgator of this curriculum, which, except for the last proviso, remains the basis of the Vassar education, was not a gentleman of parts or a social reformer, but a self-educated Poughkeepsie brewer, the keeper of an ale and oyster house. Matthew Vassar's farming parents had migrated from England to Dutchess County, New York, when the boy was four years old. He left school at the age of ten to go to work for a neighboring farmer, carrying his few small belongings tied up in a cotton handkerchief. Persistence and hard work had their storied rewards: at forty, he was a successful Poughkeepsie businessman with a good-sized brewery on the river, membership in the Baptist church, an urge toward foreign travel, and strong philanthropic inclinations. Having no children, he determined to attach his name to some lasting benevolent enterprise and settled on woman's education after cautious shopping and advice-seeking. Once, however, he had been fixed in the notion, his plan became clothed in rhetoric and in philosophic axioms: "Woman, having received from her Creator the same intellectual constitution as man, has the same right as man to intellectual culture and development...The mothers of a country mold the character of its citizens, determine its institutions, and shape its destiny. Next to the influence of the mother is that of the female teacher..." His maiden speech to the Board of Trustees at the initial meeting in February, 1861, had the resonance of a sovereign pronouncement: "I have come to the conclusion, that the establishment and endowment of a College for the education of young women is a work which will satisfy my highest aspirations, and will be, under God, a rich blessing to this city and State, to our country and the world."

The authoritative tone is characteristic; it is as though, speaking through the mouth of the elderly, didactic brewer, were the first, fresh Vassar girl. The stiff, exact provisions evoke the basic architecture of the Vassar campus, different from the colonial republicanism of the early men's colleges and from the collegiate Gothic of the late big philanthropy—something purposive and utilitarian: dark-red brick, plainly set-out buildings in the prevailing factory style of the late nineteenth century. In the phraseology also, candidly revealed, is the first note of Vassar emulation, of the passion for public service coupled with a yearning for the limelight, a wish to play a part in the theatre of world events, to perform some splendid action that will cut one's name in history like a figure eight in ice.

The essence of Vassar is mythic. Today, despite much competition, it still figures in the public mind as the archetypal woman's college. Less intellectual than Radcliffe or Bryn Mawr, less social and weekendish than Smith, less athletic than Wellesley, less Bohemian than Bennington, it is nevertheless the stock butt of musical-comedy jokes and night-club wheezes. It has called down thunder from the pulpit, provided heroines for popular ballads; even a girdle bears its name. Like Harvard, it is always good for a knowledgeable smile from members of the population who have scarcely heard the name of another college. It signifies a certain *je ne sais quoi*; a whiff of luxury and the ineffable; plain thinking and high living. If a somehow know-it-all manner is typical of the Vassar student, the public has a way of winking that it knows all about Vassar, though this sly wink only intimates that there is something to know. For different people, in fact, at different periods, Vassar can stand for whatever is felt to be wrong with the modern female: humanism, atheism, Communism, short skirts, cigarettes, psychiatry, votes for women, free love, intellectualism. Pre-eminently among American college women, the Vassar girl is thought of as carrying a banner. The inscription on it varies with the era or with the ideas of the beholder and in the final sense does not matter—the flushed cheek and tensed arm are what count.

I myself was an ardent literary little girl in an Episcopal boarding school on the West Coast, getting up at four in the morning to write a seventeen-page medieval romance before breakfast, smoking on the fire-escape and thinking of suicide, meeting a crippled boy in the woods by the cindery athletic field, composing a novelette in study hall about the life of a middle-aged prostitute ("Her eyes were turbid as dishwater") when the name, *Vassar*, entered my consciousness through the person of an English teacher. She symbolized to me the critical spirit, wit, cool learning, detachment—everything I suddenly wished to have and to be, from the moment I first heard her light, precise, cutting voice score some pretension, slatternly phrase or construction on the part of her pupils. With blond buns over her ears, gold-rimmed glasses and a teacher's taste in dress, Miss A——was severe and formidable, yet she smoked, as I knew, on the side, read *The American Mercury* and was shocked by nothing. She advised me to send my novelette to H. L. Mencken for criticism. The idea of going to Vassar and becoming like Miss A—— immediately dominated my imagination. I gave up a snap course in domestic science and registered for Latin. I tutored in Caesar during the summer and coaxed my family. To go east to college was quite a step in Seattle.

What Vassar represented at that time to the uninitiated person can be gathered from the attitude of my Catholic grandmother in Minneapolis, whom I stopped to visit on my way east to Poughkeepsie. She sent for the parish priest to armor me against the "heresy" I should be exposed to. The priest was as embarrassed as I was at the task set him. He contented himself with a few rumbling remarks about the efficacy of prayer and the sacraments, and then admonished the old lady that at Vassar I would find the very best of Western thought, contemporary and classical—I ought to be proud to be going there. Listening breathlessly, I hardly knew whether to be more thrilled by the priest's liberal commendation or by my grandmother's conservative disapproval.

For the majority, perhaps, of the freshmen swarming through Taylor Gate that year for their first interview with the dean, Vassar had some such overtones. Its high, iron-runged, Gothic gate, which swung open on this day to receive the stream of cars laden with luggage, tennis rackets, phonographs, lamps, and musical instruments, was for most of us outlanders, still in our neat cloche hats and careful little traveling suits, a threshold to possibility. (It was the autumn, though we could not foresee it, of the Wall Street crash.) Bucolically set in rolling orchard country just outside the town of Poughkeepsie, with the prospect of long walks and rides along curving back roads and cold red apples to bite; framed by two mirror-like lakes, by a lively off-campus street full of dress shops, antique stores, inns, which were brimming now with parents, brothers, and fiancés, Vassar, still warm and summery, gave the impression of a cornucopia overflowing with promises. The bare-headed Yale boys in roadsters parked outside Taylor Gate; the tall, dazzling girls, upper-classmen, in pale sweaters and skirts, impeccable, with pearls at the throat and stately walks, like goddesses; the vaulted library; the catalogue already marked and starred for courses like Psychology and Philosophy ("The Meaning of Morals, Beauty, Truth, God—open to freshmen by special permission"); the trolley tracks running past the spiked fence downtown to further shopping, adventure, the railroad station, New York, plays, concerts, night clubs, Fifth Avenue bus rides—all this seemed to foretell four years of a Renaissance lavishness, in an academy that was a Forest of Arden and a Fifth Avenue department store combined.

The dean, in her opening address, told us that we were the smallest class ever to be admitted (in recent years, I presume) and hence the most highly selected. She spoke to us of the responsibilities that thereby devolved on us, but to this part I hardly listened, being so filled with the pride and glory of belonging to the very best class in the very best college in America. This feeling did not really leave me during four years in college; Vassar has a peculiar power of conveying a sense of excellence.

After October, 1929, some of us had smaller allowances; my roommate and I no longer went off-campus every night for a dinner beginning with *canapé* of anchovies and going on to artichokes and mushrooms under glass. More of us were on scholarships or using some form of self-help. Typing papers for others, waking friends in the morning, for the first time became regular industries. Some students' fathers were rumored to have shot themselves or to have had nervous breakdowns, but the off-campus shops still prospered, selling grape lemonade, bacon-and-tomato sandwiches, and later 3.2 beer. New York department stores brought dress exhibitions once or twice a year to the tearooms; we bought more than we could afford and charged it. Yale boys came down weekly for the Saturday-night "J" dance, at which the girls were stags and cut in on them. At these times the more prosperous went out to eat at roadhouses, tearooms, or inns in twos, fours, sixes, or eights. The boys carried whiskey in flasks, and sometimes there were gin picnics. One of my friends had an airplane; another girl kept a pet goat, very white and pretty; in the spring of senior year, when cars were permitted, a few roadsters appeared. In New York, we went to plays, musicals, and speakeasies, two or three girls together on a Saturday day leave; on weekends, alone with our beaux. Many of us were engaged.

During our junior year, the word "Communist" first assumed an active reality: a plain girl who was a science major openly admitted to being one. But most of our radicals were Socialists, and throughout that election year they campaigned for Norman Thomas, holding parades and rallies, though in most cases they were too young to vote. We of the "aesthetic" camp considered them jejune and naïve; we were more impressed when we heard, after a poll, that a plurality (as I recall) of the faculty were voting for Thomas that year.

The inert mass of the student body was, as usual, Republican; we aesthetes did not believe in politics, but slightly favored the Democrats. Then our trustee, Franklin Roosevelt, was elected President. Miss Newcomer of the Economics Department went off to serve on a committee at Albany. Doctor MacCracken, our president, had lunch with Roosevelt off a tray in the White House—and we undergraduates felt more than ever that Vassar was at the center of everything.

With the impetus of the New Deal and memories of the breadlines behind us, even we aesthetes began reading about Sacco and Vanzetti and Mooney. We wrote papers for Contemporary Prose Fiction on Dos Passos. The pretty blue-eyed Republican girls looked troubled when you talked to them about these things; *their* favorite book was *Of Human Bondage*, which we despised. The Socialists made friends with us, though they swore by Miss Lockwood's press course, and we by Miss Sandison's Renaissance or by Miss Rindge's art or by a course in Old English or in verse writing: our group, being aesthetes, was naturally more individualistic. But by the end of our senior year the Socialists, the aesthetes, and the pretty Republican girls had been drawn closer together.

We all drank 3.2 beer at night in Mrs. Cary's tearoom, discussed term papers and politics, sang songs of farewell to each other in half-mocking, half-tender accents. We were happy to be together, our differences of origin and opinion reconciled in the fresh May darkness, but our happiness rested on the sense that all this was provisional and transitory. "Lost now in the wide, wide world," we sang fervently, but actually almost all of us were joyous to be leaving college, precisely because we had loved it, for Vassar had inspired us with the notion that the wide, wide world was our oyster.

A few years later, a census was taken, and it was discovered that the average Vassar graduate had two-plus children and was married to a Republican lawyer.

This finding took by surprise even that section of the alumnae—Vassar Club activists, organizers of benefits and fund-raising drives—who looked upon it as providential. Here, at last, they felt, was something concrete to offset newspaper stories of students picketing during a strike in nearby Beacon, students besieging the state legislature in Albany, that would put an end to the rumors of immorality, faddishness, and Bohemianism that, because of a few undergraduates, had clung to the college's public persona for two decades or more. What these figures proved, the alumnae apologists were really implying, was that the Vassar education had not "taken" or had taken only on a small group who were not at all typical of Vassar and who by their un-Vassarish behavior were getting the college a bad name. And yet the statistical Average herself would have been the first to protest (with that touch of apology so characteristic of Vassar women who have not "done" anything later on) that she was not at all representative of Vassar standards and point to some more unconventional classmate as the real Vassar thing.

A wistful respect for the unorthodox is ingrained in the Vassar mentality. The Vassar freshman still comes through Taylor Gate as I did, with the hope of being made over, redirected, vivified. The daughter of a conservative lawyer, doctor, banker, or businessman, she will have chosen Vassar in all probability with the idea of transcending her background. And if she does not have such plans for herself, her teachers have them for her. If she is, say, a Vassar daughter or a girl from a preparatory school like Chapin or Madeira who chose Vassar because her friends did, her teachers, starting freshman year, will seek to "shake her up," "emancipate" her, make her "think for herself." This dynamic conception of education is Vassar's hallmark.

The progressive colleges have something similar, but there the tendency is to orient the student in some preconceived direction—toward the modern dance or toward "progressive" political thinking, while at Vassar, by and large, the student is almost forbidden to take her direction from the teacher. "What do *you* think?" is the question that ricochets on the student if she asks the teacher's opinion; and the difference between Vassar and the traditional liberal college (where the teacher is also supposed to keep his own ideas in the background) is that at Vassar the student is obliged, every day, to proffer hers.

Thus at a freshman English class I recently visited, the students were discussing Richard Hughes' *The Innocent Voyage*, a book whose thesis is that children are monsters, without moral feeling in the adult sense, insane, irresponsible, incapable of conventional grief or remorse. This idea was very shocking to perhaps half the class, well-brought-up little girls who protested that children were not "like that," indignant hands waved in the air, anguished faces grimaced, while a more detached student in braids testified that her own experience as a baby-sitter bore Mr. Hughes out. The teacher took no sides but merely smiled and encouraged one side and then the other, raising a hand for quiet when the whole class began shouting at once, and interrupting only to ask, "Do you really know children? Are you speaking from what you have seen or remember, or from what you think *ought* to be so?" This book plainly was chosen not because it was a favorite with the professor or even because of its literary merits but because it challenged preconceptions and disturbed set ideas.

The effect of this training is to make the Vassar student, by the time she has reached her junior year, look back upon her freshman self with pity and amazement. When you talk to her about her life in college, you will find that she sees it as a series of before-and-after snapshots: "When I came to Vassar, I thought like Mother and Daddy... I was conservative in my politics... I had race prejudice... I liked academic painting." With few exceptions, among those who are articulate and who feel that the college has "done something" for them, the trend is from the conservative to the liberal, from the orthodox to the heterodox, with stress on the opportunities Vassar has provided for getting to know "different" people, of opposite opinions and from different backgrounds.

Yet the statistical fate of the Vassar girl, thanks to Mother and Dad and the charge account, is already decreed. And the result is that the Vassar alumna, uniquely among American college women, is two persons—the housewife or matron, and the yearner and regretter. The Vassar graduate who has failed to make a name for herself, to "keep up," extend her interests, is, because of her training, more poignantly conscious of backsliding than her contemporary at Barnard or Holyoke. And unlike the progressive-college graduate, on the other hand, who has been catered to and conciliated by her instructors, the Vassar girl who drifts into matronhood or office work is more inclined to blame herself than society for what has happened, and to feel that she has let the college down by not becoming famous or "interesting." The alumnae records are full of housewives, doctors, teachers, educators, social workers, child-welfare specialists, public-health consultants. But the Vassar dream obdurately prefers such figures as Inez Milholland, '09, who rode a white horse down Fifth Avenue campaigning for woman suffrage; Edna St. Vincent Millay, '17, the *révoltée* girl-poet who made herself a byword of sexual love and disenchanted lyricism; Elizabeth Hawes, '25, iconoclastic dress designer, and author of *Fashion Is Spinach*. The Vassar romanticism will pass over a college president in favor of an author or journalist—Constance Rourke, '07, pioneer folklorist and author of *American Humor*; Muriel Rukeyser, ex-'34, Eleanor Clark, Elizabeth Bishop, '34, poets and writers, Jean Poletti, '25, Lois ("Lipstick" of *The New Yorker*) Long,

'22, Beatrice Berle, '23, noted for her opinions on marriage and for the twin bathtubs she and her husband, Adolf A. Berle, Jr., shared in their Washington house—and it will recognize as its own even such antipodal curiosities as Elizabeth Bentley, '30, the ex-Communist spy queen, and Major Julia Hamblet, '37, the first woman to enlist in the Marines.

The incongruities on this list are suggestive. An *arresting performance* in politicis, fashion, or art is often taken by the Vassar mind to be synonymous with true accomplishment. The Vassar dynamism drives toward money and success and the limelight in a truly Roman fashion, when it is not yoked to their opposite—service. With its alertness, its eagerness to *do* things, it tends, once the academic restraints are removed, to succumb to a rather journalistic notion of what constitutes value.

In the arts, after the first few intransigent gestures, Vassar talent streams into commercial side lines—advertising, fashion writing, publicity, promotion—and here assurance and energy case the Vassar success woman in an elephant-hide of certainties—a sort of proud flesh. This older Vassar career woman is nearly as familiar to American folklore as the intrepid young Portia or Rosalind she may at one time have passed for. Conscious of being set apart by a superior education, confident of her powers in her own field of enterprise, she is impervious to the universe, which she dominates, both mentally and materially. On the campus, she is found at vocational conferences, panel discussions, committee meetings—she is one of those women who are always dominating, in an advisory capacity. In the world, she is met in political-action groups, consumers' leagues, on school boards and in charitable drives, at forums and round-tables. Married, almost professionally so, the mother of children, she is regarded as a force in her community or business, is respected and not always liked. Vassar, of course, has no patent on this model of the American woman, but there is a challenge in the Vassar atmosphere that makes her graduates feel that they owe it as a positive duty to the college and to the human community to be outstanding, aggressive, and secure.

All this is still far away from the current undergraduate. She has heard vaguely through the alumnae magazine that some Vassar graduates are unhappy and frustrated because college did not prepare them for a life of dishwashing and babies, but this prospect for herself appears to have no relevance, though she may be planning to marry immediately on graduation and to begin having children at once. The Vassar career woman she is aware of, without self-identification. Vassar girls today, even more than most young people, seem to live in an ideal present; the alumnae they are heading to become seem as remote to them as the freshmen selves they have transcended. They knit, play bridge, attend classes and lectures, looking decorous and polite, with smooth, soft coiffures and tranquil faces. Their plans are made—one will be a doctor; one will work for the UN; another will take up journalism. There is none of the conflict and indecision that harried us in the thirties; they have decided to help the world, but not to change or destroy it. They prepare their work with competence, recite with poise and credit; in mastery of assigned material, some of it quite difficult, they outdo any group of college students I have had experience with. In the classroom, a serene low voice begs elucidation of a point in a Platonic dialogue: "I'm not sure I understand what Socrates means to say here." The difficulty is explained—"Thank you," and a note is taken. Among the upperclassmen, these nods of illumination and swift scribbles on the note pad are frequent; the college is businesslike.

They read Sartre and Tennessee Williams as part of their work in the drama; a class in Aesthetics is popular; they listen to music in the dormitories; but, despite competence, civility, and even deferential interest, they have an air of placid aloofness from what is currently going on in the world of arts and letters. All that appears distant to them; they ask about the names of current authors in the same tone of dreamy, faraway curiosity as they ask about the Vassar of fifteen or twenty years ago. Has the college changed much, they inquire, certain that it has changed immeasurably because *they* are there. The so-called literary renaissance of Vassar during the thirties is something they now hear of with amazement and for the

very first time. Reversing the situation in most colleges, the faculty
is ahead of the student body in its awareness of the times. To the
student, the immediate Vassar is the planet.

If you ask a Vassar undergraduate today to define what a Vassar
girl essentially is, she will repulse the thought of a Vassar *stereotype*,
as she calls it, and tell you that Vassar is a collection of very different
"individuals." Yet this reply, to the ears of an alumna, is a highly Vassar
remark, indicating a certain virtuous superiority of popular error.

In many ways, Vassar *has* changed. The campus remains the
same—the two lakes; the walk through the pines; Sunset Hill; the
deserted golf course; the six spare buildings of the Quadrangle;
the Main Hall with its porte-cochere, busy Message Center and
post office, dark parlors, and bright bulletin boards; the old riding
academy housing the theatre and the classics department; the old
observatory; the hemlocks; the new gymnasium; the bulging field-
stone Gothic of the Euthenics Building; the Circle with its brilliant
rim of spring flowers, where class picnics are held; the two subur-
banish faculty dormitories; the Shakespeare Garden; the outdoor
theatre, a great green stadium overlooking the lake; the Students'
Building, scene of lectures and dances; Taylor Gate. Poughkeepsie
and the railroad station by the Hudson are reached by bus along
the track where the old trolley once ran, but the burgher town, with
its twisting streets, melancholy river light, somber Hudson Valley
mansions and tinny store façades, is still held at a distance. Some of
the students, as always, do welfare work in the various Community
Centers; Luckey-Platt, the serviceable family-style department
store, still offers charge accounts to students; Poughkeepsie citizens attend Vassar lectures and plays, and Poughkeepsie matrons
hold luncheon parties in the dining room of Alumnae House; but
the off-campus life, in the main, centers about a street or two in
Arlington, the outlying section in which the campus is located. And
this itself is less lively than formerly; a Peck & Peck, a drugstore, an
eating place or two, and the Vassar Bank are the principal remains
of a once-spirited commercial area, where teashops, inns, and dress
shops once flourished on Vassar extravagance.

Today, "off-campus" for the students is mainly represented by Alumnae House, a tall stucco and brown-beamed building that stands on a hill overlooking the college and that plays, significantly, more and more of a part in campus life and politics. Where, in my day, the roadster, the trolley car, and the taxi bore us off the campus and away from the supervisory eye—downtown in groups to a speakeasy, or off with our dates to a road-house or a picturesque old inn—today's undergraduates flock up the hill to Alumnae House for beer, Cokes, hamburgers, and Vassar devils (a sort of fudgy cake sundae) in the Pub on week nights; and on weekends, they join their young men in the big lounge-living room for a cocktail or two, under the watchful eyes of the alumnae secretary or her assistants, who see that the young men do not get too much to drink, that there is no necking, that somebody plays the piano or sings during the bigger cocktail parties (thus slowing down the consumption of liquor) and that, on such occasions, the bar is shut down in ample time to speed the girls and their escorts off to an early dinner in the dining halls before the evening dance.

There is no compulsion on the part of the college that off-campus social life should be conducted under these auspices—the students apparently prefer it so. This increasing dependency on the college and its auxiliary agencies to furnish not only education but plea-sure, emotional guidance, and social direction is reflected in nearly every sphere of the current Vassar life. Two hundred and sixteen Yale freshmen, for example, were imported last year by the college for a Saturday-night freshman dance—in former years the Vassar neophyte was dependent on her own initiative, the kindness of her brother or her roommate, to get herself "started." For girls from the West or from small-town high schools, this could be a source of misery, yet in my day any attempt on the part of the administra-tion to pair us off with male wallflowers in a similar predicament was met with groans. I well remember, as a freshman member of the Vassar debate squad, being paired off with a poor freshman from Wesleyan (six and a half feet tall and chinless) when their team came to debate us on censorship and how my six roommates followed us about, laughing and drawing satirical caricatures, as we danced, ate, and walked around the campus together.

In the same way, the college's Vocational Bureau has multiplied its activities of mercy, so that the senior now who goes out into the world will be counseled, fortified, and supplied with letters of introduction by a network of Vassar alumnae. The college is a miniature welfare state. During the early thirties, a single psychiatrist, a psychologist, and a visiting consultant from Riggs Institute took care of the emotional problems of 1,250 students. Now Vassar's 1,350 girls have been endowed with a two-million-dollar grant by Paul Mellon (in memory of his wife, an alumna) for a guidance and counseling program under the direction of Dr. Carl Binger, the psychiatrist who testified in the second Alger Hiss trial.

These fresh, pink-cheeked girls in neatly turned-up blue jeans, flannel culottes, tweed jackets, well-cut shirts appear both too well adjusted and too busy to take any more guidance or counseling. The extracurricular side of Vassar life has already expanded to the point where solitude and self-questioning seem regulated out of existence. Lectures, symposia, recitals, dance programs, foreign movies compete with each other and with organized camping trips, bicycle trips, square dances, factory tours, Hall Plays, for the students' spare time. The student is always "signed up" for some activity, afternoons, evenings, weekends. There are two competing newspapers to be got out, plus the usual literary magazine, yearbook and scholarly magazine. Then there is the radio workshop, the Outing Club, the "Swupper" Club, the travel bureau. Every student is required to give four hours a week to the cooperative work program in the kitchens, dining rooms, or Message Center; slackers are put on a "blacklist" and given demerits of additional hours, which are meted out also for improper dress.

There are Student Council Meetings and Student Curriculum Committee meetings, meetings of the United World Federalists, of the Student Liberal Association, and the Students for Democratic Action. Nearly every afternoon and evening, besides the usual athletics, besides the scheduled lectures, forums, and recitals given for

the college at large, there are tryouts for something or other: the
Hall Play, one of the two newspapers, the literary magazine, the
Flora Dora Girls, or the Gold Dusters (all Vassar music makers),
the choir, the orchestra, or the Glee Club. There is scenery to be
made for the Theatre (not to be confused with the Hall Plays, which
are extracurricular), costumes to be sewed. There are meetings of
the Thekla Club, the *Cercle Français*, the Classics Club, the Spanish
Club, Philosophers' Holiday, the Psychology Club, the Russian
Club, the Science Club, the German Club.

Nehru is speaking at Hyde Park; a New York doctor is discussing "Whither Medicine?" at the Dutchess County Social Planning
Council; the Yale Outing Club is visiting; the Senior or Junior Prom
Committee must meet; the Daisy Chain has to be chosen from
the sophomore class. Founder's Day must be planned for, and the
Tree Ceremonies; a note-topic is due. Jeans must be changed for
dinner (only skirts are permitted in the dining room). After dinner,
if no lecture or recital is impending, if there are no interviews or
rehearsals, or last-minute dummying of the newspaper, if there is
no reading to be done in the library, no quiz to prepare for or letters
to write, there are the endless bridge and knitting in the common
rooms or a hurried excursion to the Pub for beer or Cokes and conversation. And in the morning, there is the Mail Rush, the central
event of the day, a jostle and scramble for love letters, letters from
home, campus mail, bills, in that order of preference.

This intensification of the extracurricular life, in which every
hour is planned for and assigned to some scheduled group activity,
in which no one is left out or discriminated against (there are no
secret societies or sororities), is the most striking feature of the current scene at Vassar. To the returning alumna whose college years
were both more snobbish and sectarian, on the one hand, and more
Bohemian, rebellious, and lyrical, on the other, the administrative
cast, so to speak, of the present Vassar mold is both disquieting
and praiseworthy. A uniform, pliant, docile undergraduate seems
to be resulting from the stress on the group and the community
that prevails at Vassar today. The outcast and the rebel are almost

equally known. There has been a leveling-off in the Vassar geography of what was once a series of ranges, peaks, and valleys, so that Vassar, formerly known for the extremities of her climate, is now a moderate plateau. The vivid and extraordinary student, familiar to the old teachers and the alumnae, is, at least temporarily, absent from the scene.

The idea of excellence, the zest for adventure, the fastidiousness of mind and humanistic breadth of feeling that were so noticeable at Vassar during the long reign of the *emeritae* (as its retired female teachers are styled—a name that evokes a wonderful extinct species of butterfly) seem somehow to have abandoned the college, even though many of the courses that used to be given by the senior faculty have been passed on in their classic form to younger women from the graduate schools. What is missing is a certain largeness of mind, an amplitude of style, the mantle of a calling, a sense of historical dignity. I think of old Miss Haight, Elizabeth Hazelton Haight, of the Latin Department—tall, deep-voiced, Sabine, with olive skin and a mass of white hair piled high and a stately classroom delivery: her romantic attachment to Horace and Apuleius, her Augustan lecture style ("When Theseus came to Athens [pause] as it were [pause] *in medias res...*") and the letter she wrote the student chief justice when a group of my friends took two statues from the old Music Hall (which, together with Classics, was in the old Riding Academy), to celebrate with wine and garlands the opening of the new Music Building ("I regret to report the rape of Venus and Minerva from the Classics Department"). And robust, flushed, warm-hearted Anna Kitchel with her Middle-Western accent and schoolgirlish way of smoking a cigarette, which she held at a perpendicular to the orifice of her lips, puffing mightily away like a choo-choo in a child's picture book; her sympathy with George Eliot in her common-law marriage with Mr. Lewes; her sympathy with Annette, Wordsworth's abandoned light-of-love and yet her hearty relish for this un-Wordsworthian lapse ("Oh, he was a *rare bird!*"). And slight, gray-haired, pretty Helen Sandison, the Elizabethan specialist, like an Elizabethan heroine herself, with

her mettlesome sharpness, her hatred of imprecision and of bowd-
lerization of texts... At the present Vassar salary level, it is hard to
attract young women fired with the ardor of teaching and capable
of all the renunciations that the unmarried teacher who lives with
a few books and prints in a faculty dormitory must make. For the
gifted young woman today, such a life, even with summers off and
sabbaticals, is not a destiny but a fate.

The problem posed by the passing of the *emeritae* is not unique,
of course, to Vassar; it is felt throughout the teaching profession, wherever fine women of the old liberal school reigned—in
private academies and public schools, from the big-city high
school to the one-room country schoolhouse. The pioneers are
gone, and who is to take their places? Other private colleges have
turned to the literary avant-garde and found Abelards to substitute for the Héloïses—young male critics, philosophers, poets,
novelists, short-story writers, trained, for the most part, in the
New Criticism, a scholastic discipline of its own. But Vassar is
committed to the *woman teacher*. That is, it considers women a
discriminated-against minority in the college teaching field, and,
as a woman's college, believes that it has a duty to hire women in
preference to men. This principle, which worked well in the past,
today creates a number of dilemmas—among them the dilemma
of defining what a woman is or ought to be. Is she a child-bearing
animal, as some ultra-modern theorists, represented on the Vassar
faculty, now contend? If so, is a spinster a woman? Is a feminist
a woman? In its hiring policy, Vassar today has compromised on
these questions. The faculty at present has a larger proportion of
men and of married women with children than it had in former
years, but now for the first time Vassar's president is a woman, and
an unmarried woman, Miss Sarah Gibson Blanding, a Kentuckian,
former head of the Department of Home Economics at Cornell,
an economist and one-time athlete—unconventional, direct, liberal, dynamic, outspoken, hospitable. The choice of Miss Blanding
a few years ago seems on the surface a victory for feminism, but
at bottom it is probably a defeat. The old humanistic curriculum,

which flourished under the paternal administration of President MacCracken, a Chaucerian and a classics scholar who once played Theseus in Greek for a college production of the *Hippolytus*, is slowly yielding to "education-for-living," as literature and the arts give way to the social sciences, and "pure" scholarship cedes to preparation for civic life and marriage.

Miss Blanding has gone on record as saying that college should not be "an ivory tower"; she is noted for her championship of the Negro, both in word and in deed; and Vassar, under her leadership, prides itself on its advances in social democracy. "Field work" among the people of Dutchess County is given prominence in the social sciences. The college points to the fact that, unlike most private colleges, including some progressive ones, it has no Jewish quota or geographical quota (a device for limiting, without acknowledging it, the proportion of Jewish students); it points to the three Negro girls in this year's freshman class and to the unusually high number of students recruited from public high schools, to its interdenominational church using ritual from various faiths, to its student self-government, its fixed room rate, its cooperative work program and new cooperative dormitory, to its interdepartmental course, *The City*, a sort of living documentary, given a few years ago under the spurring of Helen Lockwood, the militant of sociology within the English department.

These, taken together, are indices of progress within the field of private education, yet it must be pointed out that the progress is relative: Vassar, after having been incorporated for more than seventy-five years, has now achieved the degree of democracy that prevails in most free state universities.

That maximum of social protection once afforded by the private college to the daughters of the well-to-do is here being withdrawn in favor of a more "open" environment that will better prepare the student for those realities of modern life that the CCNY or Hunter student faces from birth. Meanwhile, a new questionnaire answered by 7,915 alumnae discloses that 61 per cent of those answering still favor the Republican Party and that 36 per cent think that Vassar could have helped them "to adjust to life" more than it did; 67 per cent, however, would choose Vassar all over again.

The adjustment-to-life question is typical of Vassar and perhaps, more generally, of feminine insularity and self-centeredness—it is impossible to imagine such a question being asked by Harvard or Chicago. But it reflects the preoccupations of the alumnae and of certain powerful faculty figures of the new dispensation; in particular, of Mrs. Dorothy Lee, '27, of Anthropology, the most controversial person on today's campus—dark, short-haired, vibrant, abrupt, boyish, speaking with a slight foreign accent, photographed with her four children by the alumnae magazine making meatballs, a cultural anthropologist of the school that emphasizes childbearing as the crucial activity in woman's life. Careers for women in the old sense are abhorrent to Mrs. Lee and her followers; she believes in a faculty of homemakers, in an extension of the cooperative principle for training in group betterment. She detests institutional living. Her views are dynamic, integralist, and puritanical; she would sacrifice the part to the whole and believes that the one-sided person is the enemy of society. In her own way, she is a pioneer, like the spinsters who preceded her, and an iconoclast, like the suffragettes she spurns.

For the present college mood, her temper is too radical, and she is as far, perhaps, from that element in the alumnae which feels itself cheated by dishwashing and diaper-changing as from the traditionalists on the faculty who fear her influence on the students. The preparation-for-life controversy that rages in the alumnae magazine and in alumnae panel discussions reaches the undergraduate body in a somewhat muted form. The superior students do not yet demand courses in the techniques of home-making or a serious revision of the curriculum. Rather, unlike their rebellious sisters of the twenties and thirties, they look forward to "working within their community" for social betterment, while being married and having babies. As the *Vassar Alumnae Magazine* puts it, speaking of the normative Vassar woman revealed by the new questionnaire:

She is the woman who changed the local school situation from a political machine to an educational institution. She is the woman behind the League of Women Voters, Planned Parenthood, and, yes, the 4-H Club. She won't very often be found sitting at the luncheon bridge table. She'll be found actively, thoughtfully, even serenely, playing her role as an intelligent citizen.

III

LITERATURE AND THE ARTS

Recalled to Life, *or*, Charles Dickens at the Bar

March, 1953

IN THE EIGHTY-ODD years since his death, Charles Dickens has been summoned again and again from the tomb to face the verdict of history. The latest qualified expert to view the body and announce his findings is Edgar Johnson, a professor at City College, the author of an eleven-hundred-page biography that reads like the report of some officially constituted commission that hands in its verdict as follows: the deceased is cleared of the charge of sentimentality (finding: healthy emotion), chidden for his domestic conduct, and awarded a place among the world's great authors, in recognition of his social vision.

Dickens hated officials, but his critics and biographers, almost inevitably, feel called upon to assume an official air when dealing with his "case." Each critic clears his throat with a vast administrative harumph and scans the expectant courtroom before imparting his conclusions. Attorneys for the defense scribble while listening to the prosecution's summation; on the bench a hanging judge peers over the bar to anathematize the quivering defendant; alienists and character witnesses succeed each other on the stand. Advocates of Dickens like Mr. Johnson have the anxious note of apologists, now glossing over and extenuating, now reprobating stoutly, lest they be charged with undue partiality. His assailants, on the other hand, present themselves as inquisitors, text in hand, eager to convict poor Dickens out of his own mouth of crimes of bad writing, crudity, unreality, unfriendliness to the proletariat, to business, to the Jews, to foreigners; "he could not paint a gentleman," and it is "questionable" whether he regarded the poor as equals.

Here, as in most inquisitions, the metonymic principle is at work—the part is substituted for the whole, and a single "incriminating" utterance is produced in court to lay bare the man in his totality. This desire to criminate has singled Dickens out uniquely among great writers; Dostoevsky sometimes wrote badly; he was virulently anti-Semitic, anti-Polish, anti-Catholic; but nobody seeks to indict him for it. And Dickens' defenders accept the criminative method when they produce a good Jew, Riah, to offset the bad Fagin, sympathetic aristocrats and proletarians to offset their opposite numbers; in their eagerness to give Dickens a clean bill of health, they are willing to strip him down to a few inoffensive platitudes.

Perhaps this zeal, however, merely testifies to the fact that Dickens is still alive—a burning issue. Certainly, the performance of Anthony West in *The New Yorker* recently suggests that it is a living man who is being collared and haled before justice. Reviewing Mr. Johnson's biography becomes, for Mr. West, an occasion for a violent attack on Dickens—the most violent attack, to my knowledge, in all Dickens literature.

He was *not* a great writer, proclaims Mr. West, but a mere entertainer, an artist who sold his birthright for popular applause. Furthermore, he was a pious fraud and a hypocrite, a veritable Pecksniff. He was not really interested in industrial reforms, but jumped on the band wagon when he saw that Mrs. Gaskell and others were making a good thing of the cause. When he attacked social abuses, he was merely following in the wake of his audience, which was way ahead of him in its clamor for social change. Far from being a critic of imperialism, he was guilty of being an imperialist of the lesser-breeds-without-the-law order; his "real" feelings about this subject are embodied not in his novels but in a private letter to a philanthropic lady written at the time of the Indian Mutiny. "...the attack on heartless economic theory," as embodied in Scrooge, was "a safety play that can be relied upon to ruffle nobody." Another attack on heartless economic theory, *Hard Times*, is "dubious social criticism…childish in its ignorance of what businessmen are like or were like as it is in its conception of industrial problems.

"Dickens's imagination, in matters of finance, never got beyond petty cash. None of his rich men are really wealthy, and none of them are engaged in credible affairs. *Hard Times* is, however, wholehearted in its attack on two things—education and Parliament—that were the really effective instruments of social reform…"

What is bewildering in this violence is first of all the fact that it seems to issue from an almost insensate ignorance of Dickens' writing and life—is it education that Dickens is attacking in *Hard Times* or "education"? Compare the dates of Mrs. Gaskell's *Mary Barton* (1848) and *The Old Curiosity Shop* (1841), where Dickens first assailed the factory system—who was following whom? "Petty cash"—Mr. Merdle's transactions? Dombey not wealthy, or Jarndyce of *Bleak House* or Mr. Boffin, the golden dustman? And if Dickens was cut off "from easy intercourse with his intellectual equals all through his life" and surrounded himself "with an entourage of second-raters," is this meant to be a judgment on Thackeray, the Carlyles, Mrs. Gaskell, Lord John Russell, George Eliot and George Henry Lewes, Tennyson, Landor, Mazzini, Lamartine, and Victor Hugo—Dickens' friends and intimates? If Dickens was following in the wake of his audience, how did that audience make its views felt? Not in legislation, certainly, which lagged far behind Dickens. Was it Parliament or Dickens that was the really effective instrument of social reform?

It has been argued that Dickens the social reformer and pamphleteer swamped Dickens the artist. Edward Sackville-West put this case at its strongest when he declared that Dickens' bathos was required to awaken pity in the hardened Victorian heart. But if this was a sin, it was a generous sin, as most of Dickens' critics have conceded. Mr. West is the first, so far as I know, to pretend that Dickens' art was a calculated untruth aimed to swell the volume of sales.

Yet a child (to take Dickens' own favorite touchstone of truth and purity of response) has only to read a single chapter of *Oliver*

Twist, say, to perceive that here is both a heated critic of society and a ready sentimentalist. We do not need a biographer to tell us that Dickens wrote his "affecting" passages with tears in his eyes; that is precisely what makes us wish to turn our own dry eyes away from the moist spectacle of the author. George Eliot also underwent a hysterical transformation as she wrote her climactic pages, the very pages we cannot read today without mortification for that gaunt, moralistic dame.

And the highbrow reader of the era was attuned to these vibrations. Daniel O'Connell, the Irish political leader, was so affected by the death of Little Nell that he burst into sobs and threw the book out the window of the railway carriage he was traveling in, groaning, "He should not have killed her." Walter Savage Landor, Macready the actor, Carlyle, and Jeffrey the critic were all overcome by the chapter; in Jeffrey's case, a visitor, perceiving his condition, feared she was intruding on a real bereavement. I do not agree with Mr. Johnson that this was healthy emotion; rather it has the eerie quality of a mass phenomenon, like the possession of the nuns of Loudun.

In any case, it was genuine enough, of its kind. The excessive suggestibility of the Victorians probably had something to do with "alienation," with the transformations being wrought in man and countryside by the process of mechanization. Already, in the eighteenth century, in the early stages of the Industrial Revolution, there appeared that taste for prodigies, for the august and the sublime, that the Victorians brought to fulfillment in their passion for mountain-climbing, for gorges and precipices, for the abysmal vertigo of crime and innocence, horror and bathos. Feeling, shrinking before the industrial vistas, sought to accommodate itself to the new scale of things by developing its own kinetics. Popular authors like Dickens and George Eliot differed from the ordinary public in that they possessed an internal self-starter of emotion.

Yet if Dickens was the prosperous owner of such a gadget or patent, he was also, of all his contemporaries, the man who looked upon the new mechanized human being with the greatest sense of fear and astonishment. For this is what many of his famous "characters" are: wind-up toys, large or small, that move in jerks and starts, whose machinery whirs toilsomely before they begin to speak. How a man can become a monster or a mechanical marvel is the question that preoccupies Dickens throughout the whole of his work. And these mechanical marvels he shows us are not travesties of men invented by a satirical author; they are appallingly true to life. Mr. Dorrit, Pecksniff, Uriah Heep—these are the travesties man has made of himself.

Leaving aside the heroes and heroines, Dickens' world is divided into two kingdoms: the kingdom of metal, which is dominated by the hunchback Quilp, that malignant Vulcan, armored and carapaced, who eats hard-boiled eggshells and prawns with their heads and tails on and cools his brazen throat by drinking boiling grog straight from the saucepan; and the kingdom of vegetables, presided over by Mr. Dick, Mr. Wemmick, and the Aged P.

The vegetable kingdom is more amiable; its inhabitants have lapsed into nature and present themselves as botanical curiosities— harmless on the whole, except for an occasional flycatcher plant. But they too have lost their humanity, which stirs in them only as a rum memory. They have obdurately become things, like the men of brass and iron, and they differ from the latter principally in that they do not treat other men as things but are content to soliloquize mystifyingly, in their own patch of ground. This obduracy is typical of all true Dickens creations: a true Dickens character never listens to the protests of reality; he inflexibly orates. In short, he has officialized himself, like Mr. Dorrit, the Father of the Marshalsea, receiving his testimonials; or Mr. Bounderby, who has invented his own authorized biography; or Mrs. Gamp, who has invented her own reference, the imaginary Mrs. Harris. All these people live in shatterproof hierarchical structures.

The thingification of man, to use Kant's term, is Dickens' inexhaustible subject and the source of his power and fascination. To treat another man as a thing, you must first become a very large thing yourself—an impervious thing. This was Dickens' discovery about character, and he remains the only writer (outside of Gogol, whom in many ways he resembles) to have this dreadful insight, not as an abstract theorem but as a concrete apprehension of a process, like the processes of manufacturing that were being developed with such rapidity in his day. "There's a young man hid with me, in comparison with which young man I am a Angel," says the convict Magwitch, impressively, to frighten the boy Pip in the churchyard. This passage has been criticized on the ground that Magwitch, realistically, would not look upon himself as a horrid apparition. But this casual self-knowledge, precisely, is what transfixes not only the boy Pip but the reader: the man Magwitch—how is it possible?—sees what he has become and uses himself as a bogy to terrify a child in a graveyard; and the fact of the frank perception prepares for Magwitch's redemption, the change of heart on which Dickens places so many hopes. Otherwise, the accents are those of Marlowe's Mephistophilis: "Why this is hell, nor am I out of it."

When Dickens tries to create virtue or manliness, he often fails (though he is very good at a kind of boyish manliness—Nicholas Nickleby, Martin Chuzzlewit, David Copperfield—with a blush still on its cheek). And yet this quality is not absent from his work, for it is present in wonderful abundance in the author himself. *This was a man*—again and again one is halted in the midst of a page to make this wondering observation, as though Dickens himself, and not his characters, were the marvel.

The author does not mean to display his manliness, as he displays, say, the virtue of Little Dorrit or Nell; it takes the reader unawares. He did not mean to display it in his life, but time and again the reader of any Dickens biography is halted by the blaze of energy, the bravery, the spontaneous anger, the magnanimity, the quick assumption of responsibility.

Can it be that this is what is amiss? Are today's critics and biographers sincerely disturbed to find a *man* entombed in the Westminster Abbey grave? A *man* entombed in the novel—the last place, apparently, they would expect to find one today? Is this why even the best of Dickens' recent critics approach him in such a gingerly fashion, as if they feared to be held accountable for any slip of the pen concerning him?

In a certain sense, of course, they are right to take these precautions, to keep their distance from Dickens and display him as a specimen that has come under official notice. Mr. West's outburst in *The New Yorker* is evidence that there exists a profound hostility to Dickens that may break out anywhere without warning, though not, as one might think, in highbrow circles, where the charge "mere entertainer" might have some appropriateness, but in commercial journalism: Orville Prescott in the New York *Times* promptly echoed Mr. West's judgment, and *Time* magazine found a citation from Lenin to prove that Dickens was not "a social revolutionary." Like the mysterious utterances of Mr. F.'s aunt, this animus of Mr. West's spouts up from arcane caverns that perhaps underlie the whole of modern "humanistic" culture.

A book review of Charles Dickens: His Tragedy and Triumph, *by Edgar Johnson.*

Settling the Colonel's Hash

February, 1954

SEVEN YEARS AGO, WHEN I taught in a progressive college, I had a pretty girl student in one of my classes who wanted to be a short-story writer. She was not studying writing with me, but she knew that I sometimes wrote short stories, and one day, breathless and glowing, she came up to me in the hall, to tell me that she had just written a story that her writing teacher, a Mr. Converse, was terribly excited about. "He thinks it's wonderful," she said, "and he's going to help me fix it up for publication."

I asked what the story was about; the girl was a rather simple being who loved clothes and dates. Her answer had a deprecating tone. It was just about a girl (herself) and some sailors she had met on the train. But then her face, which had looked perturbed for a moment, gladdened.

"Mr. Converse is going over it with me and we're going to put in the symbols."

Another girl in the same college, when asked by us in her sopho-more orals why she read novels (one of the pseudo-profound questions that ought never to be put) answered in a defensive flurry: "Well, *of course* I don't read them to find out what happens to the hero."

At the time, I thought these notions were peculiar to progressive education: it was old-fashioned or regressive to read a novel to find out what happens to the hero or to have a mere experience empty of symbolic pointers. But I now discover that this attitude is quite gen-eral, and that readers and students all over the country are in a state of apprehension, lest they read a book or story literally and miss the presence of a symbol. And like everything in America, this search for meanings has become a socially competitive enterprise; the best reader is the one who detects the most symbols in a given stretch of prose. And the benighted reader who fails to find any symbols humbly assents when they are pointed out to him; he accepts his mortification.

I had no idea how far this process had gone until last spring, when I began to get responses to a story I had published in *Harper's*. I say "story" because that was what it was called by *Harper's*. I myself would not know quite what to call it; it was a piece of reporting or a fragment of autobiography—an account of my meeting with an anti-Semitic army colonel. It began in the club car of a train going to St. Louis; I was wearing an apple-green shirtwaist and a dark-green skirt and pink earrings; we got into an argument about the Jews. The colonel was a rather dapper, flashy kind of Irish-American with a worldly blue eye; he took me, he said, for a sculptress, which made me feel, to my horror, that I looked Bohemian and there-fore rather suspect. He was full of the usual profound clichés that anti-Semites air, like original epigrams, about the Jews: that he could tell a Jew, that they were different from other people, that you couldn't trust them in business, that some of his best friends were Jews, that he distinguished between a Jew and a kike, and finally that, of course, he didn't agree with Hitler: Hitler went too far; the Jews were human beings.

All the time we talked, and I defended the Jews, he was trying to get my angle, as he called it; he thought it was abnormal for anybody who wasn't Jewish not to feel as he did. As a matter of fact, I have a Jewish grandmother, but I decided to keep this news to myself: I did not want the colonel to think that I had any interested reason for speaking on behalf of the Jews, that is, that I was prejudiced. In the end, though, I got my comeuppance. Just as we were parting, the colonel asked me my married name, which is Broadwater, and the whole mystery was cleared up for him, instantly; he supposed I was married to a Jew and that the name was spelled B-r-o-d-w-a-t-e-r.

I did not try to enlighten him; I let him think what he wanted; in a certain sense, he was right; he had unearthed my Jewish grandmother or her equivalent. There were a few details that I must mention to make the next part clear: in my car, there were two nuns, whom I talked to as a distraction from the colonel and the moral problems he raised. He and I finally had lunch together in the St. Louis railroad station, where we continued the discussion. It was a very hot day. I had a sandwich; he had roast-beef hash. We both had an old-fashioned.

The whole point of this "story" was that it really happened; it is written in the first person; I speak of myself in my own name, McCarthy; at the end, I mention my husband's name, Broadwater. When I was thinking about writing the story, I decided not to treat it fictionally; the chief interest, I felt, lay in the fact that it happened, in real life, last summer, to the writer herself, who was a good deal at fault in the incident. I wanted to embarrass myself and, if possible, the reader too.

Yet, strangely enough, many of my readers preferred to think of this account as fiction. I still meet people who ask me, confidentially, "That story of yours about the colonel—was it really true?" It seemed to them perfectly natural that I would write a fabrication, in which I figured under my own name, and sign it, though in my eyes this would be like perjuring yourself in court or forging checks. Shortly after the "story" was published, I got a kindly letter from a man in Mexico, in which he criticized the menu from an artistic point of view: he thought salads would be better for hot weather and it would be more in character for the narrator-heroine to have a Martini. I did not answer the letter, though I was moved to, because I had the sense that he would not understand the distinction between what *ought* to have happened and what *did* happen.

Then in April I got another letter, from an English teacher in a small college in the Middle West, that reduced me to despair. I am going to cite it at length.

"My students in freshman English chose to analyze your story, 'Artists in Uniform,' from the March issue of *Harper's*. For a week

I heard oral discussions on it and then the students wrote critical analyses. In so far as it is possible, I stayed out of their discussions, encouraging them to read the story closely with your intentions as a guide to their understanding. Although some of them insisted that the story has no other level than the realistic one, most of them decided it has symbolic overtones.

"The question is: how closely do you want the symbols labeled? They wrestled with the nuns, the author's two shades of green with pink accents, with the 'materialistic godlessness' of the colonel... A surprising number wanted exact symbols; for example, they searched for the significance of the colonel's eating hash and the author eating a sandwich... From my stand point, the story was an entirely satisfactory springboard for understanding the various shades of prejudice, for seeing how much of the artist goes into his painting. If it is any satisfaction to you, our campus was alive with discussions about 'Artists in Uniform.' We liked the story and we thought it amazing that an author could succeed in making readers dislike the author—for a purpose, of course!"

I probably should have answered this letter, but I did not. The gulf seemed to me too wide. I could not applaud the backward students who insisted that the story has no other level than the realistic one without giving offense to their teacher, who was evidently a well-meaning person. But I shall try now to address a reply, not to this teacher and her unfortunate class, but to a whole school of misunderstanding. There were no symbols in this story; there was no deeper level. The nuns were in the story because they were on the train; the contrasting greens were the dress I happened to be wearing; the colonel had hash because he had hash; materialistic godlessness meant just what it means when a priest thunders it from the pulpit—the phrase, for the first time, had meaning for me as I watched and listened to the colonel.

But to clarify the misunderstanding, one must go a little further and try to see what a literary symbol is. Now in one sense, the colonel's hash and my sandwich can be regarded as symbols; that is, they typify the colonel's food tastes and mine. (The man in Mexico had

different food tastes which he wished to interpose into our reality.)
The hash and the sandwich might even be said to show something
very obvious about our characters and bringing-up, or about our
sexes; I was a woman, he was a man. And though on another day
I might have ordered hash myself, that day I did not, because the
colonel and I, in our disagreement, were polarizing each other.

The hash and the sandwich, then, could be regarded as symbols
of our disagreement, almost conscious symbols. And underneath
our discussion of the Jews, there was a thin sexual current running,
as there always is in such random encounters or pickups (for they
have a strong suggestion of the illicit). The fact that I ordered something conventionally feminine and he ordered something conventionally masculine represented, no doubt, our awareness of a sexual
possibility; even though I was not attracted to the colonel nor he to
me, the circumstances of our meeting made us define ourselves as
a woman and a man.

The sandwich and the hash were our provisional, *ad hoc* symbols of ourselves. But in this sense all human actions are symbolic
because they represent the person who does them. If the colonel
had ordered a fruit salad with whipped cream, this too would
have represented him in some way; given his other traits, it would
have pointed to a complexity in his character that the hash did not
suggest.

In the same way, the contrasting greens of my dress were a
symbol of my taste in clothes and hence representative of me—all
too representative, I suddenly saw, in the club car, when I got an
"artistic" image of myself flashed back at me from the men's eyes. I
had no wish to stylize myself as an artist, that is, to parade about
as a symbol of flamboyant unconventionality, but apparently I had
done so unwittingly when I picked those colors off a rack, under
the impression that they suited me or "expressed my personality"
as salesladies say.

My dress, then, was a symbol of the perplexity I found myself
in with the colonel; I did not want to be categorized as a member
of a peculiar minority—an artist or a Jew; but brute fate and the

colonel kept resolutely cramming me into both those uncomfortable pigeonholes. I wished to be regarded as ordinary or rather as universal, to be anybody and therefore everybody (that is, in one sense, I wanted to be on the colonel's side, majestically above minorities); but every time the colonel looked at my dress and me in it with my pink earrings I shrank to minority status, and felt the dress in the heat shriveling me, like the shirt of Nessus, the centaur, that consumed Hercules.

But this is not what the students meant when they wanted the symbols "labeled." They were searching for a more recondite significance than that afforded by the trite symbolism of ordinary life, in which a dress is a social badge. They supposed that I was engaging in literary or artificial symbolism, which would lead the reader out of the confines of reality into the vast fairy tale of myth, in which the color green would have an emblematic meaning (or did the two greens signify for them what the teacher calls "shades" of prejudice), and the colonel's hash, I imagine, would be some sort of Eucharistic mincemeat.

Apparently, the presence of the nuns assured them there were overtones of theology; it did not occur to them (a) that the nuns were there because pairs of nuns are a standardized feature of summer Pullman travel, like crying babies, and perspiring businessmen in the club car, and (b) that if I thought the nuns worth mentioning, it was also because of something very simple and directly relevant: the nuns and the colonel and I all had something in common—we had all at one time been Catholics—and I was seeking common ground with the colonel, from which to turn and attack his position.

In any account of reality, even a televised one, which comes closest to being a literal transcript or replay, some details are left out as irrelevant (though nothing is really irrelevant). The details that are not eliminated have to stand as symbols of the whole, like stenographic signs, and of course there is an art of selection, even in a newspaper account: the writer, if he has any ability, is looking for the revealing detail that will sum up the picture for the reader in a flash of recognition.

But the art of abridgment and condensation, which is familiar to anybody who tries to relate an anecdote, or give a direction—the art of natural symbolism, which is at the basis of speech and all representation—has at bottom a centripetal intention. It hovers over an object, an event, or series of events and tries to declare what it is. Analogy (that is, comparison to other objects) is inevitably one of its methods. "The weather was soupy," i.e., like soup. "He wedged his way in," i.e., he had to enter, thin edge first, as a wedge enters, and so on. All this is obvious. But these metaphorical aids to communication are a far cry from literary symbolism, as taught in the schools and practiced by certain fashionable writers. Literary symbolism is centrifugal and flees from the object, the event, into the incorporeal distance, where concepts are taken for substance and floating ideas and archetypes assume a hieratic authority.

In this dream-forest, symbols become arbitrary; all counters are interchangeable; anything can stand for anything else. The colonel's hash can be a Eucharist or a cannibal feast or the banquet of Atreus, or all three, so long as the actual dish set before the actual man is disparaged. What is depressing about this insistent symboliza-tion is the fact that while it claims to lead to the infinite, it quickly reaches very finite limits—there are only so many myths on record, and once you have got through Bulfinch, the Scandinavian, and the Indian, there is not much left. And if all stories reduce themselves to myth and symbol, qualitative differences vanish, and there is only a single, monotonous story.

American fiction of the symbolist school demonstrates this mournful truth, without precisely intending to. A few years ago, when the mode was at its height, chic novels and stories fell into three classes: those which had a Greek myth for their framework, which the reader was supposed to detect, like finding the faces in the clouds in old newspaper puzzle contests; those which had symbolic modern figures, dwarfs, hermaphrodites, and cripples, illustrating maiming and loneliness; and those which contained symbolic animals, cougars, wild cats, and monkeys. One young novelist, a product of the Princeton school of symbolism, had all three elements going at once, like the ringmaster of a three-ring circus, with the freaks, the animals, and the statues.

The quest for symbolic referents had as its object, of course, the deepening of the writer's subject and the reader's awareness. But the result was paradoxical. At the very moment when American writing was penetrated by the symbolic urge, it ceased to be able to create symbols of its own. Babbitt, I suppose, was the last important symbol to be created by an American writer; he gave his name to a type that henceforth would be recognizable to everybody. He passed into the language. The same thing could be said, perhaps, though to a lesser degree, of Caldwell's Tobacco Road, Eliot's Prufrock, and possibly of Faulkner's Snopeses. The discovery of new symbols is not the only function of a writer, but the writer who cares about this must be fascinated by reality itself, as a butterfly collector is fascinated by the glimpse of a new specimen. Such a specimen was Mme. Bovary or M. Homais or M. de Charlus or Jupien; these specimens were precious to their discoverers, not because they repeated an age-old pattern but because their markings were new. Once the specimen has been described, the public instantly spots other examples of the kind, and the world seems suddenly full of Babbitts and Charlus, where none had been noted before.

A different matter was Joyce's Mr. Bloom. Mr. Bloom can be called a symbol of eternal recurrence—the wandering Jew, Ulysses the voyager—but he is a symbol thickly incarnate, fleshed out in a Dublin advertising canvasser. He is not *like* Ulysses or vaguely suggestive of Ulysses; he is Ulysses, circa 1905. Joyce evidently believed in a cyclical theory of history, in which everything repeated itself; he also subscribed in youth to the doctrine that declares that the Host, a piece of bread, is also God's body and blood. How it can be both things at the same time, transubstantially, is a mystery, and Mr. Bloom is just such a mystery: Ulysses in the visible appearance of a Dublin advertising canvasser.

Mr. Bloom is not a symbol of Ulysses, but Ulysses-Bloom together, one and indivisible, symbolize or rather demonstrate eternal recurrence. I hope I make myself clear. The point is transubstantiation:

Bloom and Ulysses are transfused into each other and neither reality is diminished. Both realities are locked together, like the protons and neutrons of an atom. *Finnegans Wake* is a still more ambitious attempt to create a fusion, this time a myriad fusion, and to exemplify the mystery of how a thing can be itself and at the same time be something else. The world is many and it is also one.

But the clarity and tension of Joyce's thought brought him closer in a way to the strictness of allegory than to the diffuse practices of latter-day symbolists. In Joyce, the equivalences and analogies are very sharp and distinct, as in a pun, and the real world is almost querulously audible, like the voices of the washerwomen on the Liffey that come into Earwicker's dream. But this is not true of Joyce's imitators or of the imitators of his imitators, for whom reality is only a shadowy pretext for the introduction of a whole *corps de ballet* of dancing symbols in mythic draperies and animal skins.

Let me make a distinction. There are some great writers, like Joyce or Melville, who have consciously introduced symbolic elements into their work; and there are great writers who have written fables or allegories. In both cases, the writer makes it quite clear to the reader how he is to be read; only an idiot would take *Pilgrim's Progress* for a realistic story, and even a young boy, reading *Moby Dick*, realizes that there is something more than whale-fishing here, though he may not be able to name what it is. But the great body of fiction contains only what I have called natural symbolism, in which selected events represent or typify a problem, a kind of society or psychology, a philosophical theory, in the same way that they do in real life. What happens to the hero becomes of the highest importance. This symbolism needs no abstruse interpretation, and abstruse interpretation will only lead the reader away from the reality that the writer is trying to press on his attention.

I shall give an example or two of what I mean by natural symbolism and I shall begin with a rather florid one: Henry James' *The Golden Bowl*. This is the story of a rich American girl who collects European objects. One of these objects is a husband, Prince Amerigo, who proves to be unfaithful. Early in the story, there is a visit to an antique shop in which the Prince picks out a gold bowl for his fiancée and finds, to his annoyance, that it is cracked. It is not hard to see that the cracked bowl is a symbol, both of the Prince himself, who is a valuable antique but a little flawed, morally, and also of the marriage, which represents an act of acquisition or purchase on the part of the heroine and her father. If the reader should fail to notice the analogy, James calls his attention to it in the title.

I myself would not regard this symbol as necessary to this particular history; it seems to me, rather, an ornament of the kind that was fashionable in the architecture and interior decoration of the period, like stylized sheaves of corn or palms on the façade of a house. Nevertheless, it is handsome and has an obvious appropriateness to the theme. It introduces the reader into the Gilded Age attitudes of the novel. I think there is also a scriptural echo in the title that conveys the idea of punishment. But having seen and felt the weight of meaning that James put into this symbol, one must not be tempted to press further and look at the bowl as a female sex symbol, a chalice, a Holy Grail, and so on; a book is not a pious excuse for reciting a litany of associations.

My second example is from Tolstoy's *Anna Karenina*. Toward the beginning of the novel, Anna meets the man who will be her lover, Vronsky, on the Moscow-St. Petersburg express; as they meet, there has been an accident; a workman has been killed by the train. This is the beginning of Anna's doom, which is completed when she throws herself under a train and is killed; and the last we see of Vronsky is in a train, with a toothache; he is off to the wars. The train is necessary to the plot of the novel, and I believe it is also symbolic, both of the iron forces of material progress that Tolstoy hated so and that played a part in Anna's moral destruction, and also of those iron laws of necessity and consequence that govern human action when it remains on the sensual level.

One can read the whole novel, however, without being conscious that the train is a symbol; we do not have to "interpret" to feel the import of doom and loneliness in the train's whistle—the same import we ourselves can feel when we hear a train whistle blow in the country, even today. Tolstoy was a deeper artist than James, and we cannot be sure that the train was a conscious device with him. The appropriateness to Anna's history may have been only a *felt* appropriateness; everything in Tolstoy has such a supreme naturalness that one shrinks from attributing contrivance to him, as if it were a sort of fraud. Yet he worked very hard on his novels—I forget how many times Countess Tolstoy copied out *War and Peace* by hand.

The impression one gets from his diaries is that he wrote by ear; he speaks repeatedly, even as an old man, of having to start a story over again because he has the wrong tone, and I suspect that he did not think of the train as a symbol but that it sounded "right" to him, because it was, in that day, an almost fearsome emblem of ruthless and impersonal force, not only to a writer of genius but to the poorest peasant in the fields. And in Tolstoy's case I think it would be impossible, even for the most fanciful critic, to extricate the train from the novel and try to make it say something that the novel itself does not say directly. Every detail in Tolstoy has an almost cruel and viselike meaningfulness and truth to itself that make it tautological to talk of symbolism; he was a moralist and to him the tiniest action, even the curiosities of physical appearance, Vronsky's bald spot, the small white hands of Prince Andrei, told a moral tale.

It is now considered very old-fashioned and tasteless to speak of an author's "philosophy of life" as something that can be harvested from his work. Actually, most of the great authors did have a "philosophy of life" which they were eager to communicate to the public; this was one of their motives for writing. And to disentangle a moral philosophy from a work that evidently contains one is far less damaging to the author's purpose and the integrity of his art than to violate his imagery by symbol-hunting, as though reading a novel were a sort of paper-chase.

The images of a novel or a story belong, as it were, to a family, very closely knit and inseparable from each other; the parent "idea" of a story or a novel generates events and images all bearing a strong family resemblance. And to understand a story or a novel, you must look for the parent "idea," which is usually in plain view, if you read quite carefully and literally what the author says.

I will go back, for a moment, to my town story, to show how this can be done. Clearly, it is about the Jewish question, for that is what the people are talking about. It also seems to be about artists, since the title is "Artists in Uniform." Then there must be some relation between artists and Jews. What is it? They are both minorities that other people claim to be able to recognize by their appearance. But artists and Jews do not care for this categorization; they want to be universal, that is, like everybody else. They do not want to wear their destiny as a badge, as the soldier wears his uniform. But this aim is really hopeless, for life has formed them as Jews or artists, in a way that immediately betrays them to the majority they are trying to melt into. In my conversation with the colonel, I was endeavoring to play a double game. I was trying to force him into a minority by treating anti-Semitism as an aberration, which, in fact, I believe it is. On his side, the colonel resisted this attempt and tried to show that anti-Semitism was normal, and he was normal, while I was the queer one. He declined to be categorized as anti-Semite; he regarded himself as an independent thinker, who by a happy chance thought the same as everybody else.

I imagined I had a card up my sleeve; I had guessed that the colonel was Irish (i.e., that he belonged to a minority) and presumed that he was a Catholic. I did not see how he could possibly guess that I, with my Irish name and Irish appearance, had a Jewish grandmother in the background. Therefore when I found I had not convinced him by reasoning, I played my last card; I told him that the Church, his Church, forbade anti-Semitism. I went even further; I implied that God forbade it, though I had no right to do this, since I did not believe in God, but was only using Him as a whip to crack over the colonel, to make him feel humble and inferior, a raw Irish Catholic lad under discipline. But the colonel, it turned out, did not believe in God, either, and I lost. And since, in a sense, I had been cheating all along in this game we were playing, I had to concede the colonel a sort of moral victory in the end; I let him

think that my husband was Jewish and that that "explained" everything satisfactorily.

Now there are a number of morals or meanings in this little
tale, starting with the simple one: don't talk to strangers on a train.
The chief moral or meaning (what I learned, in other words, from
this experience) was this: you cannot be a universal unless you
accept the fact that you are a singular, that is, a Jew or an artist or
what-have-you. What the colonel and I were discussing, and at the
same time illustrating and enacting, was the definition of a human
being. I was trying to be something better than a human being; I
was trying to be the voice of pure reason; and pride went before a
fall. The colonel, without trying, was being something worse than
a human being, and somehow we found ourselves on the same
plane—facing each other, like mutually repellent twins. Or, put in
another way: it is dangerous to be drawn into discussions of the
Jews with anti-Semites: you delude yourself that you are spreading
light, but you are really sinking into muck; if you endeavor to be
dispassionate, you are really claiming for yourself a privileged position, a little mountain top, from which you look down, impartially,
on both the Jews and the colonel.

Anti-Semitism is a horrible disease from which nobody is
immune, and it has a kind of evil fascination that makes an enlightened person draw near the source of infection, supposedly in a
scientific spirit, but really to sniff the vapors and dally with the
possibility. The enlightened person who lunches with the colonel
in order, as she tells herself, to improve him, is cheating herself,
having her cake and eating it. This attempted cheat, on my part, was
related to the question of the artist and the green dress; I wanted
to be an artist but not to pay the price of looking like one, just as I
was willing to have Jewish blood but not willing to show it, where it
would cost me something—the loss of superiority in an argument.

These meanings are all there, quite patent, to anyone who con-
sents to look *into* the story. They were *in* the experience itself, waiting to be found and considered. I did not perceive them all at the
time the experience was happening; otherwise, it would not have

taken place, in all probability—I should have given the colonel a wide berth. But when I went back over the experience, in order to write it, I came upon these meanings, protruding at me, as it were, from the details of the occasion. I put in the green dress and my mortification over it because they were part of the truth, just as it had occurred, but I did not see how they were related to the general question of anti-Semitism and my grandmother until they *showed* me their relation in the course of writing.

Every short story, at least for me, is a little act of discovery. A cluster of details presents itself to my scrutiny, like a mystery that I will understand in the course of writing or sometimes not fully until afterward, when, if I have been honest and listened to these details carefully, I will find that they are connected and that there is a coherent pattern. This pattern is *in* experience itself; you do not impose it from the outside and if you try to, you will find that the story is taking the wrong tack, dribbling away from you into artificiality or inconsequence. A story that you do not learn something from while you are writing it, that does not illuminate something for you, is dead, finished before you started it. The "idea" of a story is implicit in it, on the one hand; on the other hand, it is always ahead of the writer, like a form dimly discerned in the distance; he is working *toward* the "idea."

It can sometimes happen that you begin a story thinking that you know the "idea" of it and find, when you are finished, that you have said something quite different and utterly unexpected to you. Most writers have been haunted all their lives by the "idea" of a story or a novel that they think they want to write and see very clearly: Tolstoy always wanted to write a novel about the Decembrists and instead, almost against his will, wrote *War and Peace*; Henry James thought he wanted to write a novel about Napoleon. Probably these ideas for novels were too set in their creators' minds to inspire creative discovery.

In any work that is truly creative, I believe, the writer cannot be omniscient in advance about the effects that he proposes to produce. The suspense in a novel is not only in the reader, but in the novelist himself, who is intensely curious too about what will happen to the hero. Jane Austen may know in a general way that Emma will marry Mr. Knightley in the end (the reader knows this too, as a matter of fact); the suspense for the author lies in the how, in the twists and turns of circumstance, waiting but as yet unknown, that will bring the consummation about. Hence, I would say to the student of writing that outlines, patterns, arrangements of symbols may have a certain usefulness at the outset for some kinds of minds, but in the end they will have to be scrapped. If the story does not contradict the outline, overrun the pattern, break the symbols, like an insurrection against authority, it is surely a still birth. The natural symbolism of reality has more messages to communicate than the dry Morse code of the disengaged mind.

The tree of life, said Hegel, is greener than the tree of thought; I have quoted this before but I cannot forbear from citing it again in this context. This is not an incitement to mindlessness or an endorsement of realism in the short story (there are several kinds of reality, including interior reality); it means only that the writer must be, first of all, a listener and observer, who can pay attention to reality, like an obedient pupil, and who is willing, always, to be surprised by the messages reality is sending through to him. And if he gets the messages correctly he will not have to go back and put in the symbols; he will find that the symbols are there, staring at him significantly from the commonplace.

This was given first as a talk at the Breadloaf School of English, in Middlebury, Vermont. Cf. "Artists in Uniform."

An Academy of Risk

Summer, 1959
"*THIS MAN IS DANGEROUS*"—the old post-office ads alerting the community to a malefactor at large, armed and with a record, are joyously brought to mind by the bold figure of Harold Rosenberg in his book of collected essays, *The Tradition of the New*. The man who invented the term action painting is an actionist critic. All his life, as these essays show, he has been interested only in action, in the "act," a favorite word with him, succinct as a pistol-shot. Before action painting, there was the action poem (the poem as destructive agent—Baudelaire, Rimbaud, Rilke, Valéry), and political action (Marxism). To Mr. Rosenberg, action and the imitation of an action—drama—are essentially the same. He is exhilarated by the hero in history, which means that he sees history as a stage of sublime or ridiculous gestures; the hero's historical "task," what used to be called the deed, is finding the appropriate gesture. This requires a willed transformation of the merely given self, as in the evolution of the dramatic character of the Bolshevik, a secular convert; in some instances, the "transformation" may be only a disguise for a bald spot, like a toupée, which turns the historical drama into comedy. In either case, Mr. Rosenberg, who has commandeered a loge seat for the performance by the authority of his intellect, genially applauds. He knows that the problem of action is serious, dead serious for our pistol-point time, and yet his very fascination with the problem makes him also a critical spectator, indeed an ideal connoisseur of the spectacle. His geniality, which has something of the pirate in it, is a product of detachment, a

quality which, contrary to common belief, is often found in the true actionist in his moments of leisure—the balletomane commissar, the bandit-chief in the forest watching a Cossack sword-dance. The performer of deeds can be objective, just because he appreciates acting. Hamlet, with the Players, got the pun too, which runs like a mystification through language.

The great joy of this book is its zestful freedom, again the result of objectivity. The essays, written over the past twenty years, have been assembled in four sections, on painting, poetry, politics, and intellectual history, and are interrelated in a way that at first appears casual, until the light dawns and the reader becomes aware that he is following the greatest show on earth—the international human comedy of modern times, a mixture of genres, from tragedy to vaudeville, whose only heroes, finally, are artists. Thanks to his detachment, Mr. Rosenberg views the twentieth century as all of a piece: a century of the new, of invention, transformation, remaking, fresh gestures. In other words, Mr. Rosenberg's idea is that if you don't remake yourself in this century, somebody else will remake you—in a gas chamber. If modern history is a panoramic stage, it is also a scientific laboratory for the production of new human beings, new identities. The action painter who "gesticulates" on canvas so that he may see himself, as it were, in silhouette and discover who he is, is experimenting on himself just as Rimbaud did, and as the Communists did to manufacture, out of the "iron" process of logic, the figure of the Bolshevik, and the Nazis in their concen-tration-camp workshops, to make a new "scientific" humanity—as well, incidentally, as a new kind of lampshade. The purge indeed (Mr. Rosenberg does not happen to mention this, but he would surely agree) is the first obligatory step, whether it is the infantile castor-oil purge of Mussolini, the mass purges of the Soviet Union, the brainwashing of the Korean prisoners-of-war, the pseudo-purge of religious conversion, the prefrontal lobotomy, or the self-pur-gation of the artist. Mr. Rosenberg is not afraid of this amalgam, as it would have been called in the thirties. When Anthony West declared in *The New Yorker* that the poems of Baudelaire led straight to the death-camps, he was asserting in a hysterical way a Philistine and semi-totalitarian doctrine of "responsibility"; Mr. Rosenberg sees a connection between all these modern events that is neither causal nor criminal. His detachment permits him to observe a likeness-in-difference without feeling obliged to confess up and withdraw his support from Rimbaud, Baudelaire, or De Kooning.

Similarly, Mr. Rosenberg's eagle's-eye view of the twentieth century has made him the first to discern tendencies and correspondences that became only slowly visible, if visible at all, to other critics. In an essay on the Fall of Paris, written in 1940, he rapidly sketches out the whole idea of Malraux's *Musée Imaginaire* (1949); it might be objected that Mr. Rosenberg did not "do" anything with his idea while Malraux made a book out of it, but a better way of putting it is that Malraux "got" a book out of it, i.e., labored it to yield him a return. Mr. Rosenberg was also the first to see through the guilty-liberal racket and the mass-culture racket; in a number of essays now grouped under the general heading, "The Herd of Independent Minds." This new body of parasitic literature—the *True Story* confessions of ex-Communists and ex-liberals and the mass-culture symposia—produced for kicks for a mass audience, is itself of course a sociological phenomenon, reflecting the vast growth of a class of professional intellectuals who are the tour-directors of modern society on a cruise looking for itself. The architects, designers, psychiatrists, museum men, questionnaire sociologists, "depth" sociologists, students of voting habits and population patterns, are all engaged in providing identities ("Tell me how you voted and I'll tell you who you are" or vice versa), showing their publics how they can yet be somebody through art-appreciation, music appreciation, good-design-appreciation, self-appreciation, i.e., knowing Values. As Mr. Rosenberg says, "Today everybody is already a member of some intellectually worked-over group, that is, an audience."

Mr. Rosenberg himself is a permanent revolutionist in politics and the arts. Still, sitting in his loge seat in the intervals of partisanship, he enjoys the farce by which the New is converted into the

Old, by being turned into a profit-commodity, as modern painting has been by fashion designers, educators, and wallpaper firms; this in fact is the Handwriting on the Wall. Art movements "sold" to the consumer are consumed in both senses. The position of the revolutionary critic is itself comically subject to erosion under these circumstances—a point Mr. Rosenberg has noted.

His sense of proportion and balance prevents him, almost everywhere ("Politics as Dancing" is the exception), from being mastered by one of his ideas so that he would fail to see its implications. This knowing what you are letting yourself in for constitutes audacity. Take action painting; while arguing strenuously for it, Mr. Rosenberg perceives where the hitch is. Action painting cannot lay claim to being judged aesthetically; by being an act, an experiment, it deliberately renounces the aesthetic as its category, for it cannot be recognized by the pleasure-faculty as objects of beauty are. If, indeed, by some accident—the passage of time or fading—such a painting became beautiful, it would cease to be an act, since the element of risk and hazard would depart from it, and it would come, as it were, to rest. In the same way, an act in history by becoming strikingly beautiful or noble slides out of the historical arena into a constructed frame—such actions, incidentally, are usually acts of sacrifice or heroic immolation. They become, precisely, a picture: a tableau or a statue. But if an action painting cannot be judged aesthetically, how can it be judged? Not at all, cheerfully admits Mr. Rosenberg, though he qualifies this somewhat by saying that a genuine action painting can be told from a fake by the amount of struggle in it. This criterion, though, is highly arbitrary—how is the struggle to be measured and who is to be the judge? Mr. Rosenberg, then, is taking a risk, with his eyes open, of polemicizing for a kind of art of which no one can say whether it is beautiful or ugly or in between, but only that it is something, that it exists and represents a decision. This decisive coming into existence, in fact, is action painting's best plea for itself—a plea entered in history's court, which is where Mr. Rosenberg always argues. And it is true that the most convincing argument that can be made, really, for action painting

(Mr. Rosenberg does not make it) is that Mr. Rosenberg himself, in his earlier essays on poetry, described exactly those qualities that action painting would later have. This suggests either that Mr. Rosenberg like a god invented action painting out of his own brain (and the movement certainly seems to have clarified from the date of his naming it) or that its appearance was inevitable in the history of art; that is, Mr. Rosenberg's prediction or hypothesis validates the painting, and the painting validates Mr. Rosenberg's hypothesis. This is perhaps untenable logically, but in practice such a coincidence really does hint that there is something to action painting.

In Mr. Rosenberg's opinion, this painting has assumed the binding authority of a historical necessity. We are forced to accept it as we accept other historical changes and advances. If we don't, we admit ourselves to the Academy, which (excuse me, Mr. Rosenberg) seems to me another version of the ash-can of history; if we don't accept it, in short, we are dead. Mr. Rosenberg is at once allured and repelled by the ever-present dead; the problem of burial is central to his book. Some of its finest passages touch on this theme; for example this, about Melville: "…while from the silent recesses of the office files, he drew forth the white-collared tomb deity, Bartleby." The spectral death-in-life of other contemporary critics, moreover, is made clammily apparent by contrast with Mr. Rosenberg's own vitality. His phrasing is a gleeful boyish exploit: "it would be just as well to bump the old mob off the raft"; "…to the tattoo artist on Melville's Pacific Island who covered the village headman with an overall design previously tried out on some bottom dog used as a sketch pad, the problem [of the audience] did not present itself." He is picturesque without forcing, like some veteran trapper or scout chatting on in the American lingo. The range of the voice is remarkable, and so is the control of volume. The accusation sometimes made against him, that he is abstract, is absolutely untrue of his writing, which moves from graphic image to graphic image (sometimes as in a really great comic strip) and is sensitive as a hearing-aid to sound. This plain talk nearly persuades you that he is right, not only in general, but in every particular of his reasoning, for what he presents is the picture of a man in a state of buoyant health. To resist his theories at any point it is necessary to draw back from this blast of vitality and ask, for instance, whether the theory of action painting is not just a new costuming of the old Marxist myth, in which the proletariat, having so long been acted on by history, decides to act into history and abolish it. By the violence of his "attack" on the canvas, the action painter abolishes art. But is it really possible to abolish art? Will not the aesthetic as a category of human experience perversely assert itself, as history did in the Soviet Union by refusing to come to an end? This in fact is happening to the school of action painters and was bound to happen regardless of the activities of museum people and popularizers. Once you hang an act on your living-room wall, a weird contradiction develops, which is inherent in the definition (or myth) of action painting itself; an "event" or gesture becomes, at worst, just as much an art-object as the piece of driftwood on the coffee table or the seashell on the Victorian whatnot. At best, it becomes art. The truth is, you cannot hang an event on the wall, only a picture, which may be found to be beautiful or ugly, depending, alas, on your taste. This applies to a Cimabue "Crucifixion" just as much as to a Pollock or an African mask. You can decide of a new painting or a painting new to you that it is "interesting," but this only means that you are postponing, for the moment, the harder decision as to whether it is good or bad; a painting cannot stay "interesting," or if you keep on calling it that you have made "interesting" into an aesthetic judgment—a judgment, by the way, which leads, by the broad path, to the populous cemetery of the Academy, where all but the immortal are buried by Father Time.

A review of The Tradition of the New, *by Harold Rosenberg.*

The Fact in Fiction

Summer, 1960

I AM SCHEDULED, I find, to talk to you about "Problems of Writing a Novel." Where this title originated no one seems to know—doubtless in the same bureau that supplies titles for school children's compositions: "How I Spent My Summer Vacation" or "Adventures of a Penny" or simply "Why?" The problems of writing a novel, to those who do not write, can be reduced to the following questions: "Do you write in longhand or on the typewriter?" "Do you use an outline or do you invent as you go along?" "Do you draw your characters from real life or do you make them up or are they composites?" "Do you start with an idea, a situation, or a character?" "How many hours a day do you spend at your desk?" "Do you write on Sundays?" "Do you revise as you go along or finish a whole draft first?" And, finally, "Do you use a literary agent or do you market your stuff yourself?" Here curiosity fades; the manufacture and marketing of the product complete the story of a process, which is not essentially different from the "story" of flour as demonstrated to a class of boys and girls on an educational trip through a flour mill (from the grain of wheat to the sack on the grocer's shelf) or the "story" of a bottle of claret or of a brass safety pin. This is the craft of fiction, insofar as it interests the outsider, who may line up, after a lecture like this, to get the author's autograph, in lieu of a free sample—a miniature bottle of wine or a card of "baby" safety pins.

Now I am not going to talk about the problems of the novel in this sense at all but rather to confront the fact that the writing of a novel has become problematic today. Is it still possible to write novels—in

longhand or on the typewriter, standing or sitting, on Sundays or
weekdays, with or without an outline? The answer, it seems to me,
is certainly not yes and perhaps, tentatively, no. I mean real novels—
not fairy tales or fables or romances or *contes philosophiques*, and I
mean novels of a high order, like *War and Peace* or *Middlemarch* or
Ulysses or the novels of Dickens, Dostoevsky, or Proust. The manufacture of second-rate novels, or, rather, of facsimiles of the novel, is
in no state of crisis; nor is there a difficulty in marketing them, with
or without an agent. But almost no writer in the West of any consequence, let us say since the death of Thomas Mann, has been able
to write a true novel; the exception is Faulkner, who is now an old
man. What was the last novel, not counting Faulkner, that was written in our day? *Ulysses*? *Man's Fate*? Camus' *The Stranger*? Someone
might say *Lolita*, and perhaps it is a novel, a freak, though, a sport
or wild mutation, which everyone approaches with suspicion, as if
it were a dangerous conundrum, a Sphinx's riddle.

What do I mean by a "novel"? A prose book of a certain thick-
ness that tells a story of real life. No one could disagree with that,
and yet many will disagree with much that I am going to say before
I am through, so I shall try to be more specific. The word "prose"
and "real" are crucial to my conception of the novel. The distinctive
mark of the novel is its concern with the actual world, the world
of fact, of the verifiable, of figures, even, and statistics. If I point
to Jane Austen, Dickens, Balzac, George Eliot, Tolstoy, Dostoevsky,
the Melville of *Moby Dick*, Proust, the Joyce of *Ulysses*, Dreiser,
Faulkner, it will be admitted that they are all novelists and that,
different as they are from a formal point of view, they have one
thing in common: a deep love of fact, of the empiric element in
experience. I am not interested in making a formal definition of
the novel (it is really a very loose affair, a grabbag or portmanteau,
as someone has said) but in finding its *quidditas* or whatness, the
essence or binder that distinguishes it from other species of prose
fiction: the tale, the fable, the romance. The staple ingredient present in all novels in various mixtures and proportions but always in
fairly heavy dosage is fact.

If a criterion is wanted for telling a novel from a fable or a tale or a romance (or a drama), a simple rule-of-thumb would be the absence of the supernatural. In fables and fairy tales, as everyone knows, birds and beasts talk. In novels, they don't; if you find birds and beasts talking in a book you are reading you can be sure it is not a novel. That takes care, for example, of *Animal Farm*. Men in novels may behave like beasts, but beasts in novels may not behave like men. That takes care of *Gulliver's Travels*, in case anyone were to mistake it for a novel. The characters in a novel must obey the laws of nature. They cannot blow up or fly or rise from the dead, as they can in plays, and if they talk to the devil, like Ivan Karamazov, the devil, though he speaks French, is not real like Faust's Mephistopheles, but a product of Ivan's derangement or fissionization. The devil is a part of Ivan. In the same way, in Mann's *Dr. Faustus,* the devil is no longer a member of the cast of characters but resident, you might say, in the fatal spirochete or syphilis germ. This is not a difference in period; Goethe did not believe in real devils either, but he could put one on the stage, because the stage accepts devils and even has a trapdoor ready for them to disappear through, with a flash of brimstone, just as it used to have a machine, up in the flies, for the gods to descend from. There are no gods in the novel and no machinery for them; to speak, even metaphorically, of a *deus ex machina* in a novel—that is, of the entrance of a providential figure from above—is to imply a shortcoming; Dickens is always criticized on this score. But a tale almost requires the appearance of a *deus ex machina* or magic helper. The devil can appear in person in a tale of Hawthorne's like "Young Goodman Brown," but not in Hawthorne's novel, *The Scarlet Letter*, though he may be there in spirit.

The novel does not permit occurrences outside the order of nature—miracles. Mr. Krook's going up in spontaneous combustion in his junkshop is a queer Punch-and-Judy note in *Bleak House,* Actually, Dickens thought science had found out that people could explode of their own force, but now it seems that they can't, that Mr. Krook couldn't; it would be all right in a fantasy or a pantomime but not in a novel. You remember how in *The Brothers Karamazov* when

Father Zossima dies, his faction (most of the sympathetic characters in the book) expects a miracle: that his body will stay sweet
and fresh because he died "in the odor of sanctity." But instead he
begins to stink. The stink of Father Zossima is the natural, generic
smell of the novel.

By the same law, a novel cannot be laid in the future, since the
future, until it happens, is outside the order of nature; no prophecy or
cautionary tale like *1984* is a novel. It is the same with public events
in the past that never happened, for example the mutiny at the end
of World War I led by a Christlike corporal in Faulkner's *A Fable*; the
title is Faulkner's warning to his readers that this volume, unlike his
"regular" books, is not to be considered a novel but something quite
different. Because the past appears, through recession, to be outside
the order of nature (think how improbable and ghostly old photographs look), most historical novels, so-called, are romances, not
novels: George Eliot's *Romola* in contrast to *Middlemarch*. This rule
is broken by Tolstoy's *War and Peace*, a novel if there ever was one,
and the reason for this is that history, as it were, has been purged by
Tolstoy's harsh and critical realism of all "historical" elements—the
flummery of costume, make-up, and accessories and the myths and
lies of historians. The time, moreover (his grandfather's day) was
not very remote from Tolstoy's own. When he experimented with
writing a novel about the days of Ivan the Terrible, he found he
could not do it. A borderline case is Stendhal's *The Charterhouse
of Parma*, where actual history (Napoleon's entry into Milan; the
Battle of Waterloo, so much admired by Tolstoy) is succeeded by
mock-history—the spurious history of Parma, complete with numbered despots, prisons, and paid assassins, a travesty invented by
Stendhal to correspond with the (literally) travestied Fabrizio in his
violet stockings and with the mock-heroics of this section of the
book. The book is a novel that turns into parody at the moment
that history, in Stendhal's opinion, ceased to make sense and turned
into a parody of the past. That moment was the triumph of reaction
in Europe after 1815.

I ought to make it clear that these distinctions are in no way pejorative; I do not mean "Novel good, fable bad," merely "Novel novel; fable fable." *Candide* is not a novel, but to say so is not a criticism of *Candide*. Indeed, there are certain masterpieces—Rameau's *Nephew*, Gogol's *Dead Souls*, *The Charterhouse of Parma* itself—so quicksilver in their behavior that it is impossible to catch them in a category; these are usually "destructive" books, like *Candide*, where the author's aim is, among other things, to elude the authorities' grasp. When people nowadays tell you something is "not a novel," as they are fond of saying, for instance, about *Dr. Zhivago*, it is always in a querulous tone, as though someone had tried to put something over on them, sell them the Empire State Building or Trajan's Monument or the Palace of Culture, when *they* know better; they were not born yesterday. That is not my intention; I am not speaking as an aggrieved consumer of modern literature (and I admire *Dr. Zhivago* too passionately to demand its identity papers before I will let it pass); I am only trying to see why a special kind of literature, a relatively new kind, what we call the novel, is disappearing from view. To do that, I must know what the novel is; it is like advertising for a missing person; first you need a description of what he looked like when last seen.

Let me begin with the birthmarks. The word novel goes back to the word "new," and in the plural it used to mean news—the news of the day or the year. Literary historians find the seed or the germ of the novel in Boccaccio's *Decameron*, a collection of tales set in a frame of actual life. This frame of actual life was the Great Plague of 1348 as it affected the city of Florence, where more than a hundred thousand people died between March and August. The figures and dates come from *The Decameron*, along with a great deal of other factual information about the Black Death: its origin in the East, some years before; its primary and secondary symptoms, differing from those in the East; the time between the appearance of the first symptoms—the tumors or buboes in the groin or armpits, some the size of a common apple, some of an egg, some larger, some smaller—and the onset of death; the means of contagion; the sanitary precautions taken; the medical theories current as to the proper diet and

mode of life to stave off infection; the modes of nursing; the rites
and methods of burial; and, finally, the moral behavior (very bad)
of the citizens of Florence during the scourge. Boccaccio's account
is supposed to be a pioneer contribution to descriptive medicine;
it is also a piece of eyewitness journalism, not unlike the Younger
Pliny's account of the eruption of Mount Vesuvius; the difference is
that Pliny wrote his report in a letter (a classic literary form) and
that Boccaccio's report is used in a new way, as a setting for a collection of fictions. The "realism," also new, of the separate tales, is
grounded, so to speak, in the journalistic frame, with the dateline
of a certain Tuesday morning, of the year 1348, when seven young
ladies, between the ages of eighteen and twenty-eight, and three
young men, the youngest twenty-five, met in the Church of Santa
Maria Novella.

If Boccaccio is the ancestor, the "father of the modern novel" is
supposed to be Defoe, a Grub Street journalist, and the author of
Robinson Crusoe, *Moll Flanders*, and many other works, including
The Journal of the Plague Year (not Boccaccio's; another one—1664–
1665). *Robinson Crusoe* was based on "a real life story," of a round-
the-world voyage, which he heard described by the returned traveler
and which he pieced out with another, a written account. Not only
was the "father of the modern novel" a journalist, but he did not
distinguish, at least to his readers, between journalism and fiction.
All his stories pretend to be factual reports, documents, and one
perhaps is—the life of a famous criminal "as told to Daniel Defoe,"
i.e., ghostwritten. This pretense, which might be called the reverse
of plagiarism, the disclaiming, that is, of authorship rather than the
claiming of it, was not a special pathological kink of Defoe's. The
novel in its early stages almost always purports to be true. Where
a fairy tale begins, "Once upon a time, in a certain kingdom," a
tale of Boccaccio (chosen at random) begins: "You must know that
after the death of Emperor Frederick II, the crown of Sicily passed
to Manfred, whose favor was enjoyed to the highest degree by a
gentleman of Naples, Arrighetto Capece by name, who had to wife
Madonna Beritola Caracciola, a fair and gracious lady, likewise a

Neapolitan. Now when Manfred was conquered and slain by King Charles I at Benevento... Arrighetto, etc., etc..." The effect of this naming and placing makes of every story of Boccaccio's a sort of deposition, and this is even truer when the sphere is less exalted and the place is a neighboring village and the hero a well-known lecherous priest.

Many of the great novelists were newspaper reporters or journalists. Dickens had been a parliamentary reporter as a young man; in middle age, he became a magazine editor, and the scent of a "news story" is keen in all his novels. Dostoevsky, with his brother, edited two different magazines, one of which was called *Time* (*Vremya*); he supplied them with fiction and feature stories, and his specialty, you might say, was police reporting—he visited suspects (usually female) in prison, interviewed them, and wrote up his impressions; he also reported trials. Victor Hugo too was a confirmed prison-visitor; his "impressions" of prisons and of current political events— demonstrations, tumults, street-fighting—are collected in *Choses Vues*. Tolstoy first became widely known through his reports from Sebastopol, where he was serving as a young officer in the Crimean War; he was telling the news, the true, uncensored story of the Siege of Sebastopol, to the civilians back home, and throughout Tolstoy's work, most noticeably in *War and Peace* but in fact everywhere, there is heard the scathing directness of the young officer's tone, calling attention to the real facts behind the official dispatches—the real facts of war, sex, family life, glory, love, death. As he wrote in his second sketch from Sebastopol (which was immediately suppressed by the Czar), "The hero of my story... is—the Truth." Coming to the twentieth century, you meet the American novelist as newspaperman: Dreiser, Sinclair Lewis, Hemingway, O'Hara, Faulkner himself. The American novelist as newspaperman, in the twenties, became a stock figure in the American myth, so much so that the terms could be inverted and every obscure newspaperman, according to popular belief, had in his desk drawer, besides a pint of whiskey, the great American novel he was writing in his spare time.

There is another kind of "fact" literature closely related to the novel, and that is the travel book, which tells the news of the exotic. Melville's first book, *Typee*, was a book of travel, and you find something of the travelogue in Conrad, Kipling, and a good deal of D. H. Lawrence: *Aaron's Rod, The Plumed Serpent, Kangaroo*, "The Woman Who Rode Away." There is very little difference, really, between *Kangaroo*, a novel about Australia, and *Sea and Sardinia*, a travel book about Lawrence himself and Frieda in Sardinia. Hemingway remains half a war correspondent and half an explorer; *The Green Hills of Africa* is his "straight" travel book. The type seems to go back to *Robinson Crusoe*; most of Conrad's heroes, one could say, are stranded Robinson Crusoes, demoralized by consciousness. In a more conventional way, Dickens, Stendhal, Henry James all published journals of travel—"impressions." Mark Twain, Henry Miller, George Orwell (*Down and Out in Paris and London, Shooting an Elephant*)—the list is even more arresting if you consider the theatre and try to imagine Ibsen, Shaw, or O'Neill as the authors of travel books. Yet Ibsen spent years abroad, in Italy and Germany, and O'Neill, like Melville and Conrad, went to sea as a young man.

The passion for fact in a raw state is a peculiarity of the novelist. Most of the great novels contain blocks and lumps of fact—refractory lumps in the porridge of the story. Students often complain of this in the old novels. They skip these "boring parts" to get on with the story, and in America a branch of publishing specializes in shortened versions of novels—"cut for greater reading speed." Descriptions and facts are eliminated, and only the pure story, as it were the scenario, is left. But a novel that was only a scenario would not be a novel at all.

Everyone knows that Balzac was a lover of fact. He delighted in catalogues of objects, inventories, explanations of the way institutions and industries work, how art is collected, political office is bought, fortunes are amassed or hoarded. One of his novels, *Les Illusions Perdues*, has a chapter which simply describes the way paper is made. The chapter has nothing to do with the action of the novel (it comes in because the hero has inherited a paper factory); Balzac put it in because he happened at the time to know something about the paper business. He loved facts of every kind indiscriminately—straight facts, curious facts, quirks, oddities, aberrations of fact, figures, statistics. He collected them and stored them, like one of his own misers, intending to house them in that huge structure, *The Human Comedy*, which is at once a scale model of the real world and a museum of curios left to mankind as though by a crazy hermit who could never throw anything away.

This fetishism of fact is generally treated as a sort of disease of realism of which Balzac was the prime clinical exhibit. But this is not the case. You find the splendid sickness in realists and non-realists alike. *Moby Dick*, among other things, is a compendium of everything that was to be known about whaling. The chapters on the whale and on whiteness, which are filled with curious lore, truths that are "stranger than fiction," interrupt and "slow down" the narrative, like the excursus on paper. Yet they cannot be taken away (as the excursus on paper certainly could be) without damaging the novel; *Moby Dick* without these chapters (in the stage and screen versions) is not *Moby Dick*. Or think of the long chapter on the Russian Monk in *The Brothers Karamazov*. Father Zossima is about to enter the scene, and, before introducing him, Dostoevsky simply stops and writes a history of the role of the elder in Russian monasticism. In the same way, in *War and Peace*, when Pierre gets interested in Freemasonry, Tolstoy stops and writes an account of the Masonic movement, for which he had been boning up in the library. Everyone who has read *War and Peace* remembers the Battle of Borodino, the capture and firing of Moscow, the analysis of the character of Napoleon, the analysis of the causes of war, and the great chapter on Freedom and Necessity, all of which are non-fiction and which constitute the very terrain of the novel; indeed, it could be said that the real plot of *War and Peace* is the struggle of the characters not to be immersed, engulfed, swallowed up by the landscape of fact and "history" in which they, like all human beings, have been placed: freedom (the subjective) is in the fiction, and necessity is in the fact. I have already mentioned the first chapter of *The Charterhouse of Parma* describing Napoleon's entry into Milan. In *The Magic Mountain*, there are the famous passages on tuberculosis, recalling Boccaccio's description of the plague, and the famous chapter on time, a philosophical excursus like the chapter on whiteness in *Moby Dick* and the chapter on Freedom and Necessity in Tolstoy. Closer to Balzac is Dreiser's picture of the hotel business in *An American Tragedy*; when Clyde becomes a bellhop, Dreiser (though this is not "important" to the story) stops and shows the reader how a hotel, behind the scenes, works.

In newspaper jargon, you might call all this the boiler plate of the novel—durable informative matter set up in stereotype and sold to country newspapers as filler to eke out a scarcity of local news, i.e., of "plot." And the novel, like newspaper boiler plate, contains not only a miscellany of odd facts but household hints and how-to-do-it instructions (you can learn how to make strawberry jam from *Anna Karenina* and how to reap a field and hunt ducks).

The novel, to repeat, has or had many of the functions of a newspaper. Dickens' novels can be imagined in terms of headlines: "Antique Dealer Dies by Spontaneous Combustion in Shop," "Financial Wizard Falls, Panic Among Speculators," "Blackleg Miner Found Dead in Quarry." Henry James, who did his best to exclude every bit of boiler plate from his books and who may have killed the novel, perhaps with kindness (consider the unmentionable small article manufactured by the Newsomes in *The Ambassadors*; what was it? Garters? Safety pins?), even James has the smell of newsprint about him, the smell of the Sunday supplement. His international plots recall the magazine section of the old Hearst newspaper chain, in which every Sunday, after church, Americans used to read about some international marriage between an American heiress and a titled fortune-hunter: Anna Gould and Count Boni de Castellane.

Novels, including James's, carried the news—of crime, high society, politics, industry, finance, and low life. In Dickens you find a journalistic coverage of the news on all fronts and a survey of all the professions from pickpocket to banker, from lawyer to grave-robber. His books tell the whole story of Victorian society, from the front page to the financial section. This ideal of coverage requires him, in fairness, to print, as it were, corrections; a bad Jew is followed by a good Jew, a bad lawyer by a good one, a bad school by a good one, and so on. Or, to put it another way, it is as though he were launching a great roomy Noah's Ark with two of each species of creation aboard. In a single book, *Middlemarch*, George Eliot "covers" English life and institutions, as found at their median point—a middling provincial town. The notion of coverage by professions was taken up, somewhat mechanically, by the American novelists Dreiser and Sinclair Lewis. You can hear it in Dreiser's titles: *The Titan*, *The Financier*, *The Genius*, *Twelve Men*. Lewis ticked off the housewife (*Main Street*), the realtor (*Babbitt*), the scientist (*Arrowsmith*), the preacher (*Elmer Gantry*), the social worker (*Ann Vickers*), the retired businessman (*Dodsworth*). A similar census, though of more mobile social types, is seen in Dos Passos. It is Faulkner, however, the most "mythic" of recent American novelists, who has documented a society more completely than any of the realists. Like Dickens, he has set himself the task of a Second Creation. Yoknapatawpha County (capital, Jefferson), Mississippi, is presided over by its courthouse (*Requiem for a Nun*), where its history and vital statistics are on file; we know its population of lawyers, storekeepers, business men, farmers, black and white, and their forebears and how they made or lost their money; we know its idiots and criminals and maniacs, its geology and geography, flora and fauna (the bear of that story and the cow of *The Hamlet*); some editions of Faulkner include a map of Yoknapatawpha County, and a letter addressed to Faulkner at Jefferson, Mississippi, would almost certainly reach him, although there is no such place.

The more poetic a novel, the more it has the air of being a factual document. I exaggerate when I say this, but if you think of Faulkner, of *Moby Dick* of *Madame Bovary* or Proust, you will see there is something in it. Joyce's *Ulysses* is a case in point. There is no doubt that Joyce intended to reconstruct, almost scientifically, twenty-four hours of a certain day in Dublin; the book, among other things, is an exercise in mnemonics. Stephen and Mr. Bloom, in their itineraries, cover certain key points in the life of the city—the beach, the library, the graveyard, the cabman's stand, Nighttown—and a guide to Joyce's Dublin has been published, with maps and a key. Nor is it by chance that the peripatetic Mr. Bloom is an advertising *canvasser*. He travels back and forth and up and down in society like Ulysses, who explored the four corners of the known world. The epic, I might put in here, is the form of all literary forms closest to the novel; it has the "boiler plate," the lists and catalogues, the circumstantiality, the concern with numbers and dimensions. The epic geography, like that of the novel, can be *mapped*, in both the physical and the social sense.

This clear locative sense is present in all true novels. Take Jane Austen. *Emma* and *Pride and Prejudice* contain few facts of the kind I have been speaking of—nothing like the paper business or the history of the Russian monk. Yet there are facts of a different sort, documents like Mr. Collins' letters, charades, riddles, menus, dance programs ("'Then the two third he danced with Miss King, and the two fourth with Maria Lucas, and the two fifth with Jane again, and the two sixth with Lizzy, and the *Boulanger*—'")—feminine facts, so to speak—and a very painstaking census-taking of a genteel class within the confines of a certain income range, marked off, like a frontier. One difference between Jane Austen and Henry James is that the reader of *Pride and Prejudice* knows exactly how much money the characters have: Mr. Bingley has four or five thousand a year (with a capital of nearly one hundred thousand); Mr. Bennet has two thousand a year, ENTAILED, while Mrs. Bennet brought him a capital of four thousand from her father, an attorney at Meryton; Mr. Darcy has ten thousand a year; his sister, Georgiana, has a capital of thirty thousand. The same with distances, ages, and time. Mr. and Mrs. Bennet have been married twenty-three years; Mrs. Weston, in *Emma*, has been Emma's governess for sixteen years; Mr. Knightley is about seven or eight and thirty; Emma is nearly twenty-one; Jane and Elizabeth, when they are finally married, live thirty miles apart; Highbury is about a mile from Mr. Knightley's property. Whenever the chance arises, Jane Austen supplies a figure. Everything is lucid and perspicuous in her well-charted world, except the weather, which is often unsettled, and this fact too is always noted ("The shower was heavy but short, and it had not been over five minutes when…"). The names of persons who are never seen in the story, like that of "Miss King" just now, are dropped as if artlessly to attest the veracity of the narrative—inviting the reader to clothe these names himself with the common identities of real life.

This air of veracity is very important to the novel. We do really (I think) expect a novel to be true, not only true to itself, like a poem, or a statue, but true to actual life, which is right around the corner, like the figure of "Miss King." We not only make believe we believe a novel, but we do substantially believe it, as being continuous with real life, made of the same stuff, and the presence of fact in fiction, of dates and times and distances, is a kind of reassurance—a guarantee of credibility. If we read a novel, say, about conditions in postwar Germany, we expect it to be an accurate report of conditions in postwar Germany; if we find out that it is not, the novel is discredited. This is not the case with a play or a poem. Dante can be wrong in *The Divine Comedy*; it does not matter, with Shakespeare, that Bohemia has no seacoast, but if Tolstoy was all wrong about the Battle of Borodino or the character of Napoleon, *War and Peace* would suffer.

The presence of a narrator, writing in the first person, is another guarantee of veracity. The narrator is, precisely, an eyewitness, testifying to the reader that these things really happened, even though the reader knows of course that they did not. This is the function of the man called Marlow in Conrad's books; he is there to promise the reader that these faraway stories are true, and, as if Marlow himself were not enough, the author appears as a kind of character witness for Marlow, testifying to having met him in reliable company, over cigars, claret, a polished mahogany table, and so on. The same function is served by the narrator in Dostoevsky's *The Possessed*, who writes in the excited manner of a small-town gossip ("Then I rushed to Varvara Petrovna's") telling you everything that went on in that extraordinary period, which everybody in town is still talking about, that began when young Stavrogin bit the governor's ear. He tells what he saw himself and what he had on hearsay and pretends to sift the collective evidence as to what exactly happened and in what order. Faulkner's favorite narrator is Gavin Stevens, the lawyer, chosen obviously because the town lawyer, accustomed to weighing evidence, would be the most reliable witness—one of the first sources a newspaper reporter sent to do a story on Yoknapatawpha County would be likely to consult.

There is the shadow of an "I" in *The Brothers Karamazov*, but *The Possessed* is the only important novel of Dostoevsky's that is told straight through in the first person, i.e., by a local busybody who seems to have seized the pen. *The Possessed* (in Russian *The Devils*) is the most demonic of all Dostoevsky's novels—the most "unnatural," unfilial, "Gothic." It would seem that the device of the narrator, the eyewitness "I," like Esther Summerson in *Bleak House* (not the autobiographical "I" of *David Copperfield* or of Proust's Marcel, who is something more than a witness), is more often used in novels whose material is exotic or improbable than in the plain novel of ordinary life, like *Middlemarch* or *Emma* or any of Trollope. These novels of ordinary life put no strain on the reader's credulity; he believes without the testimony of witnesses. The first-person narrator is found in Conrad, in Melville, and in *Wuthering Heights*, *Bleak House*, *Jane Eyre*, all of which center around drafty, spooky old houses and are related to the ghost story. In the same way James, who rarely used the first-person narrator, does so with the governess in his ghost story, *The Turn of the Screw*. In other words, on the periphery of the novel, on the borderline of the tale or the adventure story you find a host of narrators. And you arrive, finally, at *Lolita* and meet Humbert Humbert, telling his own story (which you might not have believed otherwise), having been first introduced by another narrator, his "editor," who authenticates his manuscript; Humbert himself has been executed. In short, you are back with Defoe and his "true biographies" of great criminals who were hanged, back at the birth of the novel, before it could stand without support.

Even when it is most serious, the novel's characteristic tone is one of gossip and tittletattle. You can hear it in the second sentence (originally the first sentence) of *Anna Karenina*: "Everything was upset at the Oblonskys." The cook, it seemed, had left; the under-servants had given notice; the mistress was shut up in her bedroom because the master had been sleeping with the former French gov-erness. This (I think) is a classic beginning, and yet some person who had never read a novel, coming on those sentences, so full of blunt malice, might conclude that Tolstoy was simply a common scandal-monger. The same might be thought of Dostoevsky, of Flaubert, Stendhal, and (obviously) of Proust, of the earnest George Eliot and the lively Jane Austen and the manly Charles Dickens. Most of these writers were people of high principle; their books, without exception, had a moral, ethical, or educational purpose. But the voice we overhear in their narratives, if we stop to listen for a minute, putting aside preconceptions, is the voice of a neighbor relating the latest gossip. "You will hardly believe what happened next," the novelists from Jane Austen to Kafka (yes indeed) seem to be exclaiming. "Wait and I'll tell you." The whole narrative method of Dostoevsky could be summed up in those two sentences. In Conrad, more ruminative, there can be heard the creaking of chairs as the men around the table settle down to listen to the indefati-gable Marlow, who only halts to wet his whistle: "Pass the bottle." The scandals the novelists are primed with are the scandals of a village, a town, or a province—Highbury or Jefferson, Mississippi, or the Province of O——; the scandals of a clique—the Faubourg St. Germain; of a city—Dublin or Middlemarch; or of a nation— Dickens' England; or of the ports and hiring offices—London or Nantucket, where news of the high seas is exchanged and a black mark put against a man's name or a vessel's. Here is another cri-terion: if the breath of scandal has not touched it, the book is not a novel. That is the trouble with the art-novel (most of Virginia Woolf, for instance); it does not stoop to gossip.

The scandals of a village or a province, the scandals of a nation or of the high seas feed on facts and breed speculation. But it is of the essence of a scandal that it be finite, for all its repercussions and successive enlargements. Indeed, its repercussions are like the echo produced in an enclosed space, a chambered world. That is why institutions ("closed corporations") are particularly prone to scandal; they attempt to keep the news in, contain it, and in doing so they magnify it, and then, as people say, "the lid is off." It is impossible, except for theologians, to conceive of a world-wide scandal or a universe-wide scandal; the proof of this is the way people have settled down to living with nuclear fission, radiation poisoning, hydrogen bombs, satellites, and space rockets. Nobody can get them excited about or even greatly interested in what-will-happen-next to the world; the plot does not thicken. In the same way, Hiroshima, despite the well-meant efforts of journalists and editors, probably caused less stir than the appearance of comets in the past; the magnitude of the event killed even curiosity. This was true, to some extent, of Buchenwald and Auschwitz too.

Yet these "scandals," in the theological sense, of the large world and the universe have dwarfed the finite scandals of the village and the province; who cares any more what happens in Highbury or the Province of O——? If the novelist cares, he blushes for it; that is, he blushes for his parochialism. *Middlemarch* becomes *Middletown* and *Middletown in Transition*, the haunt of social scientists, whose factual findings, even in the face of Auschwitz or a space-satellite, have a certain cachet because they are supposed to be "science"; in science, all facts, no matter how trivial or banal, enjoy democratic equality. Among novelists, it is only Faulkner who does not seem to feel an itch of dissatisfaction with his sphere, and there are signs of this even in him—*A Fable*, for example.

But it is not only that the novelist of today, in "our expanding universe," is embarrassed by the insignificance (or lack of "significance") of his finite world. A greater problem is that he cannot quite believe in it. That is, the existence of Highbury or the Province of O—— is rendered improbable, unveracious, by Buchenwald and Auschwitz, the population curve of China, and the hydrogen bomb. Improbable when "you stop to think"; this is the experience of everybody and not only of the novelist; if we stop to think for one second, arrested by some newspaper story or general reflection, our daily life becomes incredible to us. I remember reading the news of Hiroshima in a little general store on Cape Cod in Massachusetts and saying to myself as I moved up to the counter, "What am I doing buying a loaf of bread?" The coexistence of the great world and us, when contemplated, appears impossible.

It works both ways. The other side of the picture is that Buchenwald and Auschwitz are and were unbelievable, and not just to the German people, whom we criticize for forgetting them; we all forget them, as we forget the hydrogen bomb, because their special quality is to stagger belief. And here is the dilemma of the novelist, which is only a kind of professional sub-case of the dilemma of everyone: if he writes about his province, he feels its inverisimilitude; if he tries, on the other hand, to write about people who make lampshades of human skin, like the infamous Ilse Koch, he feels still more the inverisimilitude of what he is asserting. His love of truth revolts. And yet this love of truth, ordinary common truth recognizable to everyone, is the ruling passion of the novel. Putting two and two together, then, it would seem that the novel, with its common sense, is of all forms the least adapted to encompass the modern world, whose leading characteristic is irreality. And that, so far as I can understand, is why the novel is dying. The souped-up novels that are being written today, with injections of myth and symbols to heighten or "deepen" the material, are simply evasions and forms of self-flattery.

I spoke just now of common sense—the prose of the novel. We are all supposed to be born with it, in some degree, but we are also supposed to add to it by experience and observation. But if the world today has become inaccessible to common sense, common sense in terms of broad experience simultaneously has become inaccessible to the writer. The novelists of the nineteenth century had, both as public persons and private figures, great social range; they "knew everybody," whether because of their fame in the great capitals of London, Paris, St. Petersburg, or in their village, province, or county, where everybody knows everybody as a matter of course. Today the writer has become specialized, like the worker on an assembly line whose task is to perform a single action several hundred times a day or the doctor whose task is to service a single organ of the human body. The writer today is turning into a *machine à écrire*, a sort of human typewriter with a standardized mechanical output: hence the meaning of those questions ("How many hours a day?" "How long does it take you?" "Have you ever thought of using a dictaphone?"). This standardization and specialization is not only a feature of his working hours but of his social existence. The writer today—and especially the young American writer—sees only other writers; he does not know anyone else. His social circle comprises other writers and his girl friends, but his girl friends, usually, are hoping to be writers too. The writer today who has a painter for a friend is regarded as a broad-ranging adventurer, a real man of the world. If he teaches in a university, his colleagues are writers or at any rate they "publish," and his students, like his girl friends, are hoping to write themselves. This explains the phenomenon, often regarded as puzzling, of the "one-book" American writer, the writer who starts out with promise and afterward can only repeat himself or fade away. There is nothing puzzling about it; he wrote that first book before he became a writer, while he was still an ordinary person. The worst thing, I would say, that can happen to a writer today is to become a writer. And it is most fatal of all for the novelist; the poet can survive it, for he does not need social range for his verse, and poets have always clubbed together with other poets in exclusive coteries, which is perhaps why Plato wanted them banned from the Republic.

The isolation of the modern writer is a social fact, and not just the writer's own willful fault. He cannot help being "bookish," which cuts him off from society, since practically the only people left who read are writers, their wives and girl friends, teachers of literature, and students hoping to become writers. The writer has "nothing in common" with the businessman or the worker, and this is almost literally true; there is no common world left in which they share. The businessman who does not read is just as specialized as the writer who writes.

To throw off this straitjacket is the recurrent dream of the modern novelist, after the age, say, of thirty or thirty-five; before that, his dream was the opposite: to come to New York (or Paris or London) to meet other writers. Various ways out are tried: moving to the country, travel, "action" (some form of politics), the resolute cultivation of side-interests—music, art, sport, gardening; sport is very popular with American men novelists, who hold on to an interest in baseball or a tennis racket or a fishing-rod as a relic of the "complete man" or complete boy they once were. But if these steps are sufficiently radical, their effect may be the reverse of what was intended. This is what seems to have happened to Gide, D. H. Lawrence, Malraux, Camus, George Orwell. Starting as novelists, they fled, as it were, in all directions from the tyranny of the novelist's specialization: into politics, diary-keeping, travel and travel-writing, war, art history, journalism, "engagement." Nor did they ever really come back to the novel, assuming that was what they wanted to do. Gide stopped with *The Counterfeiters*; Lawrence with *Women in Love*; Malraux with *Man's Fate*; Orwell with his first book, *Burmese Days*; Camus with *The Stranger*. Their later books are not novels, even if they are called so, but fables of various kinds, tracts, and parables. But they did not settle down to a single form or mode, and this perpetual restlessness which they have in common seems a sign of an unrequited, unconsummated love for the novel, as though in the middle of their *oeuvre* there were a void, a blank space reserved for the novel they failed to be able to write. We think of them as among the principal "novelists" of our time, but they were hardly novelists at all, and in each case their work as a whole has an air of being unfinished, dangling.

They are certainly key modern figures. Allowing for differences in talent, their situation is everybody's; mine too. We are all in flight from the novel and yet drawn back to it, as to some unfinished and problematic relationship. The novel seems to be dissolving into its component parts: the essay, the travel book, reporting, on the one hand, and the "pure" fiction of the tale, on the other. The center will not hold. No structure (except Faulkner's) has been strong enough to keep in suspension the diverse elements of which the novel is made. You can call this, if you want, a failure of imagination. We know that the real world exists, but we can no longer imagine it.

Yet despite all I have been saying, I cannot, being human, help feeling that the novel is not finished yet. Tomorrow is another day. Someone, somewhere, even now may be dictating into a dictaphone: "At five o'clock in the afternoon, in the capital of the Province of Y——, a tall man with an umbrella was knocking at the door of the governor's residence." In short, someone may be able to believe again in the reality, the factuality, of the world.

This is a paraphrase of a talk or talks given to Polish, Yugoslav, and British audiences in the winter of 1960.

Characters in Fiction

March, 1961
IN BELGRADE, THE OTHER day, an interviewer asked me what book
I thought best represented the modern American woman. All I
could think of to answer was: *Madame Bovary.* It occurred to me
afterward that I might have named *Main Street* or Henry James's
A Portrait of a Lady. What else? I tried to remember women in
American books. Hester Prynne, Daisy Miller, Scott Fitzgerald's
flappers and Daisy in *The Great Gatsby,* Temple Drake in *Sanctuary,*
Dos Passos' career women, Ma Joad in *The Grapes of Wrath.* But
since then? It was like leafing through a photograph album and
coming, midway, on a sheaf of black, blank pages. Was it possible
that for twenty-five years no American woman had had her likeness
taken? "Submit a clear recent photo," as they say in job applications.
But there was none, strange as it seemed considering the dominant
role women are supposed to play in American life.

So I tried the experiment with men. The result was almost
the same. Captain Ahab, Christopher Newman in *The American,*
Babbitt, Elmer Gantry, Gatsby, Mac and Charley Anderson in
Dos Passos, Jason in *The Sound and the Fury,* Colonel Sutphen in
Absalom, Absalom, Flem and Mink Snopes, Studs Lonigan. After
that, nothing, no one, except the Catholic priests of J. F. Powers,
the bugler Prewitt in *From Here to Eternity,* and Henderson in
Henderson the Rain King.

Someone might see this as a proof of the conformity of American
life; there are no people any more, it might be claimed—only
human vectors with acceleration and force. But in my experience

this is simply not true. There are more people than ever before, at least in the sense of mutations in our national botany, and this is probably due to mobility—cross-fertilization. Take as an example a gangster who was in the slot-machine racket, decided to go straight and became a laundromat king, sent his daughter to Bennington, where she married a poet-in-residence or a professor of modern linguistic philosophy. There are three characters already sketched out in that sentence and all of them brand-new: the father, the daughter, and the son-in-law. Imagine what one of the old writers might have made of the wedding and the reception afterward at the 21 Club. The laundromat king or his equivalent is easy to meet in America; there are hundreds of him. Try teaching in a progressive college and interviewing the students' parents. And do not pretend that the laundromat king has no "inner life"; he is probably a Sunday painter, who has studied with Hans Hofman in Provincetown. What, for that matter, was the inner life of Monsieur Homais in *Madame Bovary*? People speak of the lack of tradition or of manners as having a bad effect on the American novel, but the self-made man is a far richer figure, from the novelist's point of view, than the man of inherited wealth, who is likely to be a mannered shadow.

The relations between parents and children (Turgenev's great theme) have never been so curious as in America now, where primitivism heads into decadence before it has time to turn around. America is full of Bazarovs but only Turgenev has described them. Nobody, as far as I know, has described an "action" painter, yet nearly everyone has met one. Nobody has done justice to the psychoanalyst, yet nearly everyone has gone to one. And what a wealth of material there is in that virgin field, what variety: the orthodox Freudian, the Horneyite, the Reichian, the Sullivanite ("interpersonal relations"), all the different kinds of revisionists, the lay analyst, the specialist in group analysis, the psychiatric social worker. Social workers themselves have become one of the major forces in American life, the real and absolute administrators of the lives of the poor, yet no one since Sinclair Lewis and Dos Passos has dared

write of them, unless you count the young author, John Updike, in
The Poorhouse Fair, who presents a single specimen and lays the
story in the future. Imagine what Dickens would have done with
this new army of beadles and the Mrs. Pardiggles behind them or
what he would have done with the modern architect as Pecksniff,
with the cant formula "Less is more." No serious writer since Dos
Passos, so far as I know, has had a go at the government official,
and the government official has not only multiplied but changed
(like the social worker) since Dos Passos' time, producing many
sub-varieties. And what about the foundation executive? Or the
"behavioral scientist"? The fact is that the very forces and institutions that are the agents and promoters of conformity in America—
bureaucracies public and private and the regimented "schools" and
systems of healing and artistic creation—are themselves, through
splits and cellular irritation, propagating an array of social types
conforming to no previous standard, though when we look for
names for them we are driven back, *faute de mieux*, on the old
names: Pecksniff, Mrs. Gamp, Bazarov, Mrs. Pardiggle, Babbitt.
When Peter Viereck, in a book of nonfiction, wanted to isolate a
new kind of conformist intellectual he could think of nothing better
to call him than "Babbitt Junior." It is as though a whole "culture"
of plants and organisms had sprung into being and there were no
scientists or latter-day Adams to name them.

This naming is very important, yet only two names in recent
fiction have "stuck": Gulley Jimson (Joyce Cary) and Lucky Jim
(Kingsley Amis). Some interest in character is still shown by writers in England, perhaps because it is an island and hence more
conscious of itself. But even in England the great national portrait
gallery that constituted the English novel is short of new acquisitions. The sense of character began to fade with D. H. Lawrence.
After *Sons and Lovers*, we do not remember figures in Lawrence's
books, except for a few short malicious sketches. There are hardly
any people in Virginia Woolf (Mr. Ramsay in *To the Lighthouse*
stands out) or in Forster or Elizabeth Bowen or Henry Green; they
exist in Ivy Compton-Burnett but tend to blur together like her

titles. Waugh has people, and so had Joyce Cary. You find them in the short stories of V. S. Pritchett and in the satires of Angus Wilson. But the last great creator of character in the English novel was Joyce. It is the same on the Continent. After Proust, a veil is drawn. You can speak of someone as a "regular Madame Verdurin" or a "Charlus," but from Gide, Sartre, Camus, no names emerge; the register is closed.

The meaning of this seems plain. The novel and the short story have lost interest in the social. Since the social has certainly not lost interest in itself (look at the popularity of such strange mirror-books as *The Lonely Crowd*, *The Organization Man*, *The Exurbanites*, *The Status Seekers*), what has happened must have occurred inside the novel and the short story—a technical or even technological crisis. An impasse has been reached within the art of fiction as a result of progress and experiment. You find a similar impasse in painting, where the portrait can no longer be painted and not because the artists do not know how to draw or get a likeness; they do. But they can no longer see a likeness as a work of art. In one sense, it is ridiculous to speak of progress in the arts (as though modern art were "better" than Rembrandt or Titian); in another sense, there *is* progress, an internal dynamic such as one finds in the processes of industry or in the biological process of aging. The arts have aged too, and it is impossible for them to "go back," just as it is impossible to recapture the youth or reinstitute a handicraft economy, like the one Ruskin dreamed of. These things are beyond our control and independent of our will. I, for instance, would like, more than anything else, to write like Tolstoy; I imagine that I still see something resembling the world Tolstoy saw. But my pen or my typewriter simply balks; it "sees" differently from me and records what to me, as a person, are distortions and angularities. Anyone who has read my work will be at a loss to find any connection with Tolstoy; to Tolstoy himself both I and my work would be anathema. I myself might reform, but my work never could; it could never "go straight," even if I were much more gifted than I am. Most novelists today, I suspect, would like to "go straight"; we are conscious of being twisted when we write. This is the self-consciousness, the squirming, of the form we work in; we are stuck in the phylogenesis of the novel.

The fictional experiments of the twentieth century went in two directions: sensibility and sensation. To speak very broadly, the experiments in the recording of sensibility were made in England (Virginia Woolf, Katherine Mansfield, Dorothy Richardson, Elizabeth Bowen, Forster), and America was the laboratory of sensation (Hemingway and his imitators, Dos Passos, Farrell). The novel of sensibility was feminine, and the novel of sensation was masculine. In Paris, there was a certain meeting and merging: Gertrude Stein (a robust recorder of the data of sensibility) influenced and encouraged Hemingway; Joyce, who experimented in both directions, influenced nearly everyone. The sensibility tendency today is found chiefly in such minor English writers as Henry Green and William Sansom; in America, it is represented by Katharine Anne Porter, Eudora Welty, Jean Stafford, and Carson McCullers. The masculine novel of sensation, more admired always in Europe than at home, seems to have arrived at the Beat Generation, via Caldwell, Dashiell Hammett, James M. Cain, Raymond Chandler; its attraction toward violence propelled it naturally toward the crime story. The effect of these two tendencies on the subject matter of the novel was identical. Sensation and sensibility are the poles of each other, and both have the effect of abolishing the social. Sensibility, like violent action, annihilates the sense of character.

Beginning with our own. In violence, we forget who we are, just as we forget who we are when engaged in sheer perception. Immersed in a picture, an effect of light, or a landscape, we forget ourselves; we are "taken out of ourselves"; in the same way, we forget ourselves in the dentist's chair. We are not conscious of our personality. In sensation, we are all more or less alike. Heat, cold, hunger, thirst, pain are experienced by man, not men. And sensibility is not a refinement of sensation; the sense of blue or green made on our retina is more finely discriminated in an art critic than it is in the average man or the color-blind person, but no useful division, humanly speaking, could be made between those, say, who saw turquoise as green and those who saw it as blue. The retina is not the seat of character. Nor are the sexual organs, even though they differ from person to person. Making love, we are all more alike than we are when we are talking or acting. In the climax of the sexual act, moreover, we forget ourselves; that is commonly felt to be one of its recommendations. Sex annihilates identity, and the space given to sex in contemporary novels is an avowal of the absence of character. There are no "people" in *Lady Chatterley's Lover*, unless possibly the husband, who is impotent. To cite the laundromat king again, the moment of orgasm would not be the best moment for the novelist to seize upon to show his salient traits; on the other hand, to show him in an orgone box (i.e., in the frame of an idea) would be a splendid notion. Similarly, the perambulating sensibility of Mrs. Dalloway, her quivering film of preception, cannot fix for us Mrs. Dalloway as a person; she remains a palpitant organ, like the heroine of a pornographic novel. The character I remember best from Virginia Woolf is Mr. Ramsay in *To the Lighthouse*, a man who lacks the fine perceptions of the others; i.e., from the point of view of sensibility he is impotent, without erectile aesthetic tissue.

Sensation and sensibility are at their height in the child; its thin, tender membrane of perception is constantly being stabbed by objects, words, and events that it does not understand. In lieu of understanding, the child "notices." Think of the first sections of *A Portrait of the Artist as a Young Man* and of Aunt Dante's hair-brushes (why was she called Dante?) and the quarrel about Parnell (who was Parnell?) at the Christmas dinner table. Or the beginning of *Dr. Zhivago*, where the child Yury, taken to his mother's funeral, looks out the window at the cabbages, wrinkled and blue with cold, in the winter fields. Yury, being a child, cannot comprehend the important event that has happened to him (death), but his eye takes in the shivering cabbages. Everyone experiences something like this in moments of intense grief or public solemnity, such as funerals; feelings, distracted from their real causes, attach them-selves arbitrarily to sights, smells, and sounds. But a child passes a good part of his life in this attentive state of detachment.

Now two characteristics of the child are that he cannot act (to any purpose) and he cannot talk (expressively); hence he is outside, dissociated. And it is just this state, of the dissociated outsider, that is at the center of modern literature of sensibility and sensation alike. Camus' *The Stranger* or *The Outsider* begins with the hero's going to his mother's deathbed and being unable to summon up the appropriate emotions or phrases.

It is modern but it is not new. The inability to say the appropriate thing or to feel the appropriate thing, combined with a horrible faculty of *noticing*, is an almost clinical trait in the character of Julien Sorel and in most of the Stendhalian heroes. Tolstoy was a master of the tragicomedy of inappropriate feelings, gestures, and sensations. Take the first chapter of *Anna Karenina*, where Stepan Oblonsky, who has been unfaithful to his wife with the French governess, finds a foolish smile spreading over his features when she taxes him with it—a *smile* of all things. He cannot forgive himself that awful, inadvertent smile (he ascribes it to a "reflex"), which causes her to shut herself up in her room and declare that all is over. Vronsky's toothache, near the end of *Anna Karenina*, as it were dunce-caps the climax; it is the distracted intrusion of the commonplace into a drama of tragic passion. Anna has killed herself, and Vronsky is on the train, going off to the Serbo-Turkish war as an "heroic volunteer" with a squadron equipped at his own expense; his face is drawn with suffering—and with the ache in his big tooth, which makes it almost impossible for him to speak. But "all at once a different pain, not an ache but an inner trouble, that set his whole being in anguish, made him for an instant forget his toothache." He has "suddenly remembered *her*," as he has last seen her mangled body exposed on a table in the railway shed. And he ceases to feel his toothache and begins to sob. At every station the train is seen off by patriotic society ladies with nosegays for the heroic volunteers, and these flowers, like the toothache, are ridiculous and painful—beside the point.

The point, however, is there, inescapably so (the corpse in the railway shed is more cruelly alive than the toothache), and this is the difference between Tolstoy (Stendhal too) and the fragmented impressionism of twentieth-century literature, where the real world is broken up into disparate painterly images out of focus and therefore hypnotic and trancelike. The world of twentieth-century sensibility, in contrast to that of Tolstoy, is a world in slow motion, a world which, however happy it may seem, is a world of paralyzed grief, in which little irrelevant things, things that do not belong, are noticed or registered on the film of consciousness, exactly as they are at a funeral service or by a bored child in church.

In the modern novel of sensibility the shimmer of consciousness occupies the whole field of vision. Happenings are broken down into tiny discrete sensory impressions, recalling pointillism or the treatment of light in Monet. The novel of sensation is less refined and seemingly more "factual": "It was hot"; "'Give me a drink,' I said." But these too are the *disjecta membra* of consciousness passing across a primitive perceptual screen. A child cannot talk, and the modern novel of sensation, like that of sensibility, is almost mute; these rolls of film are silent, with occasional terse flashes of dialogue, like subtitles. The only form of action open to a child is to break something or strike someone, its mother or another child; it cannot cause things to happen in the world. This is precisely the situation of the hero of the novel of sensation; violence becomes a substitute for action. In the novel of sensibility, nothing happens; as people complain, there is no plot.

Once these discoveries had been made, however, in the recording of the perceptual field (i.e., of pure subjectivity), the novel could not ignore them; there was no turning back to the objectivity of Tolstoy or the rational demonstrations of Proust. The "objective" novel of Sarraute, Robbe-Grillet, and Butor is simply a factual treatment of the data of consciousness, which are presented like clues in a detective story to the events that the reader guesses are taking place. The very notion of character is ruled out. One way, however, remains open to the novelist who is interested in character (which means in human society)—a curious back door. That is the entry found by Joyce in *Ulysses*, where by a humorous stratagem character is shown, as it were, inside out, from behind the screen of consciousness. The interior monologue every human being conducts with himself, *sotto voce*, is used to create a dramatic portrait. There is no question but that Mr. Bloom and Molly are characters, quite as much as the characters of Dickens or any of the old novelists—not mere bundles of vagrant sensory impressions but articulated wholes. Their soliloquies are really half of a dialogue—a continuous argument with society, whose answers or objections can be inferred. Mr. Bloom and Molly are pathetically social, gregarious, worldly, and lonely: misunderstood. This sense of being the victim of a misunderstanding dominates *Finnegans Wake*, where the hero is Everybody—the race itself. Nothing could be more vocal than these books of Joyce: talk, talk, talk. *Finnegans Wake* is a real babel of voices, from the past, from literature, from the house next door and the street; even the river Liffey chatters. We would know Mr. Bloom anywhere by his voice, the inmost Mr. Bloom; the same with Molly. Joyce was a master mimic of the voice of conscience, and Mr. Bloom and Molly are genuine imitations. This blind artist was the great ventriloquist of the novel. A sustained power of mimicry is the secret of all creators of character; Joyce had it while Virginia Woolf, say, did not. That is why Joyce was able to give shape and body—in short, singularity, definition—to the senseless data of consciousness.

The notion that life is senseless, a tale told by an idiot—the under-theme of twentieth-century literature—is affirmed again by Faulkner in *The Sound and the Fury*. Yet here, as in *Ulysses*, characters appear from the mists of their own reveries and sensations: the idiot Benjy, Jason, Dilsey, the Negro cook. And a plot, even, is indicated for the reader to piece together from clues dropped here and there: the story of Caddy and the castration of Benjy and Quentin's suicide. The materialization of plot and character prove that there *is* being, after all, beyond the arbitrary flux of existence. Following Joyce and Faulkner, the imitation-from-within became almost standard practice for writers who were impatient with the fragmented impressionist novel and who had assimilated nonetheless some of its techniques. To use the technique of impressionism to create something quite different—a character study—seems the

manifest intention of Joyce Cary in *The Horse's Mouth*, where the
author, as it were, impersonates the eye of Gulley Jimson, an old
reprobate painter down on his luck; the dancing, broken surface is
only a means, like the muttering of an inner dialogue, to show the
man in action, incessantly painting in his mind's eye as he boozily
peregrinates the docks and streets. Something very similar is John
Updike's *The Poorhouse Fair*, which is seen through the resentful
hyperopic eye of an old man sitting on the porch of a county poorhouse. The sign of this kind of writing, the mark of its affiliation
with the pure impressionist or stream-of-consciousness novel,
is that when you start the book you do not know where you are.
It takes you quite a few pages to get your bearings, just as if you
were bumping along inside a sack in some fairy story; then you
awake to the fact that the consciousness you have been thrust into
is named Benjy and is feebleminded or is a criminal old painter
with a passion for William Blake's poetry or a charity patient whose
eyesight, owing to the failing muscles of old age, bends and distorts
everything in the immediate foreground and can only focus clearly
on what is far off. Once you know where you are, you can relax and
study your surroundings, though you must watch out for sudden,
disorienting jolts and jerks—an indication that the character is in
movement, colliding or interacting with objective reality.

The reader, here, as in *Ulysses,* is restricted to a narrow field of
vision or to several narrow fields in succession. Now something
comparable happens in recent books that, on the surface, seem to
owe very little to the stream-of-consciousness tradition and to take
no interest in the mechanics of perception or the field of vision as
such. I mean such books as *Augie March, Henderson the Rain King,
The Catcher in the Rye, Lolita*, and two of my own novels, *The Groves
of Academe* and *A Charmed Life*. These books are impersonations,
ventriloquial acts; the author, like some prankster on the telephone,
is speaking in an assumed voice—high or deep, hollow or falsetto,
but in any case not his own. He is imitating the voice of Augie or
of Holden Caulfield and the book is written in Augie's or Holden's
"style." The style is the man (or the boy), and the author, pretending

to be Augie or Holden or Humbert Humbert, remains "in character" throughout the book, unless he shifts to another style, that is, to
another character. These books, in short, are dramatic monologues
or series of dramatic monologues. The reader, tuned in, is left in no
doubt as to where he is physically, and yet in many of these books
he finds himself puzzled by the very vocal consciousness he has
entered: is it good or bad, impartial or biased? Can it be trusted as
Huck Finn or Marcel or David Copperfield could be trusted? He
senses the author, cramped inside the character like a contortionist
in a box, and suspects (often rightly) some trick. In short, it is not
all straight shooting, as it was with the old novelists.

This is not a defect, yet it points to the defects of the method,
which can be summed up as a lack of straightforwardness. There is
something burglarious about these silent entries into a private and
alien consciousness. Or so I feel when I do it myself. It is exhilarat-
ing but not altogether honest to make believe I am a devious red-
haired man professor with bad breath and bits of toilet paper on his
face, to talk under my breath his sibilant, vindictive thought-lan-
guage and draw his pale lips tightly across my teeth. "So *this* is how
the world looks to a man like that!" I can say to myself, awestruck,
and so, I expect, John Updike, twenty-five years old, must have
felt when he discovered what it felt like to be an old pauper with
loosened eye-muscles sitting on a poorhouse porch. But I cannot
know, really, what it feels like to be a vindictive man professor, any
more than a young man can know what it is to be an old man or
Faulkner can know what it is to be a feeble-minded adult who has
had his balls cut off. All fictions, of course, are impersonations, but
it seems to me somehow less dubious to impersonate the outside
of a person, say Mrs. Micawber with her mysterious "I will never
leave Mr. Micawber," than to claim to know what it feels like to *be*
Mrs. Micawber. These impersonations, moreover, are laborious; to
come at a character circuitously, by a tour de force, means spending great and sometimes disproportionate pains on the method of
entry. I read somewhere that Salinger spent ten years writing *The
Catcher in the Rye*; that was eight years too long. Granted, the book

is a feat, but it compels admiration more as a feat than as a novel, like the performance of a one-armed violinist or any other curiosity. This could not be said of *Huckleberry Firm*; Mark Twain's imitation of Huck's language is never, so to speak, the drawing card. In the cases of Salinger, Updike, myself, one wonders whether the care expended on the mechanics of the imitation, on getting the right detail, vocabulary, and so on, does not constitute a kind of advertisement for the author, eliciting such responses as "Think of the work that went into it!" or "Imagine a twenty-five-year-old being able to take off an old man like that!" One is reminded of certain young actors whose trademark is doing character parts, or, vice versa, of certain old actresses whose draw can be summed up in the sentence "You would never guess she was sixty."

Yet you might say that it was a fine thing for a well-paid writer in his twenties to know from the inside what it was like to be an aged charity patient. Very democratic. True, and this is a real incentive for the novelist of the twentieth century. The old authors identified with the hero or the heroine, a sympathetic figure whose dreams and desires resembled the author's own. "*Madame Bovary, c'est moi*," said Flaubert, and no doubt there was quite a lot of Madame Bovary in him or of him in Madame Bovary. Allowing for the differences of circumstance and intellect, he could have been Emma Bovary; the stretch of imagination to encompass her circumstances and her intellect was a great step, of course, in the democratization of the novel, and the naturalists, English and French, pushed further in this direction, with their studies of servant girls, factory operatives, and of the submerged poor in general. Even James tried it with his poor little anarchist, Hyacinthe Robinson. Yet here, as in Flaubert, there is still the idea of a hero or a heroine—mute inglorious Cinderellas who never went to the ball; what separates the author from the hero or the heroine is fate or social destiny. Their souls are not alien. But for the writer today (the writer who has any interest in character) it has become almost obligatory not merely to traverse social barriers but to invade the privacy of a soul so foreign or so foetal as to seem beyond grasp. Take *Ulysses*. Molly Bloom is not a soulmate of Joyce's or a sister under the skin. She is as far removed from Joyce as you could get and still remain human—the antipodes. Mr. Bloom is closer, but he is not Joyce as he might have been if he were Jewish, an advertising canvasser, and married to Molly. He is an independent, sovereign world to which Joyce has managed to gain access. There is no doctrine of "sympathies" or a-touch-of-nature-makes-the-whole-world-kin underlying *Ulysses*. Or underlying *The Sound and the Fury*, where Faulkner explores the inner life of the mental defective Benjy—his own, you might say, diametrical opposite. Much of modern literature might be defined as the search for one's own diametrical opposite, which is then used as the point-of-view. The parallel would be if Dickens had tried to write *David Copperfield* from within the sensibility of Uriah Heep or *Oliver Twist* through the impressions of Fagin.

Difficulty alone (though it always exercises a charm) does not explain the appeal of such enterprises for modern writers. There is something else—a desire to comprehend, which seems to be growing stronger as the world itself becomes more incomprehensible and dubious. The older writers, when they sought their characters from among the poor and the obscure, assumed that there was a common humanity and were concerned to show this. But it is that very assumption that is being tested, tried out, by the writers of today when they start examining their own opposites. I will give an illustration from my own work to show what I mean, rather than presume to speak for others.

When I first had the idea of the book called *The Groves of Academe*, it presented itself as a plot with a single character at the center. An unsavory but intelligent professor who teaches modern literature in an experimental college is told that his contract will not be renewed for reasons not specified but because in fact he is a trouble-maker; whereupon, he proceeds to demonstrate his ability to make trouble by launching a demagogic campaign for reappointment, claiming that he is being dismissed for having been a Communist and parading himself as the victim of a witch-hunt. This claim is totally false, but it is successful, for he has gauged very well the atmosphere of

a liberal college during the period of anti-Communist hysteria
that reached a climax in Senator McCarthy. No one in that liberal
college stops to inquire whether he has really been a Communist
because everyone is too preoccupied with defending his right to
have been one and still remain a teacher; even the college president,
knowing (who better?) that politics has nothing to do with the
professor's being dropped from the faculty, yields as a professional
liberal to this blackmail. Now the normal way of telling this story
would be from the outside or from the point of view of one of the
professor's sympathizers. But I found I had no interest in telling it
that way; to me, the interest lay in trying to see it from the professor's point of view and mouthing it in the clichés and the hissing
jargon of his vocabulary. That is, I wanted to know just how it felt
to be raging inside the skin of a Henry Mulcahy and to learn how,
among other things, he arrived at a sense of self-justification and
triumphant injury that allowed him, as though he had been issued
a license, to use any means to promote his personal cause, how he
manipulated and combined an awareness of his own undesirability
with the modern myth of the superior man hated and envied by
mediocrity. To do this, naturally, I had to use every bit of Mulcahy
there was in me, and there was not very much: I am not a paranoid,
nor a liar, nor consumed with hatred, nor a man, for that matter.
But this very fact was the stimulus. If I could understand Mulcahy,
if I could make myself *be* Mulcahy, it would get me closer to the
mystery, say, of Hitler and of all the baleful demagogic figures of
modern society whom I could not imagine being. There was no
thought of "*Tout comprendre, c'est pardonner*" or of offering a mas-
ter-key to public events like *Darkness at Noon*. What I was after
was something much more simple, naïve, and childlike: the satisfaction of the curiosity we all feel when we read in the paper of
some crime we cannot imagine committing, like the case of the
man who insured his mother-in-law at the airport and then planted
a bomb in the plane she was taking. Certain crimes, certain characters, in their impudence or awfulness, have the power of making
us feel *bornés*, and in a sense I wanted to tiptoe into the interior of

Mulcahy like a peasant coming into a palace. The question was the same as between the peasant and the king: did we belong to the same species or not? The book is not an answer, but an experiment, an assaying.

There is an element of the private game, even of the private joke, in this kind of writing—a secret and comic relation between the author and his character. An arcane laughter, too infernal for the reader to hear, quietly shakes such books; the points, the palpable hits (inspired turns of phrases, *trouvailles* of vocabulary) may altogether escape the reader's notice. Indeed, it sometimes happens that the reader is quite unaware of what the author is doing and complains that the style is full of clichés, when that, precisely, is the point. Or the glee of the hidden author may produce uncanny noises, such as the giggle or whinny overheard sometimes in *Lolita* testifying to who-knows-what indecorous relations between the author and Humbert Humbert. Joyce salted his work with private jokes, hints, and references that no one but *he* could be expected to enjoy, yet with Joyce it added to the savor. Lesser writers (or at least I) find themselves constrained by the naturalistic requirements of the method, the duty to keep a straight face, stay in character, speak in an assumed voice, hollow or falsetto, as though in a game that has gone on too long and that no one knows how to stop. There are moments when one would like to drop the pretense of being Mulcahy and go on with the business of the novel.

To return to the question of character. What do we mean when we say there are "real people" in a book? If you examine the works of Jane Austen, who, everyone agrees, was a creator of characters, you will find that the "real people" in her books are not so often the heroes and heroines as the minor characters: Lady Catherine de Bourgh and Mr. Collins, Mr. and Mrs. Bennet, Lady Bertram, poor Miss Bates, Emma's friend Harriet, the timorous and valetudinarian Mr. Woodhouse. These beings are much more thoroughly and wonderfully themselves than the heroes and heroines are able to be; the reason for this is, I think, that they are comic.

Or turn to *Ulysses*. Who would deny that Stephen Dedalus, a straight character, seems less "real" than Mr. Bloom and Molly, less "real" than his father, Mr. Dedalus? In what does this "reality" consist? In the incorrigibility and changelessness of the figure. Villains may reform, heroes and heroines may learn their lesson, like Emma or Elizabeth or Mr. Darcy, or grow into the author, like Stephen Dedalus and David Copperfield, but a Lady Catherine de Bourgh or a Molly Bloom or a Mr. Dedalus, regardless of resolutions, cannot reform or change, cannot be other than they are. Falstaff is a species of eternity; that is why the Hostess' description of his death is so poignantly sad, far sadder than the pretty death of Ophelia, for Falstaff, according to the laws of his creation, should not die. This was Queen Elizabeth's opinion too when she demanded his resurrection and Shakespeare obliged with *The Merry Wives of Windsor*. "Mortal men, mortal men," Falstaff sighs speciously, but he himself is an immortal, an everlasting, like Mr. and Mrs. Micawber who, when last heard of, were still going strong in Australia. The same with Mrs. Gamp, Pecksniff, Stepan Oblonsky, Monsieur Homais, Stepan Trofimovitch, old Karamazov. Real characterization, I think, is seldom accomplished outside of comedy or without the fixative of comedy; the stubborn pride of Mr. Darcy, the prejudice of Elizabeth, the headstrongness of Emma. A comic character, contrary to accepted belief, is likely to be more complicated and enigmatic than a hero or a heroine, fuller of surprises and turnabouts; Mr. Micawber, for instance, can find the most unexpected ways of being himself; so can Mr. Woodhouse or the Master of the Marshalsea. It is a sort of resourcefulness.

What we recognize as reality in these figures is their implacable resistance to change; they are what perdures or remains—the monoliths or plinths of the world. Pierre in *War and Peace* seems more real than Levin, his opposite number in *Anna Karenina*. This is because Pierre is fat—fat and awkward and wears a funny-looking green civilian hat at the Battle of Borodino, like a sign of his irreducible innocent stoutness. Thanks to a streak of cruelty or sarcastic sharpness in Tolstoy, most of his heroes and heroines are not spared a satirical glance that picks out their weak points: Vronsky's bald spot, Prince Andrei's small white hands, the heavy step of the Princess Marya. They live as characters because Tolstoy is always conscious of their limitations, just as he is with his comic figures; he does not forget that Anna is a society woman and Vronsky a smart cavalry officer—types that in real life he disapproved of and even detested.

The comic element is the incorrigible element in every human being; the capacity to learn, from experience or instruction, is what is forbidden to all comic creations and to what is comic in you and me. This capacity to learn is the prerogative of the hero or the heroine: Prince Hal as opposed to Falstaff. The principle of growth in human beings is as real, of course (though possibly not so common), as the principle of eternity or inertia represented by the comic; it is the subjective as opposed to the objective. When we identify ourselves with the hero of a story, we are following him with all our hopes, i.e., with our subjective conviction of human freedom; on the comic characters we look with despair, in which, though, there is a queer kind of admiration—we really, I believe, admire the comic characters *more* than we do the hero or the heroine, because of their obstinate power to do-it-again, combined with a total lack of self-consciousness or shame. But it is the hero or the heroine whose fate we feel suspense for, whom we blush for when they make a mistake; we put ourselves in their place from the very first pages, from the minute we make their acquaintance. We do not have to *know* the hero or the heroine to be on their side; not even a name is necessary. We are pulling for them if they are called "K." or "he." This mechanism of identification with the hero is very odd and seems to rest, almost, on *lack* of knowledge. If a book or story begins, "He took the train that night," we are surer that "he" is the hero (i.e., our temporary double) than if it begins, "Richard Coles took the five forty-five Thursday night." Or "Count Karenin seated himself in a first-class carriage on the Moscow-Petersburg express." We would wait to hear more about this "Richard Cole" or "Count Karenin" before depositing our sympathies with him. This throws an interesting light on the question of character.

In the modern novel there is little suspense. No one reads *Ulysses* or *Finnegans Wake* or *The Sound and the Fury* or *Mrs. Dalloway* for the sake of the story, to find out what is going to happen to the hero or the heroine. The chief plot interest in these books is to try to find out what happened before the book started: what was in that letter the chicken scratched up? what had Earwicker done in Phoenix Park? why does Benjy get so excited every time he is taken near the golf course? what is biting Stephen ("agenbite of inwit")? who, really, has been Clarissa Dalloway? The absence of suspense means that the cord of identification between the reader and the hero has deliberately been cut. Or put it a different way: the reader, as I have said, wakes up in a foreign consciousness, a bundle of impressions, not knowing where he is. The first reaction is a mild panic, an attack of claustrophobia; far from the reader's identifying, say, with Stephen at the outset of *Ulysses*, his whole wish is to fight his way out of Stephen into the open world, in order to discover where Stephen is and what is going on. And even when these fears have been quieted (Stephen is in a tower; he lives with Buck Mulligan, a medical student; his mother has just died), new fears surge up and always of a locative character, so that the reader is put in the position of a perpetual outsider, hearing what Stephen hears, seeing what Stephen sees but failing to get the drift often, asking bewildered questions: "Where am I?" "Who is talking?" "What's up?" An anxiety about location (the prime clinical symptom in the reader of the modern novel) precludes interest in direction; in any case, the end is foreordained: nothing can happen to Stephen but to become Joyce. Stephen is neither subject nor object, neither hero nor comedian, but the bombarded center of a perceptual all-out attack; in this sense, *Ulysses* is a scientific study in the logistics of personality. In the laboratory of the modern novel, the author *qua* author (not *qua* character) is the spot-lit master-figure. And in science the only hero can be the white-coated scientist; the rest is data. The difference can be felt by a comparison with Proust. Proust's Marcel is still a hero, followed by the reader with suspense, to learn what will happen with his grandmother, what will happen with Gilberte, what will happen with Albertine—something more *can* happen to him than to become Proust. Marcel is a pure subject, despite the attention he pays to studying and analyzing his reactions; if the book is, in part, a reconstruction of anterior events, it is Marcel himself, not just the reader, who is trying to find out what actually took place before the book started, and this quest for certainty is itself a hero's goal.

In the old novels, there was a continual fluctuating play between the hero and the "characters," that is, between the world as we feel it to be subjectively and the world as we know it as observers. As subjects, we all live in suspense, from day to day, from hour to hour; in other words, we are the hero of our own story. We cannot believe that it is finished, that we are "finished," even though we may say so; we expect another chapter, another installment, tomorrow or next week. In moments of despair, we look on ourselves leadenly as objects; we see ourselves, our lives, as someone else might see them and may even be driven to kill ourselves if the separation, the "knowledge," seems sufficiently final. Our view of others, on the contrary, cannot but be objective and therefore tinged with a sad sense of comedy. Others are to us like the "characters" of fiction, eternal and incorrigible; the surprises they give us turn out in the end to have been predictable—unexpected variations on the theme of being themselves, of the *principio individuationis*. But it is just this principle that we cannot see in ourselves. What is happening in modern literature is a peculiar reversal of roles: we try to show the object as subject and the subject as object. That is, can I be inside Professor Mulcahy and outside me? The answer is I cannot; no one can. There can only be one subject, ourselves, one hero or heroine. The existentialist paradox—that we are subjects for ourselves and objects for others—cannot be resolved by technical virtuosity. The best efforts, far from mastering the conundrum, merely result in the creation of characters—Benjy, Jason, Molly, Mr. Bloom, and so on—who are more or less "successful" in exactly the old sense, more or less "realized," concrete, objectively existent. Choirs of such characters make up the modern novel. What has been lost, however, in the continuing experiment is the power of the author to speak in his own voice or through the undisguised voice of an alter ego, the hero, at once a known and an unknown, a bearer of human freedom. It would seem, moreover, that there was a kind of symbiosis between the hero and the "characters," that you could not have the one without the others or the others without the one. The loss of the hero upset a balance of nature in the novel, and the languishing of the "characters" followed. Certainly the common world that lies between the contemporary reader and the contemporary author remains unexplored, almost undescribed, just as queer and empty a place as Dickens' world would be if he had spent eight years recording the impressions of Fagin or the sensory data received by Uriah Heep in the slithery course of a morning's walk.

This is the substance of a talk or talks given in Yugoslavia and England in the winter of 1960.

The American Realist Playwrights

July, 1961

AS SOON AS THIS title is announced for a lecture or an article, a question pops up: who are they? Is there, as is assumed abroad, a school of realists in the American theatre or is this notion a critical figment? The question is legitimate and will remain, I hope, in the air long after I have finished. Nevertheless, for purposes of discussion, I am going to take for granted that there is such a group, if not a school, and name its members: Arthur Miller, Tennessee Williams, William Inge, Paddy Chayevsky, the Elmer Rice of *Street Scene*. Behind them, casting them in the shadow, stands the great figure of O'Neill, and opposite them, making them seem more homogeneous, are writers like George Kelly, Wilder, Odets, Saroyan. Their counterparts in the novel are Dreiser, Sherwood Anderson, James T. Farrell, the early Thomas Wolfe—which illustrates, by the way, the backwardness of the theatre in comparison with the novel. The theatre seems to be chronically twenty years behind, regardless of realism, as the relation of Beckett to Joyce, for example, shows. The theatre feeds on the novel; never vice versa: think of the hundreds of dramatizations of novels, and then try to think of a book that was "novelized" from a play. There is not even a word for it. The only actual case I can call to mind is *The Other House* by Henry James—a minor novel he salvaged from a play of his own that failed. To return to the main subject, one characteristic of American realism in the theatre is that none of its practitioners currently—except Chayevsky—wants to call himself a realist. Tennessee Williams is known to his admirers as a "poetic realist," while Arthur Miller declares that he is an exponent of the "social play" and identifies himself with the Greek playwrights, whom he describes as social playwrights also. This delusion was dramatized, if that is the word, in *A View from the Bridge*.

The fact that hardly a one of these playwrights cares to be regarded as a realist without some qualifying or mitigating adjective's being attached to the term invites a definition of realism. What does it mean in common parlance? I have looked the word "realist" up in the Oxford English Dictionary. Here is what they say. "...In reference to art and literature, sometimes used as a term of commendation, when precision and vividness of detail are regarded as a merit, and sometimes unfavorably contrasted with idealized description or representation. In recent use it has often been used with the implication that the details are of an unpleasant or sordid character." This strikes me as a very fair account of the historical fate of the notion of realism, but I shall try to particularize a little, in the hope of finding out why and how this happened. And I shall not be condemning realism but only noting what people seem to think it is.

When we say that a novel or a play is realistic, we mean, certainly, that it gives a picture of ordinary life. Its characters will be drawn from the middle class, the lower middle class, occasionally the working class. You cannot write realistic drama about upper-class life; at least, no one ever has. Aristocracy does not lend itself to realistic treatment, but to one or another kind of stylization: romantic drama, romantic comedy, comedy of manners, satire, tragedy. This fact in itself is a realistic criticism of the aristocratic idea, which cannot afford, apparently, to live in the glass house of the realistic stage. Kings and noble men, said Aristotle, are the protagonists of tragedy—not women or slaves. The same is true of nobility of character or intellect. The exceptional man, whether he be Oedipus or King Lear or one the romantic revolutionary heroes of Hugo or Musset, is fitted to be the protagonist of a tragedy, but just this tragic fitness disqualifies him from taking a leading role in a realist drama. Such figures as Othello or Hernani can never be the subject of realistic treatment, unless it is with the object of deflating them, showing how *ordinary*—petty or squalid—they are. But then the hero is no longer Othello but an impostor posing as Othello. Cut down to size, he is just like everybody else but worse, because he is a fraud into the bargain. This abrupt foreshortening is why realistic treatment of upper-class life always takes the harsh plunge into satire. No man is a hero to his valet, and Beaumarchais' Figaro is the spokesman of social satire—not of realism; his personal and private realism turns his master into a clown. Realism deals with ordinary men and women or, in extreme forms, with sub-ordinary men, men on the level of beasts or of blind conditioned reflexes (*La Bete Humaine*, *The Hairy Ape*). This tendency is usually identified with naturalism, but I am regarding naturalism as simply a variety of realism.

Realism, historically, is associated with two relatively modern inventions, i.e., with journalism and with photography. "Photographic realism" is a pejorative term, and enemies of realistic literature often dismissed it as "no more than journalism," implying that journalism was a sordid, seamy affair—a daily photographic close-up, as it were, of the clogged pores of society. The author as sheer observer likened himself to a camera (Dos Passos, Christopher Isherwood, Wright Morris), and insofar as the realistic novel was vowed to be a reflector of ordinary life, the newspapers inevitably became a prime source of material. Newspaper accounts impressed the nineteenth century with their quality of "stark objectivity," and newspapers, which appeared every day, seemed to be the repositories of everydayness and to give a multiple image of the little tragedies and vicissitudes of daily life. In America, in the early part of this century, the realistic novel was a partner of what was called "muck raking" journalism, and both were linked with populism and crusades for political reform.

Hence, perhaps, in part, the unsavory associations in common speech of the word "realistic," even when applied in nonliterary contexts. Take the phrase "a realistic decision." If someone tells you he is going to make "a realistic decision," you immediately understand that he has resolved to do something bad. The same with "Realpolitik." A "realistic politics" is a euphemism for a politics of harsh opportunism; if you hear someone say that it is time for a government to follow a realistic line, you can interpret this as meaning that it is time for principles to be abandoned. A politician or a political thinker who calls himself a political realist is usually boasting that he sees politics, so to speak, in the raw; he is generally a proclaimed cynic and pessimist who makes it his business to look behind words and fine speeches for the motive. This motive is always low.

Whatever the field, whenever you hear that a subject is to be treated "realistically," you expect that its unpleasant aspects are to be brought forward. So it is with the play and the novel. A delicate play like Turgenev's *A Month in the Country*, though perfectly truthful to life, seems deficient in realism in comparison with the stronger medicine of Gorki's *The Lower Depths*. This is true of Turgenev's novels as well and of such English writers as Mrs. Gaskell. And of the peaceful parts of *War and Peace*. Ordinary life treated in its uneventful aspects tends to turn into an idyl. We think of Turgenev and Mrs. Gaskell almost as pastoral writers, despite the fact that their faithful sketches have nothing in common with the artificial convention of the true pastoral. We suspect that there is something arcadian here—something "unrealistic."

If realism deals with the ordinary man embedded in ordinary life, which for the most part is uneventful, what then is the criterion that makes us forget Turgenev or Mrs. Gaskell when we name off the realists? I think it is this: what we call realism, and particularly dramatic realism, tends to single out the ordinary man at the moment he might get into the newspaper. The criterion, in other words, is drawn from journalism. The ordinary man must become "news" before he qualifies to be the protagonist of a realistic play or novel. The exceptional man is news at all times, but how can the ordinary man get into the paper? By committing a crime. Or, more rarely, by getting involved in a spectacular accident. Since accidents, in general, are barred from the drama, this leaves crime—murder or suicide or embezzlement. And we find that the protagonists of realistic drama, by and large, are the protagonists of newspaper stories—"little men" who have shot their wives or killed themselves in the garage or gone to jail for fraud or embezzlement. Now drama has always had an affinity for crime; long before realism was known, Oedipus and Clytemnestra and Macbeth and Othello were famous for their deeds of blood. But the crimes of tragedy are the crimes of heroes, while the crimes of realistic drama are the crimes of the nondescript person, the crimes that are, in a sense, all alike. The individual in the realistic drama is regarded as a cog or a statistic; he commits the uniform crime that sociologically he might be expected to commit. That is, supposing that 1,031 book-keepers in the state of New York are destined to tamper with the accounts, and 304 policemen are destined to shoot their wives, and 1,115 householders to do away with themselves in the garage, each individual bookkeeper, cop, and householder has been holding a ticket in this statistical lottery, like the fourteen Athenian youths and maidens sent off yearly to the Minotaur's labyrinth, and he acquires interest for the realist theatre only when his "number" comes up. To put it as simply as possible, the cop in *Street Scene* commits his crime—wife-murder—without having the moral freedom to choose to commit it, just as Willy Loman in *Death of a Salesman* commits suicide—under sociological pressure. The hero of tragedy, on the contrary, is a morally free being who identifies himself with his crime (i.e., elects it), and this is true even where he is fated, like Oedipus, to commit it and can be said to have no personal choice in the matter. Oedipus both rejects and accepts his deeds, embraces them in free will at last as *his*. It is the same with Othello or Hamlet. The distinction will be clear if you ask yourself what tragedy of Shakespeare is closest to the realistic theatre. The answer, surely, is *Macbeth*. And why? Because of Lady Macbeth. Macbeth really doesn't choose to murder the sleeping Duncan; Lady Macbeth chooses for him; he is like a middle-class husband, nagged on by his ambitious wife, the way the second vice-president of a bank is nagged on by his Mrs. Macbeth, who wants him to become first vice-president. The end of the tragedy, however, reverses all this; Macbeth becomes a hero only late in the drama, when he pushes Lady Macbeth aside and takes all his deeds on himself. Paradoxically, the conspicuous tragic hero is never free *not* to do his deed; he cannot escape it, as Hamlet found. But the mute hero or protagonist of a realistic play is always free, at least seemingly, not to emerge from obscurity and get his picture in the paper. There is always the chance that not he but some other non-descript bookkeeper or policeman will answer the statistical call.

The heroes of realistic plays are clerks, bookkeepers, policemen, housewives, salesmen, schoolteachers, small and middling businessmen. They commit crimes but they cannot be professional criminals (unlike the heroes of Genet or the characters in *The Beggars Opera*), for professional criminals, like kings and noble men, are a race apart. The settings of realistic plays are offices, drab dining rooms or living rooms, or the backyard, which might be defined as a place where some grass has once been planted and failed to grow. The backyard is a favorite locus for American realist plays, but no realist play takes place in a garden. Nature is excluded from the realist play, as it has been from the realistic novel. The presence of Nature in Turgenev (and in Chekhov) denotes, as I have suggested, a pastoral intrusion. If a realist play does not take place in the backyard, where Nature has been eroded by clothes-poles, garbage cans, bottled-gas tanks, and so on, it takes place indoors, where the only plant, generally, is a rubber plant. Even with Ibsen, the action is confined to a room or pair of rooms until the late plays like *A Lady from the Sea*, *The Master Builder*, *John Gabriel Borkman*, when the realistic style has been abandoned for symbolism and the doors are swung open to the garden, mountains, the sea. Ibsen, however, is an exception to the general rule that the indoor scene must be unattractive: his middle-class Scandinavians own some handsome furniture; Nora's house, like any doll's house, must have been charmingly appointed. But Ibsen is an exception to another rule that seems to govern realistic drama (and the novel too, for that matter)—the rule that it must not be well written. (Thanks to

William Archer's wooden translations, his work now falls into line in English.) This rule in America has the force, almost, of a law, one of those iron laws that work from within necessity itself, apparently, and without conscious human aid. Our American realists do not *try* to write badly. Many, like Arthur Miller, strive to write "well," i.e., pretentiously, but like Dreiser in the novel they are cursed with inarticulateness. They "grope." They are, as O'Neill said of himself, "fogbound."

The heroes are petty or colorless; the settings are drab; the language is lame. Thus the ugliness of the form is complete. I am not saying this as a criticism, only observing that when a play or a novel fails to meet these norms, we cease to think of it as realistic. Flaubert, known to be a "stylist," ceases to count for us as a realist, and even in the last century, Matthew Arnold, hailing Tolstoy as a realist, was blinded by categorical thinking—with perhaps a little help from the translations—into calling his novels raw "slices of life," sprawling, formless, and so on. But it is these clichés, in the long run, that have won out. The realistic novel today is more like what Arnold thought Tolstoy was than it is like Tolstoy or any of the early realists. This question of the beauty of form also touches the actor. An actor formerly was supposed to be a good-looking man, with a handsome figure, beautiful movements, and a noble diction. These attributes are no longer necessary for a stage career; indeed, in America they are a positive handicap. A good-looking young man who moves well and speaks well is becoming almost unemployable in American "legit" theatre; his best hope today is to look for work in musical comedy. Or posing for advertisements. On the English stage, where realism until recently never got a foothold, the good-looking actor still rules the roost, but the English actor cannot play American realist parts, while the American actor cannot play Shakespeare or Shaw. A pretty girl in America may still hope to be an actress, though even here there are signs of a change: the heroine of O'Neill's late play, *A Moon for the Misbegotten*, was a freckled giantess five feet eleven inches tall and weighing 180 pounds.

Eisenstein and the Italian neo-realists used people off the street for actors—a logical inference from premises which, being egalitarian and documentary, are essentially hostile to professional élites, including Cossacks, Swiss Guards, and actors. The professional actor in his greasepaint is the antithesis of the pallid man on the street. But film and stage realism are not so democratic in their principles as may at first appear. To begin with, the director and a small corps of professionals—electricians and cameramen—assume absolute power over the masses, i.e., over the untrained actors picked from the crowd; no resistance is encountered, as it would be with professional actors, in molding the human material to the director-dictator's will. And even with stars and all-professional casts, the same tendency is found in the modern realist or neo-realist director. Hence the whispered stories of stars deliberately broken by a director: James Dean and Brigitte Bardot. Similar stories of brainwashing are heard backstage. This is not surprising if realism, as we now know it, rejects as nonaverage whatever is noble, beautiful, or seemly, whatever is capable of "gesture," whatever in fact is free. Everything I have been saying up till now can be summed up in a sentence. Realism is a depreciation of the real. It is a gloomy puritan doctrine that has flourished chiefly in puritan countries—America, Ireland, Scandinavia, northern France, nonconformist England—chilly, chilblained countries, where the daily world is ugly and everything is done to keep it so, as if as a punishment for sin. The doctrine is spreading with industrialization, the growth of ugly cities, and the erosion of Nature. It came late to the English stage, long after it had appeared in the novel, because those puritan elements with which it is naturally allied have, up until now, considered the theatre to be wicked.

At the same time, in defense of realism, it must be said that its great enemy has been just that puritan life whose gray color it has taken. The original realists—Ibsen in the theatre, Flaubert in the novel—regarded themselves as "pagans," in opposition to their puritan contemporaries, and adhered to a religion of Beauty or Nature; they dreamed of freedom and hedonistic license (Flaubert) and exalted (Ibsen) the autonomy of the individual will. Much of this "paganism" is still found in O'Casey and in the early O'Neill, a curdled puritan of Irish-American stock. The original realists were half Dionysian aesthetes ("The vine-leaves in his hair") and their heroes and heroines were usually rebels, protesting the drabness and meanness of the common life. Ibsen's characters complain that they are "stifling"; in the airless hypocrisy of the puritan middle-class parlor, people were being poisoned by the dead gas of lies. Hypocrisy is the cardinal sin of the middle class, and the exposure of a lie is at the center of all Ibsen's plots. The strength and passion of realism is its resolve to tell the whole truth; this explains why the realist in his indictment of society avoids the old method of satire with its delighted exaggeration. The realist drama at its highest is an implacable exposé. Ibsen rips off the curtain and shows his audiences to themselves, and there is something inescapable in the manner of the confrontation, like a case slowly being built. The pillars of society who sit in the best seats are, bit by bit, informed that they are rotten and that the commerce they live on is a commerce of "coffin ships." The action on the Ibsen stage is too close for comfort to the lives of the audience; only the invisible "fourth wall" divides them. "This is the way we live now!" Moral examination, self-examination are practical as a duty, a protestant stock-taking, in the realist mission hall.

For this, it is essential that the audience accept the picture as true; it cannot be permitted to feel that it is watching something "made up" or embellished. Hence the stripping down of the form and the elimination of effects that might be recognized as literary. For the first time too, in the realist drama, the accessories of the action are described at length by the playwright. The details must strike home and convince. The audience must be able to place the furniture, the carpets, the ornaments, the napery and glassware as "just what these people would have." This accounts for the importance of the stage set. Many critics who scornfully dismiss the "boxlike set" of the realistic drama, with its careful disposition of furniture, do not understand its function. This box is the box or "coffin" of average middle-class life opened at one end to reveal the corpse within, looking, as all embalmed corpses are said to do, "just as if it were alive." Inside the realist drama, whenever it is genuine and serious, there is a kind of double illusion, a false bottom: everything appears to be lifelike but this appearance of life is death. The stage set remains a central element in all true realism; it cannot be replaced by scrim or platforms. In *A Long Day's Journey into Night*, surely the greatest realist drama since Ibsen, the family living room, with its central overhead lighting-fixture, is as solid and eternal as oak and as sad as wicker, and O'Neill in the text tells the stage-designer what books must be in the glassed-in bookcase on the left and what books in the other by the entrance. The tenement of Elmer Rice's *Street Scene* (in the opera version) was a magnificent piece of characterization; so was the Bronx living room of Odets' *Awake and Sing*—his sole (and successful) experiment with realism. I can still see the bowl of fruit on the table, slightly to the left of stage center, and hear the Jewish mother interrupting whoever happened to be talking, to say, "Have a piece of fruit." That bowl of fruit, which *was* the Jewish Bronx, remains more memorable as a character than many of the people in the drama. This gift of characterization through props and stage set is shared by Paddy Chayevsky in *Middle of the Night* and by William Inge in *Come Back, Little Sheba*, where an unseen prop or accessory, the housewife's terrible frowsty little dog, is a master-stroke of realist illusionism and, more than that, a kind of ghostly totem. All these plays, incidentally, are stories of death-in-life.

This urgent correspondence with a familiar reality, down to the last circumstantial detail, is what makes realism so gripping, like a trial in court. The dramatist is witnessing or testifying, on an oath never sworn before in a work of art, not to leave out anything and to tell the truth to the best of his ability. And yet the realistic dramatist, beginning with Ibsen, is aware of a missing element. The realist mode seems to generate a dissatisfaction with itself, even in the greatest masters: Tolstoy, for example, came to feel that his novels, up to *Resurrection*, were inconsequential trifling; the vital truth had been left out. In short, as a novelist, he began to feel like a hypocrite. This dissatisfaction with realism was evidently suffered also by Ibsen; halfway through his realist period, you see him start to look for another dimension. Hardly had he discovered or invented the new dramatic mode than he showed signs of being cramped by it; he experienced, if his plays are an index, that same sense of confinement, of being stifled, within the walls of realism that his characters experience within the walls of middle-class life. Something was missing: air. This is already plain in *The Wild Duck*, a strange piece of auto-criticism and probably his finest play; chafing, restless, mordant, he is searching for something else, for a poetic element, which he represents, finally, in the wild duck itself, a dramatic symbol for that cherished wild freedom that neither Ibsen nor his characters can maintain, without harming it, in a shut-in space. But to resort to symbols to make good the missing element becomes a kind of forcing, like trying to raise a wild bird in an attic, and the strain of this is felt in *Rosmersholm*, where symbols play a larger part and are charged with a more oppressive weight of meaning. In *The Lady from the Sea*, *The Master Builder*, and other late plays, the symbols have broken through the thin fence or framework of realism; poetry has spread its crippled wings, but the price has been heavy.

The whole history of dramatic realism is encapsulated in Ibsen. First, the renunciation of verse and of historical and philosophical subjects in the interests of prose and the present time; then the dissatisfaction and the attempt to restore the lost element through a recourse to symbols; then, or at the same time, a forcing of the action at the climaxes to heighten the drama; finally, the renunciation of realism in favor of a mixed mode or hodgepodge. The reaching for tragedy at the climaxes is evident in *Hedda Gabler* and still more so in *Rosmersholm*, where, to me at any rate, the climactic shriek "To the mill race!" is absurdly like a bad film. Many of Ibsen's big moments, even as early as *A Doll's House*, strike me as false and grandiose, that is, precisely, as stagey. Nor is it only in the context of realism that they appear so. It is not just that one objects that people do not act or talk like that—Tolstoy's criticism of King Lear on the heath. If you compare the mill-race scene in *Rosmersholm* with the climax of a Shakespearean tragedy, you will see that the Shakespearean heroes are far less histrionic, more natural and *ordinary*; there is always a stillness at the center of the Shakespearean storm. It is as if the realist, in reaching for tragedy, were punished for his *hubris* by a ludicrous fall into bathos. Tragedy is impossible by definition in the quotidian realist mode, since (quite aside from the question of the hero) tragedy is the exceptional action one of whose signs is beauty.

In America the desire to supply the missing element (usually identified as poetry or "beauty") seems to grow stronger and stronger exactly in proportion to the author's awkwardness with language. The less a playwright can write prose, the more he wishes to write poetry and to raise his plays by their bootstraps to a higher realm. You find these applications of "beauty" in Arthur Miller and Tennessee Williams; they stand out like rouge on a pitted complexion; it is as though the author first wrote the play naturalistically and then gave it a beauty-treatment or face-lift. Before them, O'Neill, who was too honest and too philosophically inclined to be satisfied by a surface solution, kept looking methodically for a way of representing the missing element in dramas that would still be realistic at the core. He experimented with masks (*The Great God Brown*), with the aside and the soliloquy (*Strange Interlude*), with a story and pattern borrowed from Greek classic drama (*Mourning Becomes Electra*). In other words, he imported into the American home or farm the machinery of tragedy. But his purpose was always a greater realism. His use of the aside, for example, was very different from the traditional use of the aside (a kind of nudge to the audience, usually on the part of the villain, to let them in on his true intent or motive); in *Strange Interlude* O'Neill was trying, through the aside, to make available to the realistic drama the discoveries of modern psychology, to represent on the stage the unconscious selves of his characters, at cross-purposes with their conscious selves but just as real if not realer, at least according to the psychoanalysts. He was trying, in short, to give a more complete picture of ordinary people in their daily lives. It was the same with his use of masks in *The Great God Brown*; he was appropriating the mask of Athenian drama, a ritual means of putting a distance between the human actor and the audience, to bring his own audience closer to the inner humanity of his character—the man behind the mask of conformity. The fact that these devices were clumsy is beside the point. O'Neill's sincerity usually involved him in clumsiness. In the end, he came back to the straight realism of his beginnings: *The Long Voyage Home*, the title of his young Caribbean series, could also be the title of the great play of his old age: *A Long Day's Journey into Night*. He has sailed beyond the horizon and back into port; the circle is complete. In this late play, the quest for the missing element, as such, is renounced; poetry is held to be finally unattainable by the author. "I couldn't touch what I tried to tell you just now," says the character who is supposed to be the young O'Neill. "I just stammered. That's the best I'll ever do. I mean, if I live. Well, it will be faithful realism, at least. Stammering is the native eloquence of us fog people." In this brave acknowledgment or advance acceptance of failure, there is something very moving. Moreover, the acceptance of defeat was in fact the signal of a victory. *A Long Day's Journey into Night*, sheer dogged prose from beginning to end, achieves in fact a peculiar poetry, and the relentless amassing of particulars takes on, eventually, some of the crushing force of inexorable logic that we find in Racine or in a Greek play. The weight of circumstance itself becomes a fate or nemesis. This is the closest, probably, the realism can get to tragedy.

The "stammering" of O'Neill was what made his later plays so long, and the stammering, which irritated some audiences, impatient for the next syllable to fall, was a sign of the author's agonized determination to be truthful. If O'Neill succeeded, at last, in deepening the character of his realism, it was because the

missing element he strove to represent was not, in the end, "poetry"
or "beauty" or "philosophy" (though he sometimes seems to have
felt that it was) but simply meaning—the total significance of an
action. What he came to conclude, rather wearily, in his last plays
was that the total significance of an action lay in the accumulated
minutiae of that action and could not be abstracted from it, at least
not by him. There was no truth or meaning beyond the event itself;
anything more (or less) would be a lie. This pun or tautology, this
conundrum, committed him to a cycle of repetition, and memory,
the mother of the Muses, became his only muse.

The younger American playwrights—Miller, Williams, Inge,
Chayevsky—now all middle-aged, are pledged, like O'Neill, to
verisimilitude. They purport to offer a "slice of life," in Tennessee
Williams' case a rich, spicy slab of Southern fruitcake, but still a slice
of life. The locus of their plays is the American porch or backyard or
living room or parlor or bus station, presented as typical, authentic
as home-fried potatoes or "real Vermont maple syrup." This authen-
ticity may be regional, as with Williams and Paddy Chayevsky (the
Jewish upper West side; a Brooklyn synagogue) or it may claim to
be as broad as the nation, as with Arthur Miller, or somewhere
rather central, in between the two, as with William Inge. But in any
case, the promise of these playwrights is to show an ordinary home,
an ordinary group of bus passengers, a typical manufacturer, and so
on, and the dramatis personae tend to resemble a small-town, non-
blue-ribbon jury: housewife, lawyer, salesman, chiropractor, work-
ing-man, schoolteacher…Though Tennessee Williams' characters
are more exotic, they too are offered as samples to the audience's
somewhat voyeuristic eye; when Williams' film, *Baby Doll*, was
attacked by Cardinal Spellman, the director (Elia Kazan) defended
it on the grounds that it was true to life that he and Williams had
observed, on location, in Mississippi. If the people in Tennessee
Williams were regarded as products of the author's imagination, his
plays would lose all their interest. There is always a point in any
one of Williams' dramas where recognition gives way to a feeling
of shocked incredulity; this shock technique is the source of his

sensational popularity. But the audience would not be electrified if it had not been persuaded earlier that it was witnessing something the author vouched for as a common, ordinary occurrence in the Deep South.

Unlike the other playwrights, who make a journalistic claim to neutral recording, Arthur Miller admittedly has a message. His first-produced play, *All My Sons*, was a social indictment taken, almost directly, from Ibsen's *Pillars of Society*. The coffin ships, rotten, unseaworthy vessels caulked over to give an appearance of soundness, become defective airplanes sold to the government by a corner-cutting manufacturer during the Second World War; like the coffin ships, the airplanes are a symbol of the inner rottenness of bourgeois society, and the sins of the father, as *almost* in Ibsen, are visited on the son, a pilot who cracks up in the Pacific theatre (in Ibsen, the ship-owner's boy is saved at the last minute from sailing on *The Indian Girl*). The insistence of this symbol and the vagueness or absence of concrete detail express Miller's impatience with the particular and his feeling that his play ought to say "more" than it appears to be saying. Ibsen, even in his later, symbolic works, was always specific about the where, when, and how of his histories (the biographies of his central characters are related with almost too much circumstantiality), but Miller has always regarded the specific as trivial and has sought, from the very outset, a hollow, reverberant universality. The reluctance to awaken a specific recognition, for fear that a larger meaning might go unrecognized by the public, grew on Miller with *Death of a Salesman*—a strong and original conception that was enfeebled by its creator's insistence on universality and by a too-hortatory excitement, i.e., an eagerness to preach, which is really another form of the same thing. Miller was bent on making his Salesman (as he calls him) a parable of Everyman, exactly as in a clergyman's sermon, so that the drama has only the quality—and something of the canting tone—of an illustrative moral example. The thirst for universality becomes even more imperious in *A View from the Bridge*, where the account of a waterfront killing that Miller read in a newspaper is accessorized with Greek architecture, "archetypes," and, from time to time, intoned passages of verse, and Miller announces in a preface that he is not interested in his hero's "psychology." Miller does not understand that you cannot turn a newspaper item about Italian longshoremen and illegal immigration into a Greek play by adding a chorus and the pediment of a temple. Throughout Miller's long practice as a realist, there is not only a naïve searching for another dimension but an evident hatred of and contempt for reality—as not good enough to make plays out of.

It is natural, therefore, that he should never have any interest in how people talk; his characters all talk the same way—somewhat funereally, through their noses. A live sense of speech differences (think of Shaw's *Pygmalion*) is rare in American playwrights; O'Neill tried to cultivate it ("dat ol davil sea"), but he could never do more than write perfunctory dialect, rather like that of somebody telling a Pat and Mike story or a mountaineer joke. The only American realist with an ear for speech, aside from Chayevsky, whose range is narrow, is Tennessee Williams. He does really hear his characters, especially his female characters; he has studied their speech patterns and, like Professor Higgins, he can tell where they come from; Williams too is the only realist who places his characters in social history. Of all the realists, after O'Neill, he has probably the greatest native gift for the theatre; he is a natural performer and comedian, and it is too bad that he suffers from the inferiority complex that is the curse of the recent American realists—the sense that a play must be bigger than its characters. This is really a social disease—a fear of being underrated—rather than the claustrophobia of the medium itself, which tormented Ibsen and O'Neill. But it goes back to the same source: the depreciation of the real. Real speech, for example, is not good enough for Williams and from time to time he silences his characters to put on a phonograph record of his special poetic longplay prose.

All dramatic realism is somewhat sadistic; an audience is persuaded to watch something that makes it uncomfortable and from which no relief is offered—no laughter, no tears, no purgation. This sadism had a moral justification, so long as there was the question of the exposure of a lie. But Williams is fascinated by the refinements of cruelty, which with him becomes a form of aestheticism, and his plays, far from baring a lie that society is trying to cover up, titillate society like a peepshow. The curtain is ripped off, to disclose, not a drab scene of ordinary life, but a sadistic exhibition of the kind certain rather specialized tourists pay to see in big cities like New Orleans. With Williams, it is always a case of watching some mangy cat on a hot tin roof. The ungratified sexual organ of an old maid, a young wife married to a homosexual, a subnormal poor white farmer is proffered to the audience as a curiosity. The withholding of sexual gratification from a creature or "critter" in heat for three long acts is Williams' central device; other forms of torture to which these poor critters are subjected are hysterectomy and castration. Nobody, not even the SPCA, would argue that it was a good thing to show the prolonged torture of a dumb animal on the stage, even though the torture were only simulated and animals, in the end, would profit from such cases being brought to light. Yet this, on a human level, is Tennessee Williams' realism—a cat, to repeat, on a hot tin roof. And, in a milder version, it is found again in William Inge's *Picnic*. No one could have prophesied, a hundred years ago, that the moral doctrine of realism would narrow to the point of becoming pornography, yet something like that seems to be happening with such realistic novels as *Peyton Place* and the later John O'Hara and with one branch of the realist theatre. Realism seems to be a highly unstable mode, attracted on the one hand to the higher, on the other to the lower elements in the human scale, tending always to proceed toward its opposite, that is, to irreality, tracing a vicious circle from which it can escape only by repudiating itself. Realism, in short, is forever begging the question—the question of reality. To find the ideal realist, you would first have to find reality. And if no dramatist today, except O'Neill, can accept being a realist in its full implications, this is perhaps because of lack of courage. Ibsen and O'Neill, with all their dissatisfaction, produce major works in the full realist vein; the recent realists get discouraged after a single effort. *Street Scene; All My Sons; The Glass Menagerie; Come Back, Little Sheba; Middle of the Night,* perhaps *Awake and Sing* are the only convincing evidence that exists of an American realist school—not counting O'Neill. If I add *Death of a Salesman* and *A Streetcar Named Desire,* it is only because I do not know where else to put them.

Mary McCarthy

MARY MCCARTHY (1912–1989) was an American critic, public intellectual, and author of more than two dozen books, including the 1963 *New York Times* bestseller *The Group*.

McCarthy was born on June 21, 1912, in Seattle, Washington, to Roy Winfield McCarthy and Therese ("Tess") Preston McCarthy. McCarthy and her three younger brothers, Kevin, Preston, and Sheridan, were suddenly orphaned in 1918. While the family was en route from Seattle to a new home in Minneapolis, both parents died of influenza within a day of one another.

After being shuttled between relatives, the children were finally sent to live with a great-aunt, Margaret Sheridan McCarthy, and her husband, Myers Shriver. The Shrivers proved to be cruel and often sadistic adoptive parents. Six years later, Harold Preston, the children's maternal grandfather and an attorney, intervened. The children were split up, and Mary went to live with her grandparents in their affluent Seattle home. McCarthy reflects on her turbulent youth, Catholic upbringing, and subsequent loss of faith in *Memories of a Catholic Girlhood* (1957) and *How I Grew* (1987).

A week after graduating from Vassar in 1933, McCarthy moved to New York City and married Harold Johnsrud, an aspiring playwright. They divorced three years later, but many aspects of their relationship would resurface in the unhappy marriage of Kay Strong and Harald Petersen in *The Group*. In the early 1930s she moved in "fellow-traveling" Communist circles, but by the latter half of the decade she repudiated Soviet-style communism, expressing solidarity with Leon Trotsky after the Moscow Trials, and vigorously countering playwrights and authors she considered to be sympathetic to Stalinism. During the 1940s and 1950s she became a liberal critic of both McCarthyism and communism.

In the late 1930s McCarthy garnered attention as a cutting theater and book critic, contributing to a wide range of publications, such as the *Nation*, the *New Republic*, *Harper's Magazine*, and the *New York Review of Books*. She served on the editorial staff of the Partisan Review from 1937 to 1948. Her milieu included German-born American political scientist and philosopher Hannah Arendt with whom she developed an enduring friendship.

In 1938, McCarthy married Edmund Wilson, an established writer; together, they had a son named Reuel, born the same year. Wilson encouraged McCarthy to write fiction, and her first book, a novel entitled *The Company She Keeps* (1942), satirizes the mores of bohemian New York intellectuals from the point of view of an acerbic female protagonist. Her second book, *The Oasis*, a thinly disguised roman à clef about the *Partisan Review* intellectuals, won the English monthly magazine *Horizon*'s fiction contest in 1949.

Soon after her divorce from Wilson in 1945, McCarthy married Bowden Broadwater, a staff member of the *New Yorker*, and also taught literature at Bard College and Sarah Lawrence College. *A Charmed Life* (1955), a novel about the rollercoaster experience of a shaky marriage in a quirky artists' community, is based on her life with Wilson in Wellfleet, Cape Cod. *The Groves of Academe* (1951), a campus satire informed by her teaching positions, casts an ironic gaze on the foibles of academics. Randall Jarrell's novel *Pictures from an Institution* (1954) is said to be about McCarthy's time at Sarah Lawrence, where he also taught.

In the 1950s, McCarthy took a strong interest in European history. Her two books about Italy, *Venice Observed* (1956) and *The Stones of Florence* (1959), combine art criticism, political theory, and reportage to bring the two cities' histories to life. While on a lecture tour in Poland for the United States Information Agency in 1959 and 1960, McCarthy met the public affairs officer for the

U.S. Embassy in Warsaw, James West. McCarthy and West left their respective partners and were married in 1961.

McCarthy's most popular literary success came in 1963 with the publication of her novel *The Group,* which remained on the *New York Times* bestseller list for almost two years, and was made into a movie by Sidney Lumet in 1966.

McCarthy maintained her commitment to liberal critiques of culture and power to the end of her life, opposing the Vietnam War in the 1960s and covering the Watergate scandal hearings in the 1970s. During the Vietnam War she traveled to Vietnam and wrote a series of articles for the *New York Review of Books* that were subsequently published as *Vietnam* (1967). McCarthy documented her experiences of a March 1968 visit to North Vietnam in her book, *Hanoi* (1968). Her coverage of the Watergate hearings in the 1970s is the basis for *The Mask of State* (1975). Her famous libel feud with writer Lillian Hellman, stemming from McCarthy's appearance on the *Dick Cavett Show* in 1979, formed the basis for the play *Imaginary Friends* (2002) by Nora Ephron.

McCarthy won a number of literary awards, including the *Horizon* Prize (1949) and two Guggenheim Fellowships (1949 and 1959). She also received both the Edward MacDowell Medal and the National Medal for Literature in 1984. She was a member of the American Academy and Institute of Arts and Letters, the National Institute of Arts and Letters, and the American Academy in Rome. She received honorary degrees from numerous universities including Bard College, Smith College, and Syracuse University.

McCarthy died of lung cancer on October 25, 1989. The second volume of her autobiography was published posthumously in 1992 as *Intellectual Memoirs: New York, 1936–1938. Between Friends: The Correspondence of Hannah Arendt and Mary McCarthy, 1949–1975* was published in 1995.

Printed in Great Britain
by Amazon

40551923R00162